GERMAN RESISTANCE TO....HITLER

Ethical and Religious Factors

GERMAN RESISTANCE TO....HITLER

Ethical and Religious Factors

By

MOTHER MARY ALICE GALLIN, O.S.U., M.A.

THE CATHOLIC UNIVERSITY OF AMERICA PRESS
WASHINGTON, D. C.

Nihil obstat:

MSGR. ALOYSIUS K. ZIEGLER
Censor Deputatus

Imprimatur:

✠ PATRICK A. O'BOYLE, D.D.
Archbishop of Washington

July 8, 1961

The *nihil obstat* and *imprimatur* are official declarations that a book or pamphlet is free of doctrinal or moral error. No implication is contained therein that those who have granted the *nihil obstat* and the *imprimatur* agree with the content, opinions, or statements expressed.

Reprinted April 1969

Library of Congress Catalog Card No.: 62-355
S.B.N. 8132-0261-2

SOLI DEO GLORIA

FOREWORD

In the course of considerable reading on the Resistance Movement in Germany, I came across Mother Mary Alice Gallin's work and I was so impressed by the research and thought which had gone into its preparation that I was eager to get in touch with her in order to exchange views and interpretations on this absorbing, if tragic, phase of German history.

The phenomenon of the Resistance Movement and its relation to the many other forces which operated during the Nazi period will be a matter of recurring interest to historians as well as to all who maintain their interest in the development of the modern German state. There were so many sensitive and courageous figures among those who participated in the Resistance that a study of the ethical and religious considerations of their conduct is a material factor in any attempt to understand the motivations and impulses behind the Movement.

I believe that Mother Mary Alice Gallin's analysis is a significant addition to the now rather extensive literature on the subject. In my judgment it throws a more revealing light on the moral problems faced by the participants than has appeared in any other comments which I have read.

John J. McCloy
Former United States High
Commissioner for Germany

January 16, 1961

ACKNOWLEDGMENTS

It is a pleasure to take this opportunity of thanking publicly all those who helped to make this dissertation a reality. The generosity of my religious superiors made possible my studies at Catholic University and their continued interest in the progress of my work has been a source of great encouragement. The topic for my research was suggested by Professor Engel-Janosi, and his cooperation in the preparation of it has been untiring and zealous. I am also deeply grateful to Dr. Martin R. P. McGuire and Father John Quasten who read the manuscript and offered several pertinent suggestions for its improvement. The permission for access to the necessary papers in the custody of the State Department was received through the courtesy of Dr. G. Bernard Noble of the Historical Division and the author's use of the papers was greatly facilitated by the efficiency and personal interest of Dr. E. Taylor Parks and his staff.

A debt of gratitude is also owed to the personnel of the Departmental Records Branch of the Adjutant General's Office of the Department of the Army who made accessible to the writer the records of trials at Nuremberg and the relevant captured German documents in the custody of the department. Mr. Taylor of the National Archives was extremely helpful in locating the documents used from the files of the former Office of Strategic Services.

Suggestions concerning the location of valuable information and personal comments on the persons and issues involved in this study were received in letters and/or personal interviews with the following: J. Lonsdale Bryans, Franklin L. Ford, Allen Dulles, Robert Graham S. J., Albrecht von Kessel, John Courtney Murray S. J., Gerhard Ritter, Dorothy Thompson, Federico Stallforth, and Generalmajor a. D. von Witzleben. To them the writer is particularly grateful for their unfailing courtesy and cooperation in answering her numerous questions.

Permission to quote at length from the following books has been received from the respective authors or publishers: From Atlantis Verlag for *The Von Hassell Diaries*; Bruce Publishing Co. for Max Jordan's *Beyond All Fronts*; J. Lonsdale Bryans for his *Blind Victory;* Allen Welsh Dulles for his *Germany's Underground*; Hans Bernd Gisevius for his *To the Bitter End*; The Macmillan Co. for Fabian von Schlabrendorff's *They Almost Killed Hitler*; St. Martin's Press for John W. Wheeler-Bennett's *The Nemesis of Power*; and Henry Regnery Co. for Ernst von Weizäcker's *Memoirs.*

A final word of thanks is offered to Miss Barbara Spies who read the entire manuscript and made many helpful suggestions as to both content and form. For her stimulating advice and loyal encouragement the author is particularly grateful.

TABLE OF CONTENTS

CHAPTER I

The German Fight against Hitler

The problems posed by an analysis of the German Resistance Movement are unique in scope, in structure, in ideological significance, and in solution. Resistance movements in the other countries of Europe during World War II were unanimously catalogued as patriotic refusal to submit to the invader. But patriotism is undoubtedly more easily felt than defined. Should we consider as patriots those Germans who disavowed Nazism and participated in the conspiracy to overthrow Hitler, using as they did all available means to undermine their own government, and even, in some instances, working to bring about the military defeat of the Third Reich?

Such unorthodox "patriotism" was not without its problems, especially in the fields of ethics and religion. The theoretical relation of the individual to the State and the resulting concept of the legality of a government are basic factors in the labeling of any government as tyrannical. Even ten years after the Nazi debacle it is not simple to answer the questions raised in this area by the modern totalitarian state; how much more difficult must it have been for the conspirators within Hitler's Germany.

For some time after the attempt to assassinate Hitler was made on July 20, 1944 the full story behind it was unknown. It has since been uncovered in the records of the Reich Security Office, in the diaries, memoirs, and letters of the conspirators, and in the evidence given at the Nuremberg trials. Nevertheless, the unfolding of the underground activity during the seven years preceding the attempted assassination has not in itself revealed the true significance of the Resistance Movement, for the motives of the participants remain uninvestigated and their problems of conscience unexplored.

The men of July 20 have been criticized both at home and abroad. Attempts to brand them as traitors have been made so as to strengthen the neo-Nazi efforts to reassume power in Germany. The most important case in this connection was the trial of Major-General Ernst Remer in Brunswick in 1952.[1] On the other hand, such critics as Lord Robert Vansittart have maintained that there was no resistance against Hitler in Germany and that the Germans, by their docile acceptance of such an evil government, have forfeited their right to an honorable place among the nations of the world.[2]

Between these two extremes we find another more subtle attack on the memory of the German Opposition, represented by such writers as Sir Lewis Namier [3] and J. W. Wheeler-Bennett.[4] The latter, in his comprehensive and important study of the German army, does not exclude the efforts of the Resistance Movement, but he implicitly criticizes the participants for their "patriotism."

> They were no squalid band of traitors in the pay of the enemy, plotting to destroy their country from motives of gain or pique or jealousy. Nor were they, in the main, inspired by any higher motives than the destruction of a Leader and a regime whom they had followed and tolerated as long as he brought them advantage but concerning whom, at various stages along the way, they had been disillusioned. These men were patriotic Germans who sought to save Germany by the only means in their power from the cataclysmic fate that was rapidly overtaking her under the leadership of Adolf Hitler.[5]

In this statement and in many innuendoes throughout his book, Mr. Wheeler-Bennett attributes essentially selfish motives to the men within Germany who had the fortitude to oppose the totali-

[1] For a discussion of the issues involved in the Remer trial cf. Dr. Hubert Schron, Landgerichtspräsident, *Das Widerstandsrecht in sittlicher und rechtlicher Beleuchtung*, published as a supplement to *Das Parlament*, January 28, 1953. Cf. also Guenther Wiesenborn, *Der lautlose Aufstand* (Hamburg: Rowohlt, 1953), *passim*.

[2] Lord Robert Vansittart, *Bones of Contention* (London: Hutchinson and Co., 1945).

[3] Sir Lewis Namier, *In the Nazi Era* (London: Macmillan & Co., 1952) and also his review of Erich Kordt's *Nicht aus den Akten* (Stuttgart: Union Deutsche, 1950) in an article entitled "Registers after the Event," *History Today*, I (June, 1951), pp. 13-22.

[4] John W. Wheeler-Bennett, *The Nemesis of Power: The German Army in Politics 1918-45* (New York: St. Martin's Press Inc., 1954).

[5] *Ibid.*, pp. 592-593.

tarian state. It appears to the writer that he does not consider sufficiently the problems which made their resistance so difficult—in the moral order, to justify their position, and in the practical order, to execute their plans. Perhaps the simplicity of the Anglo-Saxon tradition of defending individual rights against infringement by the government, even at the cost of revolution and civil war, mars Mr. Wheeler-Bennett's insight into the problems peculiar to the German Resistance.

In explanation of the German attitude toward resistance one of the conspirators has written:

> Germans are by nature not at all adapted to play the part of revolutionaries. They have an inborn respect for the authority of the State. Riots and civil wars have often occurred in other countries, but they have almost never occurred in German history. Anyone who attempts to interfere with the existing authorities has to reckon with strong opposition, however right he may be from the objective point of view.[6]

This analysis of the German mentality by a German is substantiated by a foreign observer who knew the group of conspirators very well. Bernardo Attolico, the Italian Ambassador to Berlin in 1939, said to Carl Burkhardt, League of Nations Commissioner in Danzig: "They have no method; they are careless, foolish; the Germans are not given to conspiracy. A conspirator needs everything they lack—patience, knowledge of human nature, psychology, tact. No, they are all going to be shot or disappear in camps. . . ."[7]

While it is true that their cooperation with one another increased as time went on, it always remained an unfortunate fact that the anti-Nazi groups failed to find a leader who had both the idealism required in a revolutionary and the power to execute his plans. Again, some who were active in the early attempts to overthrow the regime in 1938 and 1939 dropped out of the conspiratorial circle along the way, while others only became active toward the end of

[6] Ernst von Weizsäcker, *Memoirs*, trans. John Andrews (Chicago: Henry Regnery Company, 1951), p. 182.

[7] Extract from Carl Burkhardt's diary submitted as von Weizsäcker Defense Document # 499 in the Ministries case, tried at Nuremberg, 1947. The complete records of this trial are available at the Departmental Records Branch of the Adjutant General's Office, Dept. of the Army, Alexandria, Va.

the war. Such instability in membership and the subsequent need for constant realignment increased the difficulty of achieving unity.

In addition to these organizational problems, the Resistance Movement in Germany suffered from its inability to convince the Allied Powers of its sincerity and its preparedness to effect a *coup d'état,* and without foreign assurances, the civilian nucleus of the active movement could not prove to the military leaders that a successful move on their part would be rewarded by favorable treatment from abroad. As Carl Goerdeler, who has been described as the "heart of the Resistance Movement," explained it to Max Jordan, an American correspondent in Berlin: "I did not find many people abroad who understood that we Germans were the first people to be conquered by Hitler." [8]

In the early days of the Nazi regime the large majority of the nation, even if it had not voted for the National Socialist party, accepted its rise to power and looked to it and to their Fuehrer for the solution of the overwhelming economic and social problems which faced post-Versailles Germany. Only slowly, as the activity of the Gestapo increased, the demolition of political parties and trade unions progressed, and the pagan spirit of such movements as the "Strength Through Joy" became apparent, did the average man begin to wonder and then to withdraw support from the Nazis—instinctively rather than for clearly defined reasons.

Aside from the small group of fanatical Nazis, the German people were not in favor of persecuting the Jews, of abolishing religion from schools and national life, or of preparing to conquer other nations. As early as the spring of 1934 the American Consul General in Berlin had reported that although Hitler was still personally popular, the "little Hitlers" were not, and pointed out that to bolster the National Socialists by making trade agreements with them would be a mistake because the popular feeling was that a change of government was imminent.[9]

Two years later the American Ambassador to Berlin wrote to

[8] Max Jordan, *Beyond All Fronts* (Milwaukee: Bruce Publishing Co., 1944), p. 262.

[9] Letters from the American Consul General in Berlin to the Undersecretary of State. March 24, March 29, April 13, and April 27, 1934. Department of State. MS, 860/003418, 3419, 3420, 3422.

President Roosevelt concerning the attitude of the Germans toward proposed sanctions on Italy. According to him, two-thirds of the people in the fall of 1935 had been hoping and praying that sanctions would be applied.

> Germans of semi-official, University, religious and royalist relations were unanimous in their hope that one dictatorship would be broken down, especially through the cooperation of the United States. If that happened, these people thought their own miserable position would be improved, even corrected. If I were to give the names of the people who showed great concern and talked freely, you could hardly doubt my conclusions.[10]

However, he noted that a great change had taken place as a result of the Hoare-Laval agreement; by March 6, 1936 the opposition of the Generals to the sending of troops into the Rhineland had ceased, and the dictatorship was stronger than ever. Thus did every indication of weakness on the part of the Western Powers have repercussions on the internal situation in Germany.

Guilt cannot be imputed to the German people as a whole since moral responsibility is a consequence of free will and will is a faculty of the individual soul.[11] Yet there may have been many who were guilty in that they recognized evil in the power that Hitler held over the people and in his utter disregard of human freedom, believed that it ought to be resisted, and yet lacked the courage to take up the fight. In any case, in Germany as in all nations at all times, the people did not act as an entity but rather as individuals. In his opening statement at the Nuremberg trials, Chief United States Prosecutor Robert Jackson took cognizance of this fact:

> Under the clutch of the most intricate web of espionage and intrigue that any modern state has endured, and persecution and torture of a kind that has not been visited upon the world

---

[10] Letter from Ambassador Dodd to President Roosevelt, April 1, 1936. State Department. MS. No serial number.

[11] On the question of collective guilt cf. Pius XII, "Address to the Sixth International Congress on Penal Law," October 3, 1953. The problem of finding an ethical foundation for the Nuremberg trials is discussed in John Paulinus Kenny O. P., *A Philosophical Study of the International Military Tribunal* (PhD dissertation, River Forest, Illinois, 1949).

> in many centuries, the elements of the German population which were both decent and courageous were annihilated. Those which were decent but weak were intimidated. Open resistance, which had never been more than feeble and irresolute, disappeared. But resistance, I am happy to say, always remained although it was manifest in only such events as the abortive effort to assassinate Hitler on July 20, 1944.[12]

The ethical and legal reasons which lay at the root of these varying reactions will be discussed later. For those whose decision fell on the side of open resistance—and even tyrannicide—there was to be a long road of conscience-searching and group discussion before they would conclude that this was the best way to serve the interests of their fatherland.

These men who resisted the totalitarian power which overshadowed them had really little in common; they came from different social, educational, religious, economic, and political strata, and differed very frequently as to the best means of fighting Hitler as well as to the ideal state which they wished to see established after the *coup* had been effected. They found unity only in their determination to bring about a change of regime.

Some of their names are now well known and constitute a roll of honor: Colonel-General Ludwig Beck, Carl Goerdeler, Admiral Canaris, Ernst von Weizsäcker, Ewald von Kleist, Helmuth von Moltke, Adam Trott zu Stolz, Michael Cardinal Faulhaber, Hans and Sophie Scholl, Martin Niemoeller, Field Marshal Erwin von Witzleben, Hans Bernd Gisevius, Fabian Schlabrendorff, Dietrich Bonhoeffer, Alfred Delp S. J., Bishop Count von Galen, Peter Count Yorck von Wartenburg, Colonel Count Claus von Stauffenberg. Of the best known group, Dr. Gerhard Ritter has said: "On the whole, Germany has never had a conspiracy of a more purely moral character, truer patriots, more genuine liberals, more embittered adversaries of tyranny, more sincere friends of social reform, than Goerdeler and his followers." [13] The same could be applied with truth to the others who shared with Goerdeler's friends a basic hatred for all that was illegal and indecent.

[12] Robert Jackson, *The Nürnberg Case: 1947* (New York: Alfred A. Knopf, 1947), p. 66.

[13] Gerhard Ritter, "Address at the Royal Institute of International Affairs," *Contemporary Review* CLXXVII (June, 1950), p. 339.

Naturally in a study of ethical factors, the only authentic approach is one which studies the actions, ideals, and motives of the individuals concerned. But where men have grouped together for the purpose of achieving a common goal it is not incorrect to suppose that, in general, they shared in the aims and incentives expressed in the name of the group. The German Resistance, since it was an underground movement, had to remain in small isolated units to prevent detection; of these units the most important have been designated generally as the Beck-Goerdeler group, the Kreisau circle, and the Foreign Office cell, but such division by no means excludes the overlapping of membership or the final attempts at concerted action by representatives of all groups. A still smaller facet of the Resistance spirit can be seen in the formation of student or worker groups illustrated by the Scholls in Munich or in the loosely organized Solf and "Uncle Emil" groups, noteworthy because they indicate the difficulty in even a rigid police state of enforcing laws which public opinion does not support.

As we trace the development of the plans to remove Hitler from power, the activity of the Beck-Goerdeler group will become apparent immediately since its story is the best known and the easiest to describe. The Foreign Office cell is more difficult to delimit both as to membership and activity. Nevertheless it appears to the writer that the division made by Mr. Wheeler-Bennett among "resisters" in the Foreign Office is untenable.

In his opinion there was one group, whose chief was State Secretary von Weizsäcker, which "remained in the service of the Third Reich, did the work of their Nazi masters, and, to-day, having survived to tell the tale and deeply regretting their lack of initiative in the past, now vividly remember their objections to the excesses of Nazi foreign policy and even their conspiracies to restrain it."[14] "Von Weizsäcker," he continues, "was genuinely opposed to the policy of aggression, but . . . because of the risks involved." Then, Mr. Wheeler-Bennett makes the distinction between von Weizsäcker and those who followed him like Erich and Theodor Kordt, and the "real resisters" like Adam von Trott zu Solz, Otto Kiep, Hans Bernd von Haeften, Eduard Brucklmeier, and Albrecht Bernstorff, ". . . who risked all and died."[15]

[14] J. W. Wheeler-Bennett, *op. cit.*, p. 416.

[15] *Ibid.*, p. 417.

That such a distinction is arbitrary is shown by the affidavits submitted at Nuremberg on behalf of von Weizsäcker by the widows of the men in the latter group. Each one testified that her husband worked in close cooperation with the State Secretary, was convinced of his hostility to the National Socialist regime, and considered him the leader in their efforts to organize a *coup*.[16] The diary of Albrecht von Kessel, one of the chief first-hand accounts of the Resistance, is dedicated to Brucklmeier, Trott zu Solz, Ulrich von Schwerin, and Peter Yorck von Wartenburg, a dedication which surely would be strange coming from the closest associate of von Weizsäcker if there had been any real division among the anti-Nazis in the Foreign Office.[17]

One might, it is submitted, legitimately distinguish between those who worked primarily to insure peace and those whose first objective was the removal of Hitler, regardless of the international scene, but this was a question of timing and expediency, not of basic opposition to the regime. Indeed the role of the Foreign Office in the Resistance Movement was extremely important, and it was the State Secretary who used his position to fulfill that role.[18]

The question of the participation of the German military leaders in the Resistance is a difficult one to answer. Recent studies of the German army and particularly of the General Staff have borne out what was discovered in the testimony at Nuremberg and caused the judges there to exonerate the General Staff. The army was certainly not Hitler's "strong arm" as one might have imagined; rather, its whole spirit of conservatism and traditionalism impelled Hitler to conquer it first before setting out to conquer the world, and this he did effectively in the spring of 1938 by means of the nefarious Blomberg-Fritsch crisis. Of the army, Hitler himself said:

> Before I was head of the German Government I thought the German General Staff was like a butcher's dog—something to be held tight by the collar because it threatened to attack

---

[16] Affidavits of Clarita von Trott zu Solz, Klothilde Brucklmaier, Barbara von Haeften, and Countess Schwerin von Schwanenfeld are contained in the von Weizsäcker Defense Document Book # 5.

[17] Albrecht von Kessel, unpublished diary written 1944-45.

[18] *Infra.* chapters III, IV, and V.

> all and sundry. Since then I have had to recognize that the General Staff is anything but that. It has consistently tried to impede every action that I have thought necessary. It objected to the military occupation of the Rhineland, to the march into Austria, to the occupation of Czechoslovakia, and finally even to the war with Poland. It is I who have always had to goad on this butcher's dog.[19]

With very few exceptions, however, the Generals also had to be goaded on constantly by the civilian members of the Resistance Movement if any action was to be taken against Hitler. The army men who were completely convinced of the need to overthrow the Nazi regime and were ready to act were few—General Baron Kurt Hammerstein, Colonel-General Ludwig Beck, Field Marshal Erwin von Witzleben, Major-General Hans Oster, Colonel-General Erich Hoepner. The position of General Franz Halder is somewhat ambiguous, for, although he was aware of the conspiracy in its early days, he never took decisive action for a *coup*.

General Hammerstein had taken a definite stand as early as June 1934 when he protested to Hindenburg about the murder of Schleicher and von Bredow,[20] and, as a close friend of Beck, encouraged him to undertake action against Hitler. Although Halder considered Hammerstein's attitude psychologically influential on the officer corps,[21] his status as a retired officer hindered him from more effective participation in the conspiracy.

Colonel-General Beck, Chief of the General Staff from 1934 to 1938, was recognized by all elements as the real leader of the opposition, the one who held in his hands all the threads of the conspiracy, but after his resignation in August 1938 he was a general without troops, and, as such, limited in his ability to bring about the desired *coup*. General von Witzleben was indeed the only general on active duty on whom the conspirators could rely;

[19] Fabian von Schlabrendorff, *They Almost Killed Hitler*, ed. Gero v. S. Gaevernitz (New York: Macmillan Co., 1947), pp. 34-35.

[20] Wheeler-Bennett, *op. cit.*, p. 329. On Hammerstein cf. article by Otto John, *Das Parlament*, July 20, 1952.

[21] Interrogation of Franz Halder by United States Army Officers, Nuremberg, February 25, 1946 a.m., MS, Department of the Army. All the interrogations of Halder cited below are MS, Dept. of the Army.

yet even he caused them concern at one time because of his apparent loss of faith in the movement.[22]

Major-General Oster was invaluable in his consistent and daring work under the protection of Admiral Canaris, Chief of ABWEHR (Counter Intelligence), but in their positions these men had no command over troops, and if a forceful *coup* were to take place there was need of an officer in a command post. According to von Hassell, by October 1939 there were several subordinate officers who could be counted on: Rundstedt, Blaskowitz, Bock, Leeb, Witzleben, List—but none was in a position to initiate action.[23] For the needed " General with troops " the conspirators sought in vain until the latter days of their planning when von Kluge, Colonel Count Claus von Stauffenberg, Stülpnagel, and even Rommel were drawn in.

When the first rumors of threatening action against Czechoslovakia were heard in November 1937, Colonel-General Beck drew up a forceful memorandum in which he stated the belief that an invasion of Czechoslovakia would lead to world war, a war which Germany would surely lose.[24] Further memoranda along the same line culminated in his resignation in the middle of August 1938,[25] a step he took rather than lead the army into a war for which he could see no justification. He had asked for a collective resignation of the army leaders, but had to accept instead their promise that they would refuse to accept his office if he resigned.

Apparently the mounting tension of the pre-Munich days dictated a different course of action.[26] On September 1, 1938 Colonel-General Halder, with Beck's concurrence, quietly assumed

[22] Ulrich von Hassell, *The Von Hassell Diaries* ed. Hugh Gibson (New York: Doubleday & Company, 1947), pp. 244-245.

[23] *Ibid.*, p. 80.

[24] Wolfgang Foerster, *Generaloberst Ludwig Beck* (Munchen: Isar Verlag, 1953), pp. 69 ff.

[25] *Ibid.*, p. 145.

[26] Interrogation of Erich Kordt by DeWitt C. Poole Mission of Department of State, December, 1945. MS, Department of State, January 7, 1946. This interrogation was made when Erich Kordt went through Washington, D. C. on his return to Germany from his diplomatic post in China. Basically his story agrees with that of the other conspirators, but the dates he gives for Beck's meeting with the Army leaders and his resignation are incorrect. Cf. Foerster, *op. cit.*, pp. 128-146.

the duties of the Chief of Staff with the hope of being able to execute the desired *coup* as soon as the favorable moment arrived. This "moment" proved to be decidedly elusive; from this time on, the constant complaint of the civilian leaders was always the vacillation of the generals. Time after time, they approached Halder, von Brauchitsch and others, trying to convince them that the "favorable moment" was *now,* and time after time the generals found a reason not to act just then.

On September 22, 1940 von Hassell noted in his diary:

> In all conferences with Beck, Popitz, Goerdeler, Oster, et al., we keep asking ourselves in vain whether the generals do not at last sense what is going on; do they realize what a terrifying responsibility they bear, both for domestic developments and for the outcome of the war? We are agreed that we must once more attempt to do everything possible to convince them that they must not allow things to go along in this way lest we find ourselves confronted with or overwhelmed by catastrophe. . . .[27]

Two and one-half years later, he again made a relevant notation:

> The longer the war lasts the less I think of the generals. They have undoubted technical ability and physical courage, but little moral courage, absolutely no broad world vision, no inner spiritual independence or that strength of resistance which rests on a genuine cultural basis. For this reason Hitler was able to make them subservient and bind them hand and foot . . . all those on whom we set our hopes are failing, the more miserably so since they agree with all they have been told and permit themselves to indulge in the most anti-Nazi talk, but are unable to summon up enough courage to act.[28]

From this it is clear that the initiative was retained by the civilians from the time of Beck's resignation until the arrival of Colonel Count Claus von Stauffenberg on the scene. The job of maintaining liaison between civilian and military opponents of the regime was carried out chiefly by Oster and Hans von Dohnanyi who, after the Fritsch affair in February 1938, did what they could to establish unified efforts under the direction and leadership of Beck.[29] Effective exchange of information also existed

[27] Von Hassell, *op. cit.*, p. 150.

[28] *Ibid.*, p. 297.

[29] Otto John, *op. cit.*

between Canaris and von Weizsäcker; in turn the State Secretary communicated with Halder through a permanent liaison officer, Hasse von Etzdorf. Nevertheless, there are many indications that the military and civilian allies found it difficult to discover a *via media* which would lead to the desired goal.

The civilian group designated as the Beck-Goerdeler circle included, in addition to the former Mayor of Leipsig and the former Chief of the General Staff, Ulrich von Hassell, the former Ambassador to Rome, Johannes Popitz, the Prussian Finance Minister, Jens Peter Jessen, a professor of Economics at the University of Berlin, and Hans von Dohnanyi, a former Justice of the Supreme Court now working in Canaris's office. Cooperating with them, in varying degrees of intimacy and reliability, were Ewald von Kleist-Schmenzin, Hans Bernd Gisevius, Dietrich Bonhoeffer, and Hjalmar Schacht. From this civilian nucleus came the first definite attempt to overthrow the Hitler regime; the *coup d'état* planned for September 14, 1938 which, according to various accounts, came so near to fruition.[30]

Counting on the anti-war sentiment of the average German, the conspirators assumed that the issuing of the order to the army to march into Czechoslovakia would be the best psychological moment for them to strike. That they were not wrong in their estimate of the temper of the people is attested to by the British Chargé in Berlin, Sir George Ogilvie-Forbes, who reported to Lord Halifax on September 11, 1938 that public opinion was strongly against war, but that ". . . the nation is helpless in the grip of the

[30] Main sources on this are: Testimony of Hans Bernd Gisevius before the International Military Tribunal at Nuremberg, *Trials of Major War Criminals before the International Military Tribunal* (Nuremberg: Secretariat of the IMT, 1947-49), XII, 218 ff; Interrogation of Erich Kordt, MS, Department of State; Interrogation of Halder, February 25, 1946 a. m. Erich Kordt (Verlaggesellschaft Dautsche, 1950).

For acceptance of their testimony cf. Allen Dulles, *Germany's Underground* (New York: The Macmillan Company, 1947), pp. 41-49; Hans Rothfels, *The German Opposition to Hitler* (Hinsdale, Ill.: Henry Regnery Co., 1948), pp. 58-61; Winston Churchill, *The Second World War, vol. I, The Gathering Storm* (Boston: Houghton Mifflin Company, 1948), pp. 310-312.

For criticism cf. Namier, *op. cit. passim*, and Wheeler-Bennett, *op. cit.*, pp. 404-424.

Nazi system." There was no sign of animosity toward the Czechs or the Western Powers. "The people," he wrote, "are like sheep being led to the slaughter." [31]

The conspirators hoped that with the people in this frame of mind, the refusal of the army to march into Czechoslovakia, followed by the arrest and trial of Hitler and his close associates, would avert a world war without at the same time precipitating civil war. The Germans looked traditionally to the army as a check upon the government, and its assumption of power would be accepted more readily than the seizure of the government by a small band of civilians.

Colonel-General Halder, Chief of the General Staff after September 1, 1938, in agreement with the Beck-Goerdeler group, asked General Erwin von Witzleben to draw up the military plans for the *coup*. Witzleben, commander of the Berlin District, thereupon advised the arrest of Hitler when he would return from the Party Day at Nuremberg, probably on the 13th or 14th of September. One panzer division of those which would be ordered to Czechoslovakia and which was being held in Thuringia (Third Panzer Division under General Hoeppner) would enter Berlin and occupy the city with the cooperation of Major-General Brockdorf-Rantzau, commander of the Potsdam division. Meanwhile Count Helldorf, Chief of Police in Berlin, would arrest Hitler, Goering, Goebbels, and Himmler. Finally, definite plans were laid for 8 P. M. on September 14th.

Unfortunately the whole strategy was based on the presumed willingness of General von Brauchitsch, Commander-in-Chief of the Army, to issue the necessary orders. Halder had not yet informed his superior officer but felt that he knew what was being prepared and would agree to cooperate at the proper moment.[32] The plan also depended on Hitler's order to invade Czechoslovakia which would be forthcoming only if the Western Powers refused to make the demanded concessions to him.

Consequently, when word came at 4 P. M. on the chosen after-

[31] Ogilvie-Forbes to Halifax, Berlin, September 11, 1938, *Documents on British Foreign Policy, 1919-1939*, Third Series, II (London: His Majesty's Stationery Office, 1949), p. 289.

[32] Halder Interrogation, February 25, 1946 a. m.

noon of September 14th that Chamberlain was flying to Berchtesgaden, the conspiracy was endangered. Beck still felt that the plans should be maintained until they saw the outcome of the conversations, and his viewpoint prevailed.[33] As the discussions progressed, first at Berchtesgaden, then at Godesberg, the conspirators regained hope. Paul Schmidt, official translator, kept them informed of developments,[34] and when they learned of the rejection of Hitler's Godesberg demands they reformulated their plans and set a tentative date for the *coup* for the 29th. Again fate interfered when the telephone call from Mussolini came at noon on the 28th, thereby introducing Munich.

Knowledge of the plans of the Resistance Movement had been made known to the British Foreign Office in the hope of inducing the Western Powers to resist Hitler's demands so as to provide an occasion for a revolt at home.[35] This was, however, too big a gamble for the British to take, and Hitler returned home from Munich a national hero beyond challenge, and the plans for a *coup* were buried in the wake of his glory.

Between the victory without war over Czechoslovakia and the victorious war with Poland in the autumn of 1939, the Resistance Movement simmered below the surface. There it grew in numbers and in significance, for the more the Nazis widened the sphere of their activities, the more the opposition found it necessary to build constructively for the future.[36] But for the moment the exterior manifestations of resistance were fewer.

The bold and uncontested seizure of Prague in the spring of 1939, the intensified Nazification of Danzig preparing the way for its return to the Reich, and the pact with Soviet Russia ornamented Hitler with a halo of success in foreign policy which testified to his "inspired" leadership and made open resistance foolhardy.

Nevertheless, continuous conversations kept the conspiracy alive: Goerdeler and Schacht were approaching the generals; Beck and von Hassell were exchanging ideas on basic policy for a new

[33] Kordt Interrogation, January 7, 1946.

[34] *Ibid.* Cf. Interrogations of Paul Schmidt by DeWitt C. Poole Mission, October 19, 22, and 26, 1945. MS, Department of State.

[35] *Infra.* chapter III.

[36] Von Kessel diary p. 103.

Germany; von Weizsäcker was using all possible channels to counteract Ribbentrop's foreign policy. The medium of the "Mittwoch Gesellschaft" was often used as a place for debating such issues and keeping contacts alive. But the cooperation between military and civilian participants had been weakened.

General von Witzleben had been transferred to Kassel, and this not only removed the most reliable commanding officer from the Berlin area but also eliminated the connecting link between Halder and Helldorf. Schacht and Gisevius were able to see Halder only once, and Canaris maintained only indirect contact with him.[37] Only a minor attempt was made by the military men to avoid the outbreak of hostilities, and it was made by General Georg Thomas, head of the Economics and Armaments Branch of OKW [High Command of the Armed Forces]. He visited General Keitel toward the end of August 1939 and tried to impress upon him the economic unpreparedness of the army for a major war; needless to say, it had no effect.[38]

Indeed the picture of the Resistance Movement is saddest in these days preceding the attack on Poland. One might express surprise that the failure of Hitler to live up to the Munich Agreement, the brutal pogrom of November 1938, the annihilation of Czech independence, and the increasing restrictions on domestic freedom were not sufficient stimuli to revivify the plans for a *coup d'état*. But the tendency to believe that the very excesses of the regime made its disintegration inevitable led to a postponement of action in the hope that it would not be necessary.

By October 1939 two things caused greater cohesion among the resistance elements: the reports of the atrocities being committed by the SS and the army in Poland on direct orders from Hitler, and the fear of an impending invasion of the Lowlands as a prelude to a western offensive.[39] The details of the resistance

[37] Halder Interrogation, February 26, 1946 a. m.

[38] Georg Thomas, "Gedanken und Ereignisse," *Schweizer Monatschefte* XXV (December, 1945), 537-559. This memorandum was drawn up by General Thomas shortly after his release from a Nazi concentration camp; a copy of it was submitted at the Nuremberg trials as Document No. 436-PS.

[39] Halder Interrogation, February 26, 1946 p. m.; Von Hassell, *op. cit.*, p. 75.

activities during this period deal largely with attempts to achieve an early peace and will be discussed in detail elsewhere.

The conspirators once again determined upon a D day for their projected *coup*—the date which would mark the invasion of Holland.[40] Erich Kordt, one of the young officials in the Foreign Office, had gone so far as to assign Georg Bruns the task of drawing up a list of the crimes to serve as a basis for charges at the anticipated trial of Hitler and his henchmen. For this purpose Bruns was given access to the files of the department by von Weizsäcker.[41] Representatives of the Foreign Office and the army also drew up memoranda for General von Brauchitsch opposing the plan to invade the Lowlands as an unwarrented violation of their neutrality.[42] For climatic rather than political reasons the invasion was postponed several times, and when the campaign in the west materialized in May 1940 it was executed with such rapidity that the plans laid by the conspirators in November were no longer realistic.

The years of 1940-41-42 were swallowed up in one military success after another, and the activities of the Resistance Movement were confined to seeking channels through which peace could be made with the Western Powers, and discussions at home about the need to re-establish the reign of law within Germany by removing Hitler from power. Goerdeler was indefatigable and indomitably optimistic; he pursued the generals constantly, urging them to act, but his reputation as an open anti-Nazi made most of them shun his company.

Halder continued in office until December 18, 1942 when he was dismissed for what he describes as "differences about operational tactics" with the Fuehrer.[43] He then retired to the country, and indicated that it would be dangerous for members of the Resistance

[40] Von Hassell noted: "Our goal must be to go into action the minute the order for invasion is given." von Hassell, *op. cit.*, p. 83.

[41] Affidavit of Georg Bruns, von Weizsäcker Defense Document Book No. 5.

[42] Von Hassell, *op. cit.*, p. 84.

[43] Testimony of Franz Halder, *Trials of War Criminals Before the Nuernberg Military Tribunal* ed. United States Department of the Army (Washington, D. C.: Government Printing Office, 1949-53), XII, 1082. Hereafter cited as *T of WC*. Cf. Halder Interrogation, February 25, 1946 a. m.

to visit him;[44] his days with the conspiracy were now definitely over and they could no longer look to him for help. During these years the most substantial contribution to resistance was probably that of the ABWEHR where the group around Oster and Canaris did their best to end the war and bring about the downfall of Hitler by relaying information to the Allies.[45] But, on the whole, this was the time when opportunities were lost.

Meanwhile, another resistance group was taking root in eastern Germany—the so-called Kreisau circle gathered around Count Helmuth von Moltke.[46] This predominantly youthful group was interested in fundamental problems of society such as religion, social justice, and educational reforms. At his estate called Kreisau in Silesia, von Moltke met with Peter Yorck von Wartenburg, Adam Trott zu Solz, Father Alfred Delp, S. J., Pastor Eugen Gerstenmaier, Franz Reisert, Theodor Haubach, Theodor Steltzer, Paulus van Husen, Hans Lukaschek, Franz Sperr, Josef Ernst Fugger zu Glott, Adolf Reichwein, Julius Leber, Hans von Haeften, Carlo Mierendorff, Pastor Harald Poelchau, Horst von Einsiedel, Dietrich von Trotha, Father König, and Countesses von Moltke and Yorck. Later the group expanded to include many in the workers' group around Wilhelm Leuschner.

Drawn together by their strong objections to the fundamental principles and brutal methods of the Nazi regime, these men discussed and debated the political, economic, and social issues involved in an attempt to restore the reign of law in the German state. As Pechel describes them:

> All these men felt deeply the responsibility toward Europe for what had happened and what must now happen. The

---

[44] Halder Interrogation, November 22, 1945 a. m.

[45] *Infra.* chapter IV.

[46] On the Kreisau circle cf. Theodor Steltzer, *Von Deutscher Politik*, herausgegeben von Friedrich Minssen (Frankfurt Am Main: Josef Knecht, 1949); Helmuth Moltke, *Letzte Briefe aus dem Gefängnis Tegel* (Berlin: K. H. Henssel, 1951); Rudolf Pechel, *Deutscher Widerstand* (Erlenbach-Zurich: E. Rentsch, 1947); Hans Rothfels, *op. cit.*, pp. 112-129; Dulles, *op. cit.*, pp. 81-96. The report drawn up by Kaltenbruner for Borman on the entire July 20, 1944 plot also contains much interesting material on Kreisau. Reichssicherheitshauptamt Bericht über den Juli 20, 1944, MS, Department of the Army.

> will, common to all, for a personal inner clarification of the problems lying before Germany bound them together in the effort to make live again for Germany the sources of the western spirit which had always fed Europe and on which she had grown and matured.[47]

The crimes for which these men of Kreisau were executed, following the abortive attempt on Hitler's life on July 20, 1944, were defeatism, and, as von Moltke himself put it, the fact of being "Christians."[48]

Through Adam Trott zu Solz the Kreisau group had connections with the group of resisters in the Foreign Office; Moltke was in an advantageous spot in Canaris's office, handling international law problems for OKW; later on the group joined hands with Colonel Count Claus Stauffenberg and his military supporters. Hence, although they themselves were not planning a violent overthrow of the government they were part of the whole pattern of resistance and did not work in isolation. We might consider their role as that of a post-war planning board, concerned with an "*attentat*" only in so far as it paved the way for their "new Germany." By joint discussions with the Beck-Goerdeler group some of the differences in their concepts of an ideal Christian state were ironed out.

While these plans were being created in the fall of 1942 and spring of 1943, the entrance of Colonel Count Claus von Stauffenberg into the resistance picture put new life into the whole movement. A battle hero, wounded in North Africa, this young officer had long been known to his fellow-officers as anti-Nazi. In the summer of 1943 he was brought to Berlin as Chief of Staff to General Olbricht in the Replacement Army [*Allgemeines Heeresamt*]. There he was able to work with his chief and with Major-General Henning von Tresckow in drawing up plans for the military occupation of Berlin, urgently needed in case of a *putsch*.

The importance of von Stauffenberg's adhesion to the group of conspirators lies not only in his willingness to attempt the assassination of Hitler but, even more, in the dynamic quality in his

[47] Pechel, *op. cit.*, p. 120. Translation mine.
[48] Letter to his wife, January 11, 1945. Moltke, *op. cit.*, p. 56.

personality which infused confidence into others and thus re-invigorated the entire movement. This effect is witnessed in his meeting with Adam Trott zu Solz in January 1944 of which one author has written:

> There is evidence that this association was the polarizing of two dynamic convictions, from which a disciplined new energy was released. Stauffenberg's passionate resolution and Trott's deeper grasp of political realities produced a unity of purpose and initiated a train of action that had so long been absent although earlier attempts on Hitler's life had been made.[49]

Thus it happened that the culmination of the efforts and plans of the German Resistance Movement—July 20, 1944—was largely the work of these younger men in the different groups. Beck was still nominally the leader, but the serious operation which he had undergone in 1943 had left him in very poor health; Goerdeler was by now too well known to the Gestapo to permit him much freedom of movement and, besides, the younger elements considered him an ultra-conservative; Moltke was already in jail. Nevertheless it would be a serious mistake to consider the final attempt on Hitler's life apart from all that had gone before it, for the young men had been led and inspired by the courage and foresight of those who had begun what they were now to finish. The structural unity of the Resistance Movement did not depend on individual personalities as much as on unanimity of spirit.

Von Stauffenberg as Chief of Staff for the Replacement Army had frequent access to Hitler's presence and was thus in the best position to undertake the actual assassination. After two or three planned moments proved unsuitable, the date was set for July 20, 1944. The story has been told at length in several works;[50] it represents the desperation of men, who, although they knew the war was lost and "unconditional surrender" lay before them, took the last chance offered to them to show the world that "another Germany" than that of the Nazi war-lords still existed. Un-

[49] David Hopkinson, "The Lesson of the German Resistance," *The Contemporary Review*, CLXXV (January, 1949), 18.

[50] Reichssicherheitshauptamt Bericht, über den 20 Juli, MS, Department of the Army. Hereafter cited as RSHA report. Wheeler-Bennett, *op. cit.*, pp. 635-693. Allen Dulles, *op. cit.*, pp. 175-194.

doubtedly they hoped for the success of the *coup,* but apparently considered it morally necessary even if it failed. The general mood may well be expressed in the words of von Tresckow to von Schlabrendorff before taking his own life after the plot failed:

> Everybody will now turn upon us and cover us with abuse. But my conviction remains unshaken—we have done the right thing. Hitler is not only the archenemy of Germany, he is the archenemy of the whole world. In a few hours' time I shall be before God, answering for my actions and my omissions, and I shall uphold with a clear conscience all that I have done in the fight against Hitler. God promised Abraham to spare Sodom should there be found ten just men in the city. He will, I trust, spare Germany for our sake, and not destroy her. Whoever joined the Resistance movement had to realize that his life was doomed. A man's moral value begins only when he is prepared to sacrifice his life for his convictions.[51]

That the attempted assassination failed may well have altered the course of German history, but it could not change the essential element in the whole story of resistance. The men whom we have been discussing were willing to sacrifice their lives, if necessary, to redeem the soul of Germany. The failure of the *coup* made the offered sacrifice a reality for most of the conspirators; hence, with July 20, 1944 the German Resistance Movement came to an end.

But an analysis of resistance within Germany would be incomplete without a brief reference to the smaller groups outside the main stream with which we have been concerned. Of great interest, in attempting an ethical and religious study of opposition to Hitler, is the Scholl group at the University of Munich.[52] Taking its name from a young medical student, Hans Scholl, the circle of friends included his sister, Sophie, Christl Probst, Alexander Schmorell, and Willi Graf (all fellow students) and Kurt Huber, professor of philosophy.

These young students in their early twenties had learned from their experiences in the army and from their observation of the SS that the freedom and honor of which the Hitler Youth leaders had boastfully taught them were far from true liberty. Influenced

[51] Von Schlabrendorff, *op. cit.*, p. 120.

[52] Inge Scholl, *Die weisse Rose* (Frankfurt am Main: Frankfurter Hefte, 1952).

by his home training and his reading of the classical philosophers and the Christian Fathers, Hans became convinced that the true answer to the questions which disquieted him were contained in Holy Scripture and not in Nazi ideology.

In discussions with his friends and Professor Huber, the fundamental evil of the Nazi system became more clear and the will to resist it was born. In the spring of 1942 these courageous students began to write, mimeograph, and distribute pamphlets which were designed to arouse opposition to the Hitler regime. Kurt Huber summarized their purpose thus:

> Our task will be to cry out the truth as clearly and as audibly as possible in the German night. We must seek to enkindle the spark of resistance which glimmers in millions of honest German hearts so that it will glow bright and courageous. The individual who stands alone and isolated in his rejection of Hitler must receive through such an action the feeling that there stands near him a large band of like-minded men. That will strengthen his courage and perseverance. Beyond that, we seek to clarify the issue for that part of the Germans who are still not clear about the bad intentions of our regime, and moreover to awaken in them the spark of resistance and an upright defence. Perhaps we shall succeed in shaking off the common tyranny in the final hour and together with the other people of Europe in recognizing in that hour a wonderful moment for building up a new humane world in which the nations and states will feel themselves to be neighbors and not enemies.[53]

After attending regular classes during the day, they worked most of the night printing and distributing their *Flugblätter der weissen Rose.* They urged the Germans to abandon the Nazi way of life and return to fundamental Christian principles of law, justice, and peace, and insisted that passive resistance would no longer suffice if the atheistic Nazi war machine were to be stopped. Into Munich, Linz, Salzburg, Wien, Frankfurt on Main, Stuttgart and elsewhere went their pamphlets, and in those cities others again mimeographed copies and spread them further abroad.

Such denunciations of the government could not go unnoticed by the omnipresent Gestapo. On February 16, 1943 the Gauleiter of

[53] *Ibid.*, p. 44. Translation mine.

Bavaria, Paul Giesler, who had already seen some of the pamphlets prepared by the Scholls, gave a lecture on patriotism to the students at the University of Munich. Urging the young men to spurn defeatism because of military set-backs, he went on to say that each young woman's patriotic duty while a student was to present the Fuehrer ". . . with an annual testimonial in the form of a son." He would be glad, he added, to furnish the fathers. Such an immoral purpose was greeted, incredibly in fear-ridden Nazi Germany, with howls and shouts from the students, leading to rioting in the streets of Munich.[54]

The turmoil had scarcely died down when the next publication of the Scholls appeared. Stressing the military debacle of Stalingrad, they attempted to arouse their fellow students to revolt against a government which was pulling them toward chaos, both at home and abroad.

> The day of reckoning has come, of reckoning between our German youth and the most abominable tyranny our nation has ever tolerated. In the name of the entire German people we demand back from the State of Adolph Hitler our personal freedom. . . . For us, there is but one watchword: war on the Party. . . . Even the dullest German's eyes have been opened by the dreadful blood bath that they have poured forth over Europe, and are pouring forth every day anew, in the name of German national freedom and honor. The German name will be disgraced forever unless German youth arises, avenges, and atones, at last, at once crushing its tormentors and building a new intellectual Europe.[55]

The authors were discovered and arrested without delay. A special trial court was convened under the same ignoble character who would later sit in judgment on the men of July 20—Roland Freisler—and the verdict was not difficult to predict. They were found guilty of defeatism, incitement to sabotage, and preparation for a new way of life based on the presupposition that Hitler would be removed from power. On February 22, Hans, Sophie, and

[54] Wheeler-Bennett, *op. cit.*, p. 540.

[55] " Flugblätter der weissen Rose " printed in Scholl, *op. cit.*, pp. 108-110. The translation used is from Ruth Andreas-Friedrich, *Berlin Underground, 1938-45*, trans. Barrows Mussey (New York: H. Holt and Co., 1947), p. 96.

Christl Probst were hanged; the others followed them in July and October of the same year.

While the Scholls were apparently not in direct contact with the conspirators in Berlin, they were aware of each other's activities through Karl Muth, founder and publisher of *Hochland,* a Catholic paper.[56] Von Hassell, upon hearing of their execution, wrote in his diary:

> I have read the simple, splendid, deeply ethical national appeal which brought them to their death. Himmler apparently did not want any martyrs and ordered a stay of execution, but it came several hours too late. It is important for the future that such an appeal should have seen the light of day. . . . The brave Scholls died on the gallows, courageous and upright martyrs.[57]

Finally, resistance in Germany is also to be found in such consistently anti-Nazi groups as the "Uncle Emil" and the Solf circle, to cite but two of what may well have been a large number of informal centers of opposition. The former is fully described in the diary of Ruth Andreas-Friedrich,[58] and presents a picture of persons on the periphery of government service, many of them journalists, who revolted against the suppression of freedom and the persecution of the Jews even before Hitler's aggressive foreign policy bore its natural fruit.

They had valuable contacts with persons in the government such as Erich Kordt and Helmuth von Moltke, and in so far as they could they shielded many Jews, shared rations with them, and helped them to emigrate. While not taking an active part in any of the specific plots to remove Hitler from power, they manifested deep sympathy with the conspirators and encouraged them in their efforts.

After the condemnation of von Moltke and his friends to death, Ruth Andreas-Friedrich and a companion went to the Catholic Church and requested that a Requiem Mass be offered on the morning of January 10, 1945 ". . . for fifteen souls that will be leaving

[56] Wheeler-Bennett, *op. cit.*, p. 540.

[57] Von Hassell, *op. cit.*, p. 296.

[58] Andreas-Friedrich, *op. cit.*

this world at that time without the consolation of the sacrament."[59] Moreover, it was to them that Frau Freya von Moltke came in this time of trouble and from their conversations one can easily sense the mutual devotion to the ideals of Christianity from which they drew their inspiration.[60]

Devotion to freedom and a desire to restore a sense of justice and honor to German life are also the reasons for the Solf Kreis. Frau Hanna Solf, widow of the former German Ambassador to Japan, was the center of this group of anti-Nazi men and women, including the former Consul in New York, Otto Kiep, a Rhodes scholar, Albrecht von Bernstorff, and Fräulein Elizabeth von Thadden, headmistress of a girls' school near Heidelberg.[61] Unfortunately, a Gestapo agent, Dr. Reckzeh, was taken into their confidence, and the whole group was imprisoned on January 12, 1944. Because von Moltke tried to warn Kiep of the impending danger of arrest, he too was seized; most of the members of the Solf circle were executed after the July 20 affair. Limited in influence and without means of significant protest against a regime which ruled by sheer force, this small circle of decent men and women added its voice to the spirit of protest and personified the refusal of so many to submit to the process of Nazification.

Resistance to Hitler in Germany was, then, a unique manifestation of the human passion for freedom. It drew from the ranks of the military and civilian leaders; it rose and fell in intensity and cohesion as do all human movements; it built great dreams and failed to realize them. Effective police control did much to discourage the average man from participating in these recognized groups of anti-Nazis, but the men with above-average courage and conviction worked on despite failure, discouragement, and intimidation.

What they did must indeed have been done from a higher motive than the desire for honor, power, or riches, since there was little hope for such reward. Yet, the very ethical ideals which inspired them were sadly lacking in practical clarification. The

[59] *Ibid.*, p. 186. It is interesting to note that neither she nor her companion was a Catholic. p. 187.

[60] *Ibid.*, pp. 181, 195. Cf. *Infra.* p. 96.

[61] Pechel, *op. cit.*, p. 88.

problems which confronted them in their search for a clearly delineated goal will furnish the substance of our investigation, and an attempt will be made to examine the solutions which were offered by individuals and groups, at the same time estimating the extent to which the conspirators adopted them as their own. The history of such a movement as the German Resistance would be meaningless, and even misleading, were the motives of those who participated in it to remain uninvestigated, for the line which marks off an anarchist from a legitimate revolutionary, and a traitor from a true patriot, is often a narrow one.

CHAPTER II

Resistance to Tyranny

Did the recognition of the arbitrary use of power by Hitler's police state imply to the average German a concurrent right to resist actively the authority of that government? Should it have implied that? The answers to these questions are fundamental if we wish to understand the problems in the moral order which confronted the members of the German Underground.

If the right of resistance against a tyrannical government was commonly believed and taught in German ethical and theological writings, there would be nothing remarkable about the convictions and actions of the men of the Resistance. But, obviously it was not as simple as that. Rather, the conspirators against the Hitler regime had to become rebels in a twofold sense: against the Nazi ideology, and against much of German ethical and religious thought.

Undoubtedly the average citizen of the Third Reich was more inclined to avoid critical investigation of the objectionable policies of the government and to concentrate his attention on the benefits which the Nazi rule had brought to Germany and to himself. Among these, he could cite glibly: higher rate of employment, greater respect for Germany among foreign nations, improved transportation and communication facilities, and greater educational and social opportunities for the "little man." But if, prompted by some disquietude of conscience over the vicious and brutal Gestapo methods of dealing with "enemies of the regime," he raised for himself the question of active resistance against the government, where could he have found assurance of its being morally justifiable?

One of the foremost Catholic theologians in modern Germany, Father Max Pribilla S. J., submitted a statement to the Nuremberg Tribunal on behalf of Veesenmayer, a defendent in the Ministries

Case.[1] He set forth the points which he thought should be taken into consideration in assessing the guilt of those who did not resist Hitler, and his views will be useful in our attempt to establish the general framework of reference for our problem.

Father Pribilla reminded the tribunal that the Germans of the Third Reich grew up in an authoritarian and not a democratic state and that, as a result:

> The idea that the individual citizen is responsible for the state and must supervise the government of the state is foreign to his national consciousness. On the contrary, the German expects directives from his government for his political thinking and action and is inclined to see his duty and prove his reliability in loyal adherence to these directives.

Such a point of view led them to obey the laws of the Nazi state even when they doubted the wisdom of Hitler's policies, especially his war policies. The explanation which Father Pribilla gave was that the German believed: (1) All responsibility rested on the government; (2) In a state of emergency [legally recognized in the Emergency decrees of February 28, 1934 and the Enabling Act of March 23, 1934], opposition would mean a concentration camp or death, and would therefore be useless; (3) Without access to the pertinent documents in the Foreign Office, an individual could not judge correctly the international scene and the justice of Hitler's policies; (4) The moral justification of resistance was by no means clear in the writings of moral theologians.

The last point is an extremely important one and requires some explanation. Making clear the dilemma of the Catholic in Germany who sought guidance in justifying resistance to Hitler, Father Pribilla explained that among Catholic moral theologians there are two schools of thought on the problem. Among Protestant theologians there was less division; almost all of them held resistance by an individual to be unjustifiable. We shall summarize briefly the important views of each group.

The teaching of the Catholic Church may be gathered from a study of natural law, Holy Scripture, the teaching of the Church

[1] Affidavit of Rev. Max Pribilla, S. J., Jan. 26, 1948. Veesenmayer defense document # 34. MS, Department of the Army.

Fathers, the Scholastics, and the ordinary teaching magisterium as evidenced in such pronouncements as papal encyclicals and episcopal letters. Utilizing these sources, certain conclusions are accepted by all Catholic theologians: (1) All authority comes from God and must be obeyed in so far as its laws are just; (2) A just law is one dictated by right reason, promulgated by him who has charge of the community, and designed to promote the common good; (3) If a law is unjust (because it violates one of the above standards) it may be disobeyed; (4) If a law commands something sinful it must be disobeyed.

What form should such disobedience take? Here the theologians are not unanimous. According to the Reverend Albert-Marie Mignault O. P., who has made a detailed study of the problem,[2] there are four possibilities: passive disobedience, use of legal means to have the law changed, armed self-defense against force used by the government to compel obedience, or a rebellion in which the people take the offensive against the authority from which the law emanated. While the first three are permissible, the fourth, according to Mignault, is not.

> Cette doctrine du droit de révolte et d'insurrection agressive contre un gouvernement tyrannique dans son exercise, mais légitimement constitué, n'est pas la doctrine de l'Église catholique.[3]

Two observations must be made regarding this opinion. Mignault uses the term "aggressive insurrection" but does not give an example nor does he indicate whether all popular uprisings would be included in it. Secondly, this study was made in 1921, before the rise of the modern totalitarian state, and is written in terms of resistance to certain unjust laws rather than to a state system which exercises its legally acquired power in an unlawful manner.

Saint Thomas Aquinas also condemns "aggressive insurrection" which he denotes as "sedition," but he states clearly that a revolt against a tyrannical government is not sedition.

---

[2] Albert-Marie Mignault, O. P., *La résistance aux lois injustes et la doctrine catholique* (Montreal: Bibliothèque de l'action française, 1921).

[3] *Ibid.*, p. 142.

> A tyrannical regime is never just, because it is ordained not to the good of the people, but to that of the ruler himself (this being the definition of tyrannical rule). And, therefore, to disturb a regime of this kind is not sedition . . . rather it is the tyrant who is guilty of sedition by sowing discords among the people in order that his dominion over them may be the more secure.[4]

According to some theologians who have developed this idea further, a revolt against tyranny is not, therefore, the aggressive insurrection which is always a serious sin, but an act of self-defence. To guarantee its character as such, it must fulfill certain conditions:

> (1) The government must be substantially and habitually tyrannical, and that is when it has lost sight of the common good, and pursues its own selfish objects to the manifest detriment of the subjects, especially where their religious interests are concerned; (2) when all legal and pacific means have been tried in vain to recall the ruler to a sense of his duty; (3) when there is a reasonable probability that resistance will be successful, and not entail greater evils than it seeks to remove; (4) when the judgment formed as to the badness of the government, and the prudence of resistance thereto, is not the opinion only of private persons or of a mere party, but is that of the larger and better portion of the people, so that it may morally be considered the judgment of the community as a whole.[5]

Granted that such a justification of active resistance exists in Catholic theology, to what extent was it taught in pre-Hitler Germany? Would the men who felt that " something ought to be done " to stop the Nazis have been apt to come under the influence of such ideas? Father Pribilla cited two of the best known Catholic texts in moral theology, presumably in wide use in Germany; both

[4] Thomas Aquinas, *Summa theologica,* trans. Fathers of the English Dominican Province (N. Y.: Benziger Bros., 1947), IIa, 2ae, q. 42, 2. However, in chapter VI of the *De regimine principum,* Saint Thomas cautions that " if there be not an excess of tyranny it is more expedient to tolerate for a while the milder tyranny than, by acting against the tyrant, to be involved in many perils which are more grievous than the tyranny itself." trans. Gerald B. Phelan (Toronto: St. Michael's College, 1935), p. 54.

[5] Michael Cronin, *The Science of Ethics* (2nd ed.; N. Y.: Benziger Bros., 1922), II, 542.

omit the distinction noted above between "rebellion" and "justified self-defence" against a tyrannical government. Reverend Antony Koch states:

> Laws which imperil higher rights or interests may be resisted by all legal means, such as remonstrances, appeals, petitions, agitation in the public press. To employ illegal means is tantamount to sedition. No matter what the provocation, revolution against a legitimate government is forbidden, because revolution by its very concept is an attack upon actually existing and divinely sanctioned rights. Pius IX solemnly condemned the proposition that 'It is permitted to withhold obedience from legitimate rulers, nay even to rebel against them.'[6]

Possibly it could be argued that a tyrannical ruler is no longer a "legitimate ruler" in the sense used here, but nothing in Koch's work indicates such a distinction.

In agreement with Koch is the position of the former Superior of the Eichstaett Seminary, the Reverend Johann Pruner, who states unequivocally:

> Aucune révolte, aucune résistance active n'est permise contre les souverains injustes et tyranniques qui oppriment le peuple, lorsqu'ils exercent légitimement le pouvoir souverain.[7]

Father Pruner does concede that some Catholic writers have seemed to permit rebellion against tyranny in certain cases, but the form of "rebellion" is apparently "to invoke the help of the potentate" against the ruler appointed by him. The possibility of applying this theory in Nazi Germany is obviously very questionable.

At the trial which took place after the July 20 affair, a certain Chaplain Hermann Wehrle · S. J. was called before the People's Court. It was to him that a young officer of Colonel Count Stauffenberg's staff, a Major Leonrod, had gone to ask if it would

[6] Antony Koch, *A Handbook of Moral Theology,* trans. and ed. Arthur Preuss (St. Louis: B. Herder Book Co., 1918-1921), I, 168.

[7] Johann Ev. Pruner, *Théologie morale, Bibliothèque théologique du XIX siècle,* 2 vols. trans. Abbé P. Belet (Genève; Grosset et Tremblay, 1880), I, p. 617. Father Pruner relies largely on I Peter II, 18: "Servants, be subject to your masters in all fear, not only to the good and moderate, but also to the severe."

be a sin not to reveal knowledge of a plot against the Fuehrer's life.[8] Wehrle told the court that he had consulted the *Lexicon für Theologie und Kirche* on the subject of "Tyrannenmord" before answering the young man's question. What would he have found there?

In the *Lexicon*, the article on "Tyrannenmord" was written by K. Hilgenreiner,[9] and the description of the Church's teaching on the subject of resistance is similar to that already cited from Koch and Pruner. It is granted that one who has usurped the throne—"tyrannus usurpationis" may be killed by state authority, by an individual given a mandate to do so by the state, or, in extreme danger, by a private individual on his own initiative. But the second kind of tyrant, "tyrannus regiminis"—one who has come into power legitimately but is ruling arbitrarily and despotically—may not be brought to death by "private authority" in any case.

It mentions the defense of active resistance by John of Salisbury in the twelfth century and the justification of tyrannicide by a private individual by Juan Mariana S. J. in the sixteenth. The teaching of the latter was, however, without support in Catholic circles; the Father General of the Society of Jesus, Aquaviva, forbade the members to teach this doctrine.[10] The article then points out that tyrannicide was condemned in the *Syllabus* of 1864.

From his reading of this article in the *Lexicon* Chaplain Wehrle concluded that it would not be a sin to keep secret the plot, but

[8] RSHA report, 30 Aug. 1944, Dept. of the Army. MS, 105/24. Wheeler-Bennett, *op. cit.*, p. 543 note, states that Leonrod asked Chaplain Wehrle if it would be a sin to kill a tyrant, but the RSHA report only seems to indicate that the question concerned revealing knowledge of a plan to kill him.

[9] "Tyrannenmord," *Lexicon für Theologie und Kirche* (Freiburg im Breisgau; Herder and Co., 1938), X, 346-48.

[10] Although John of Salisbury had justified tyrannicide in the case of a ruler who habitually abuses his position, his teaching does not seem to have been condemned. In his *Policraticus* he wrote: "The prince, as the likeness of the Deity is to be loved, worshipped and cherished; the tyrant, the likeness of wickedness, is generally to be even killed. *The Statesman's Book of John of Salisbury* trans. John Dickinson. (N. Y.: Alfred A. Knopf, 1927), p. 336. Frederick Copleston, S. J., in his *A History of Philosophy* vol. III (Westminster, Md.: The Newman Press, 1953), p. 347, states that although Mariana's principle was traditional his conclusions were misguided.

nevertheless he warned Leonrod not to take an active part in it.[11] When asked in court if he considered Hitler to have been a tyrant within the meaning used in this article, he replied in the affirmative. Unfortunately he did not specify which type of tyrant he had in mind.

Finally, writings and pronouncements of recent popes add nothing in the way of a clear statement on the right of active resistance. Encyclicals directed to those suffering under an unjust and persecuting government in Mexico, Spain, and Russia, as well as Germany,[12] uphold and commend those who refuse to obey the unjust laws of their country, but never encourage the citizens to open revolt.

The writings of Leo XIII lay great emphasis on the evils which result from open rebellion [13] but should not be read apart from the historical situation for which he wrote them. For in the late nineteenth and early twentieth centuries, the "rebellions" were inspired by the anti-clerical and anti-monarchist groups in the various countries of Europe. Hence, it would appear that the words of Leo XIII are directed to those who sought to overthrow their legitimate governments for selfish ends rather than for the common good.

The rise of the totalitarian state brought with it a new and complex situation. It was soon condemned by the Holy See because of its extension of controls over every facet of human life and endeavor.

---

[11] RSHA report, 19 Aug. 1944, Dept. of the Army, MS, 105/23.

[12] Pius XI, *Acerba Animi* (On Mexico), Sept. 29, 1932; *Firmissimam Constantiam* (On Mexico), Mar. 28, 1937; *Dilectissima Nobis* (On Spain), June 3, 1933; *Mit brennender Sorge* (On Germany), March 14, 1937; *Divini Redemptoris* (On Russia), March 19, 1937. All of these can be found in Joseph Husslein, S. J., *Social Wellsprings*, Vol. II (Milwaukee; Bruce Publishing Co., 1942).

[13] For example in his encyclical *Immortale Dei*, Leo XIII wrote: "To cast aside obedience and by popular violence to incite to revolt, is therefore, treason, not against man only, but against God." Yet, he also reaffirms the teaching that unjust laws which are repugnant to the natural or divine law should not be obeyed. Cf. *Diuturnum* and *Sapientiae Christianae*. For the text of these encyclicals with useful annotations cf. Joseph Husslein, S. J., *Social Wellsprings* (Milwaukee: Bruce Publishing Co., 1940).

> Once the authority of God and the sway of His law are denied in this way [i. e. by according the civil authority an unrestricted field of action] the civil authority as an inevitable result tends to attribute to itself that absolute autonomy which belongs exclusively to the Supreme Maker. It puts itself in the place of the Almighty and elevates the State or group into the last end of life, the supreme criterion of the moral and juridical order, and therefore forbids every appeal to the principles of natural reason and of the Christian conscience.[14]

That an intolerable situation existed for the citizens of the Third Reich had already been recognized by Pope Pius XI in his stinging denunciation of the Nazi regime.[15] Countless infringements on individual and parental rights, exaltation of one race and one state at the expense of international peace, and the deification of the person of the Fuehrer were all condemned. The pope complained of the repeated violations of the Concordat and praised the Catholic clergy and laity who were resisting in the face of "aggressive paganism." But, again, we find no intimation that a revolt would be mandatory or even justifiable.

Whether this hesitation to invoke a policy of open resistance is inspired by clear-cut moral doctrine, by papal desire not to interfere in the national affairs of her children, or by a disinclination to urge them to a course of action which might bring greater evils upon them in case of failure cannot be known with certainty. In any case, it appears that the general sources from which a German Catholic of the 1930's might have sought an answer to his problems were, at best, extremely confusing on this question of resistance. He would have discovered little which would have encouraged him to defend his rights against the tyrannical government, and almost nothing which would have justified tyrannicide.

On the other hand, what was offered to German Protestants from their theological teachers? The founders of the two most significant denominations, Martin Luther and John Calvin, stood on the same fundamental ground—that all resistance to rulers is wicked—resting their case largely on the quotation from Saint Paul:

> Let everyone be subject to the higher authorities, for there

[14] Pius XII, *Summi Pontificatus,* October 20, 1939. NCWC translation.
[15] Pius XI, *Mit brennender Sorge,* Mar. 14, 1937.

> exists no authority except from God, and those who exist have been appointed by God. Therefore he who resists the authority resists the ordinance of God; and they that resist bring on themselves condemnation.[16]

This doctrince was amplified in the writings of Luther and remained the traditional position of his followers [17] until the days of Martin Niemoeller and the Confessing Church. Because of historical circumstances, the persistence of this view in Germany is understandable. Luther's rupture from Rome caused him to turn to the German princes to enforce the reforms which he desired to effect. Dependent upon their active cooperation, he naturally preached the duty of unconditional obedience to them on the part of their subjects.[18]

> The princes of this world are gods, the common people are Satan, through whom God sometimes does what at other times he does directly through Satan, i. e., makes rebellion as a punishment for the people's sins. . . . I would rather suffer a prince doing wrong than a people doing right.[19]

Furthermore, he left his followers in no doubt about the evil of such rebellion:

> It is in no wise proper for anyone who would be a Christian to set himself up against his government, whether it act justly or unjustly. . . .[20]
>
> There are no better works than to obey and serve all those who are set over us as superiors. For this reason also disobedience is a greater sin than murder, unchastity, theft, and dishonesty, and all that these may include.[21]

The evolution of Lutheranism into a state-dominated church naturally meant the perpetuation of this teaching in its most

[16] Rom. XIII, 1. Cf. the discussion on this point in George H. Sabine, *A History of Political Theory* (N. Y.: Henry Holt and Co., 1950), pp. 354-398; and J. W. Allen, *A History of Political Thought in the Sixteenth Century* (London: Methuen & Co., 1928), pp. 15-30 and 52-60.

[17] Sabine, *op. cit.*, pp. 356-362.

[18] *Ibid.*, p. 356.

[19] Quoted by Preserved Smith, *The Age of the Reformation* (N. Y.: Henry Holt & Co., 1920), pp. 594-595.

[20] *Ibid.*, p. 595.

[21] Quoted in Sabine, *op. cit.*, p. 361.

rigorous form. The predominance of the Lutheran church over all others in Germany, especially in places of learning and political significance, led to a pervasion of the entire national mentality by this theory.[21a]

Meanwhile, the church of Calvin took root and developed mainly in Holland, Scotland, and America, and became "the chief medium through which the justification of resistance was spread through western Europe." [22] Calvin had taught that the civil magistrate must be regarded as the vicar of God to be obeyed as God himself, but this presupposed a church-dominated state such as that of Geneva. His ecclesiastical descendants often found themselves in a less favored position and were forced, as it were, into a camp of opposition to the government.

Calvin had taught, however, that if the constitution of a state provided for inferior magistrates charged with the duty of resisting a tyrannical ruler, then this might be accepted as a means of resistance provided by God. Such magistrates had not only a right to resist but a duty to do so: "The sovereign power is held jointly and one sharer has the duty to prevent aggression by another." [23]

It was this "loophole" which was used to justify Calvinists' action in France and Scotland of the late sixteenth century. John Knox, a rabid opponent of the Catholic Queen of Scotland, rejected completely the doctrine of passive obedience.

> For now the common song of all men is, We must obey our kings, be they good or be they bad; for God hath so commanded. But horrible shall the vengeance be, that shall be

[21a] This is true despite the Calvinism of the Hohenzollerns.

[22] Sabine, *op. cit.*, p. 362.

[23] Calvin had in mind an institution similar to the "tribunes of the people" in Rome or the Ephors who served as a check on the Lacedemonian kings. Cf. *Institutes of the Christian Religion* trans. John Allen (Phila.: Presbyterian Board of Christian Education, 1936), Book IV, Ch. XX, Sects. 30-31. This Calvinist concept was brought before the Nuremberg Tribunal by Kurt Welzendorff in his attempt to clarify the German outlook on the problem of resistance. Affidavit of Kurt Welzendorff, April 30, 1948. Vessenmayer defense document # 32. Calvin also cited examples from the Old Testament, such as Judith and Debbora who received special missions from God.

> poured forth upon such blasphemers of God, his holy name and ordinance. For it is no less blasphemy to say that God hath commanded kings to be obeyed when they command impiety, than to say that God by his precept is author and maintainer of all iniquity.[24]

Knox's position was based, however, not on a defense of the natural rights of the subjects but on the necessity to correct and repress the Catholic monarch's "idolatry." He did much, nevertheless, to undermine the inviolability of the sovereign's person.

The teachings of Knox apparently made little impression on German thought. The same can be said of the Monarchomachs, represented especially by the unknown author of the *Vindiciae contra tyrannos* (1599) and George Buchanan. The contributions of the Jesuits—Bellarmine, Suarez, and Mariana—were also without evident influence on German political theory. While civil wars and revolutions in France, Holland, Scotland, England, and America were defended by both Calvinists and Catholics (especially the Jesuits) such was not the case in Germany.[25] The strong tradition of Lutheranism, augmented by the philosophy of Kant, colored the mentality of the people as a whole regardless of their religious affiliation, and the common view favored passive acceptance of political inequity if such were the expression of God's Providence.

Thus, although the Churches themselves resisted and protested against many of the most flagrant laws of the Third Reich,[26] they did not provide in their doctrinal teaching the necessary impetus for the men of the Resistance Movement.[27] This should not be

[24] John Knox, *Appelation.* Cited in Sabine, *op. cit.*, p. 369. Cf. Allen, *op. cit.*, pp. 106-118 for discussion of Knox's break with Calvin's teaching on resistance.

[25] For the development of the theory of resistance outside of Germany cf. Sabine, *op. cit.*, pp. 372-396. Jesuits and Calvinists alike argued that power rested in the people, was derived from them by contract, and could be revoked if King became a tyrant, p. 388. Also cf. Allen *op. cit.*, passim.

[26] *Infra.* chapter VI.

[27] Present recognition within Germany of the need to restudy the question of resistance in the light of the modern totalitarian state is indicated in the formation of a group around Generalmajor Herman von Witzleben in Munich within the past few years. Military men, jurists, professors,

interpreted to mean that the Christian training which those men had received did not play a large part in motivating them to revolt against the corruption and degradation of the Nazi state; it means only that the right to overthrow that government by force was not clearly delimited in the theology of the churches.

Was there, then, perhaps a legal basis on which they could rest their case? In an affidavit submitted at Nuremberg, a distinguished authority on German constitutional law, Kurt Welzendorff, denied that there was anything in the legal tradition to justify open revolt.[28]

> A stipulation of unwritten positive law, which stipulation would exempt the resistance of the people as a special matter pertaining to constitutional law—from the general bans and prohibitions and which would declare it justified, is completely unimaginable for us, because it would stand in contrast to our present attitude of the essence of State and Law and the interconnections existing between them.

It is suggested that this statement contains the key to the German dilemma. The "present attitude of the essence of State and Law" was one which had lost touch with the fundamental Thomistic principle that "Law is a dictate of right reason."[29] Material law was the all-important aspect, and when this was transformed by the Nazis into a "theology of revelations of the Fuehrer," the only question that could arise was "whether the will of the Fuehrer was expressed in such a concrete way as to reflect the will of the State."[30] In such a legal system, law emanated from the will of the ruler, whether that be the Reichstag or the Fuehrer, without reference to objective natural law.

But the right of resistance must be predicated on the existence of an external natural law in which man finds his "rights" which

Catholic priests, and Protestant clergymen have met for several discussions on the problems involved—e. g. the oath, the problem of resistance, of tyrannicide, etc. Their discussions are being published in *Europäische Publikation.* The present writer is indebted to Gen. von Witzleben for several kind letters and for a personal interview on Feb. 22, 1954.

[28] Affidavit of Kurt Welzendorff, April 30, 1948. Veesenmayer defense document # 32.

[29] Thomas Aquinas, *Summa theologica,* Ia, 2ae, q. 90, 4.

[30] Statement of Dr. Horn, counsel for von Ribbentrop, *IMT*, XVII, 598.

are inalienable and which give him grounds for revolution against an unlawful regime. If we accept the "translation" theory of political power, advanced by such writers as Suarez and Bellarmine, we can agree that in transferring political power to the organs of the state, the people do so "in the name of the natural rights of the people, whereby they do not by any means dispose of these rights permanently by their contractual act of delegation, but on the contrary remain the perpetual and original possessors of political power."[31] Since, therefore, the social contract is the immediate source of the state authority, "the people as a whole or its authorized representatives may resort to resistance in extreme emergency, when the public welfare is in utter disarray and all legal means have been exhausted, and if necessary they may depose the monarch and change the constitution."[32]

The writer of this justification of resistance was Joseph Mausbach, the foremost among the German advocates for a return to the doctrines of natural law. Together with Peter Tischleder and Heinrich Rommen, he has "offered a profound and unassailable basis for the translation theory and consequently for the theory of the social contract and the right to resist."[33] But although these writers had voiced their opinions before Hitler came to power, they had not yet been able to permeate German thought.

Four centuries had gone by since the anti-natural law doctrines of Luther had taken root in German soil. The so-called Catholic restoration in the ninetenth century did nothing to revive a natural law basis for the legal system of Germany. On the contrary, Adam Mueller, often considered one of the leaders of this "restoration" wrote:

> We may safely deny all natural law that is supposed to exist outside or above or before positive law; we may safely declare

[31] Edgar Alexander, "Church and Society in Germany" in Joseph N. Moody (ed), *Church and Society 1789-1950* (N. Y.: Arts. Inc., 1953), pp. 506-507.

[32] *Ibid.*, p. 507. Note that the "social contract" is the immediate but not the ultimate source of authority.

[33] *Ibid.*, Mausbach (1861-1931) was the author of several important theological studies including: *Katholische Moraltheologie* and *Naturrecht und Völkerrecht*. He was professor of Moral and Apologetics at the University of Münster, and was made a Papal Chamberlain in 1912.

> all positive law to represent natural law, since all the innumerable localities which originate positive law exist by the force of nature. And because it is true that all positive law is at the same time natural law, we are in the future justified to designate with the term of natural law the endeavor to safeguard true nature with positive law.[34]

It was not until the 1880's that a genuine revival of Christian natural law began, and since it was sponsored largely by the Jesuits it was looked on with suspicion by many Catholic and non-Catholic thinkers. An interesting example of the ignorance of the Thomistic writings on natural law is given in the life of the famous German jurist, Rudolf von Ihering. In the second edition of his work, *Der Zweck im Recht,* he acknowledged his surprise upon learning that the teleological foundation of law and morality which he thought he had "discovered" in his work, had actually been described long ago by Saint Thomas Aquinas. "With amazement," he wrote, "I ask myself how it was possible that such verities, once formulated, could fall into such complete oblivion in our Protestant education."[35]

It might be suggested that the education received by at least the older members of the conspiracy against Hitler was that spoken of with such disillusionment by Ihering. The writings of Tischleder, Rommen, and Mausbach were undoubtedly very useful in building up a system of law based on natural law doctrine, but it would have taken far more than a few decades of such teaching to destroy previous errors.

The men of the Resistance Movement seldom refer directly to "natural rights," and the very diversity of reasons which they offer for fighting the Hitler regime creates the impression that they were not concerned with a rational explanation of any abstract "right" or "duty" of resistance. This can be said without in any way detracting from the probability that they acted in defense of fundamental human rights from a high ethical or religious motivation.[36]

[34] Moody, *op. cit.*, p. 379.

[35] *Ibid.*, p. 498.

[36] This is the opinion of Gen. von Witzleben's group as a result of their discussions and study. Personal interview Feb. 22, 1954. In the typescript

We come then to the core of our problem: what were the motives of the men within Germany who fought the Nazis? Because it would be impracticable to investigate the ideas and ideals of each single individual whose name has been connected with the Resistance Movement, we shall limit ourselves to a detailed study of the five major personalities around whom the others gathered: Beck, Goerdeler, von Moltke, von Weizsäcker, and von Stauffenberg. To supplement their own statements, we shall use relevant comments made by their co-conspirators, for it would not seem arbitrary to assume that the men who worked so closely together were in basic agreement on the objective to be attained and the reasons for pursuing such a goal.

All reports agree that the central figure in the conspiracy against Hitler was Colonel-General Ludwig Beck, Chief of the General Staff until August 18, 1938. He it was whom the conspirators had designated for interim Head of State if the *coup* of July 20, 1944 had succeeded.

Born June 29, 1880, in Biebrich-on-the-Rhine, he was brought up in a strongly Evangelical family and trained to a life built on good order, duty, and hard work.[37] A completely military education and active service as a young Captain in World War I combined to intensify the characteristics of his early training. Devotion to duty, silent obedience of commands, and careful abstinence from politics were impressed upon the young German soldier and, in turn, taught by him to those who later came under his jurisdiction.

The ideal of the General Staff was the efficient and unostentatious accomplishment of the assigned task, and, as Chief of the General Staff, Beck insisted on two points: his men must develop clear logical thought, and must have characters strong enough to carry out what reason dictated.[38]

of their discussions it is the conclusion reached by Professor Künneth, Father Pribilla, S. J. and Dr. Weinkauff, thus including a Protestant clergyman, Catholic priest, and lawyer.

[37] Biographical information on Beck is taken from Max Pribilla, S. J., "Ein grosser Gegenspieler Hitlers," *Stimmen der Zeit,* 149 Band (Jan., 1950), pp. 254-260.

[38] Foerster, *op. cit.*, p. 44: "Wir brauchen Offiziere, die den Weg logischer Schlussfolgerungen in geistiger Selbstzucht systematisch bis zu Ende gehen,

Although he greeted the reëstablishment of the prestige of the German Army accomplished by Hitler, he opposed using that army as an instrument of power politics. His voice was raised against the occupation of the Rhineland in 1935, and when it went through despite his protest he urged the Fuehrer to announce publicly that Germany would not fortify the area west of the Rhine.[39] From the very beginning of the Nazi rule he had little or no respect for Hitler; he later told Colonel-General Halder that at the meetings he had attended when he was Chief of the General Staff he had to sit there "facing a lunatic" while ". . . everybody present had received his [Hitler's] statements in icy silence."[40] The more insight he gained into Hitler's plans, the more his opposition crystalized.

Beck worked closely with Colonel-General von Fritsch, Commander in Chief of the Army from 1934 to February 1938. The latter was powerful in the leadership of his men, but weak in the presence of Hitler. He was willing to "defend the prerogatives of the Officer Corps before Caesar's throne, but the idea of dethroning Caesar never occurred to him."[41] Nevertheless he voiced his objection to the plans made known by Hitler at a secret conference of November 5, 1937, plans which laid bare the Fuehrer's intentions to secure "living space," cost what it would.[42]

Despite the order of silence imposed upon those present at that conference, Foreign Minister von Neurath and Colonel-General von Fritsch talked it over with Colonel-General Beck who had already been informed of the details by Colonel Hossbach.[43] Beck thereupon prepared the first of a series of memoranda opposing Hitler's policies, answering his arguments point for point. The Fuehrer

deren Charakter und Nerven stark genug sind, das zu tun, was der Verstand diktiert," Address at the 125th anniversary of the Kriegsakademie, Oct. 15, 1935.

[39] Testimony of General Jodl at Nuremberg, *IMT*, XV, 352.

[40] Halder Interrogation, Oct. 27, 1945, p. m.

[41] Wheeler-Bennett, *op. cit.*, p. 358.

[42] A record of this meeting was made from memory by Colonel Hossbach on Nov. 10, 1937. *Documents on German Foreign Policy 1918-1945* (Washington, D. C.: Government Printing Office, 1949 ff.), Series D, Vol. I, pp. 29-39.

[43] Hossbach reported that Beck was extremely shocked by this news. Foerster, *op. cit.*, p. 80.

had made "living space" his theme; Austria and Czechoslovakia must be acquired to satisfy this need, and expediency advised doing so with lightning speed lest England and France intervene. Beck answered that while living space might be required, the political enmity aroused by such aggression would lead ultimately to Germany's exclusion from international markets and economy. He denied the value of a policy of autarchy, insisting that Germany had need of world trade for her survival.[44]

His major argument was, however, the inevitable intervention of England and France. He reiterated this point on several occasions and was only to realize his error after Munich. He had visited Paris in June 1937 and had conversed with General Gamelin, M. Edouard Daladier, and Marshal Petain, and his impression was that they would definitely fight if Hitler acted forcibly against Czechoslovakia.

Some authors have hinted that Beck's arguments indicate a purely pragmatic objection to Hitler's foreign policy; the army was not yet ready to wage a victorious war and so he wished action postponed.[45] In the light of other evidence such a conclusion seems short-sighted. Certainly no moralistic or legalistic reasoning would have dissuaded the German dictator from his chosen course of action, and it was for him that Beck wrote his memorandum. The Chief of Staff was well aware that the only hope lay in convincing Hitler that, contrary to Ribbentrop's estimate of the situation, the Western Powers would defend their interests in Central Europe and would inflict a military defeat on Germany.

As early as 1934 Colonel-General Beck had written of the new regime: "It is not what we do but the way we do it that is so bad: a policy of sheer power and broken promises."[46] The code of honor and the sense of responsibility so deeply ingrained in his character inspired his criticism of the Nazis. Although he subscribed to the von Seeckt tradition that the military leaders should be aloof from the rough and tumble of politics, Beck believed that the army should serve only a political organization which was fundamentally moral. His sense of duty to the people, the state,

[44] Memoranda of Nov. 12, 1937. Foerster, *op. cit.*, pp. 80-82.

[45] Namier, *op. cit.*, p. 26.

[46] Foerster, *op. cit.*, p. 70.

and the army was such that he felt bound as a military man to fight against the war plans of a statesman who made decisions without reference to the moral aspects of problems.[47]

The von Fritsch crisis of February 1938 opened his eyes to Hitler's real designs against the army, and he fought to have a "show down" between the army and the party, but the well-timed *Anschluss* and the "not-guilty" verdict of the court martial left him with a deflated balloon.[48] On May 5, 1938 he directed a memorandum to the new Commander-in-Chief, Colonel-General Walther von Brauchitsch, pointing out the folly of Hitler's determination to settle the Sudeten problem by force. Such a program would, in his opinion, lead to a world war, a war which Germany could not win.[49]

The most comprehensive exposé of his thoughts was that of July 16, 1938 in a document drawn up for Colonel-General von Brauchitsch to read to an assembly of high officers. Beck asked for a collective demarche on the part of the generals against Hitler's war policy and the assurance of a mass resignation if their demand went unsatisfied.[50] A well known American critic of the German General Staff, General Telford Taylor AUS, conceded the fundamental basis of Beck's opposition by this time.

> At long last—unhappily, much too late—it had begun to dawn on Beck that he was confronting a problem far broader and deeper than how to put an end to *Fall Gruen* [operational plan for action against Czechoslovakia]. At last he realized that the menace of war was not simply a momentary, mad idea of Hitler's but was an intrinsic part of an evil and dangerous political and social system. Beck was face to face with the Third Reich itself.[51]

Implicit in Beck's thought at this time was a military *coup d'état* if the suggestion for collective resignation did not win approval. He wanted to put an end not only to Hitler's war plans

[47] *Ibid.*, p. 98.

[48] The affair is described in detail in Foerster, *op. cit.*, pp. 85-92 and Wheeler-Bennett, *op. cit.*, pp. 357-374.

[49] Memorandum of May 5, 1938, Foerster, *op. cit.*, pp. 90-106.

[50] Memorandum of July 16, 1938, *Ibid.*, pp. 116-121.

[51] Telford Taylor, *Sword and Swastika* (N. Y.: Simon and Schuster, 1952), pp. 198-99.

but to the "legal uncertainty and the self-assumed importance of the party."[52] In the statement which he made to the Commander-in-Chief on July 29, 1938 it was clearly explained that the unlawful character of the inner political system was uppermost in his mind. It was not yet the person of the Fuehrer which was the object of his opposition; it was the abuses within the political system which he thought could still be cured by legal methods. But, if the ordinary means failed, he was ready to head a military *putsch* against Hitler.[53]

The nonrevolutionary character of the army was apparent at once. On August 4 Colonel-General von Brauchitsch summoned the meeting that Beck desired, but he refused to read the memorandum prepared by the Chief of the General Staff. He permitted Beck to read it himself to the assembled officers who were impressed by his forthrightness and courage but who, with the exception of General Adam, refused to go along with him. In their view, the responsibility rested solely on the shoulders of the Fuehrer, and they insisted that they must avoid all semblance of political interests.[54]

When Hitler learned of this meeting and heard the details of the Beck memorandum he sent for Colonel-General von Brauchitsch and demanded an explanation. The Commander-in-Chief gave him a copy of the memorandum but added nothing of his own to support it. Hitler's answer was the meeting summoned for August 10 at the Berghof. Significantly omitting Beck from the list of guests, Hitler summoned chiefly the younger Army Chiefs and spoke to them at length of his political theories and war plans. Another meeting was called by the Fuehrer on August 15; this time he announced his decision to settle the Czech question in the fall, by force if necessary. Beck thereupon decided to resign, and submitted his resignation to von Brauchitsch on August 18th.[55]

Fabian von Schlabrendorff maintains that Beck had a personal interview with Hitler at this time, and states that Beck resigned,

[52] ". . . der Rechtsunsicherheit und der Bonzokratie der Partei." Article by Prof. Seraphim in *Das Parlament*, July 20, 1952.

[53] Foerster, *op. cit.*, p. 127.

[54] *Ibid.*, pp. 138-142.

[55] *Ibid.*, pp. 142-146; Testimony of Field Marshal von Manstein at Nuremberg, *IMT*, XX, p. 606.

saying to the Fuehrer who had insisted that the only duty the army had was to obey his orders: "This is a point of view which I cannot accept. As Chief of the General Staff I am not prepared to take the responsibility for orders of which I do not approve."[56] Whether von Schlabrendorff's report is accurate or not, the statement certainly represents Beck's position.[57] It should be remembered that Beck had reestablished the principle of military coresponsibility when he had begun his term of office, although it was clearly a concept incompatible with an authoritarian state.[58]

Beck took leave of his staff in a quiet informal manner on August 27; on September 1 Colonel-General Franz Halder succeeded to the post. The wisdom of his resignation and its effect on the conspiracy against Hitler will be discussed later,[59] but the motives which led him to resign were inextricably interwoven with his whole character. Speaking of this man who would later lead the opposition, von Schlabrendorff writes: "His whole personality radiated noble candor."[60] His inability to speak one way and act another—a trait he expected to find in all officers—is testified to by many who knew him.

Lieutenant General A. C. Wedemeyer USA, who knew him at the German War Academy, has written:

> It is not generally known that Colonel General Ludwig Beck, Chief of the German General Staff just prior to the war, and scores of other senior and junior officers deplored Nazi racial discrimination, the unscrupulous acts of aggression, and the rule of tyranny as epitomized by Hitler and his henchmen. I knew General Beck personally and considered him one of the finest men I have met in any country—a cultured gentleman, enlightened and tolerant. General Beck, General Rommel, and thousands of other patriotic Germans in the military service were understandably in a most difficult position, torn

---

[56] Schlabrendorff, *op. cit.*, p. 17.

[57] Cf. Foerster, *op. cit.*, p. 143.

[58] Walter Goerlitz, *History of the German General Staff, 1657-1945* trans. Brian Battershaw (N. Y.: Praeger, 1953), p. 293. The idea of coresponsibility was expressly dropped in the General Staff handbook for 1939. *Ibid.*, p. 342.

[59] Infra. chapter V.

[60] Schlabrendorff, *op. cit.*, p. 44.

> between sworn loyalties to those in power and their innate loyalties to principles of decency and justice in human relationships.[61]

In his testimony before the Nuremberg Tribunal, Hans Bernd Gisevius, one of the collaborators in the Beck-Goerdeler circle, paused to focus attention on the motives which prompted Beck's resignation and subsequent activity against Hitler.

> Therefore I owe it to his memory, and to my oath here, not to conceal the fact that Beck took the consequences of being the only German general to relinquish his post voluntarily, in order to show that there is a limit beyond which even generals in leading positions may not go; but at the sacrifice of their position and their life, must resign and accept no further orders. Beck was of the opinion that the General Staff was not only an organization of war technicians; he saw in the German General Staff the conscience of the German Army, and he trained his staff accordingly. He suffered immensely during the later years of his life because men whom he had trained in that spirit did not follow the dictates of their conscience. I owe it to this man to say that he was a man of inflexible character.[62]

Beck's fundamental opposition to the Hitler regime remained constant, but his conviction regarding the best way to fight it underwent a gradual change. In the early days he found it necessary to convert himself to the idea of contravening the nonpolitical tradition of the army. Possibly for this reason he took leave of his staff without emphasizing the reasons for his resignation. Gisevius attributes his submission to Hitler's wish that no publicity be given to the step he was taking to his immersion in the traditions of the Officer Corps which made unpalatable "even the faintest semblance of an attack upon the authority of the state." [63]

Yet, in less than a month he was deeply involved in the plans for the *coup* of September 15. His earlier opinion—that the very brutality of the regime portended imminent collapse—gave way to

[61] Wedemeyer's review of Hans Speidel's *Invasion* in *Annals of the American Academy*, 274: 218.

[62] Testimony of Gisevius at Nuremberg, *IMT*, XII, 208.

[63] Hans Bernd Gisevius, *To The Bitter End*, trans. Richard and Clara Winston (Boston: Houghton Mifflin Co., 1947), p. 283.

agreement with Goerdeler, Schacht, Gisevius and others for the overthrow of the government and the arrest of Hitler and the other key figures. After the failure of the plot to materialize, Beck continued to work toward the goal, becoming more and more rebellious against a regime which had so totally disregarded both domestic and international law, until in 1944 he was ready to join hands with Colonel Count von Stauffenberg in the plans for assassination.

The basis of his opposition is delineated in the conversations recorded by Ulrich von Hassell, one of his closest collaborators. In December 1938 after an afternoon spent with Beck, von Hassell noted:

> A refined and intelligent man, and a decent soldier. This whole trend disgusts him, and the irresponsible attitude of our leaders toward war angers and horrifies him.[64]

It is interesting to note here the reflection of Beck's own deep sense of responsibility in his criticism of the government on the grounds of its "irresponsible attitude."

A short time before the outbreak of the war which he had fought so hard to avoid, Beck insisted to von Hassell that there was little hope of gaining a foothold in the army. "Unfortunately," wrote von Hassell, "he has a very low opinion of the leading people in the army. . . . He is firmly convinced of the vicious character of the policies of the Third Reich."[65] Again, on February 15, 1940, von Hassell noted that he and Beck had been discussing the reported SS atrocities in Poland and that to them: "The pernicious character of the regime, above all in the ethical sense, becomes more and more apparent."[66] Beck was particularly distressed when Halder signed and distributed to the troops the orders from Hitler demanding illegal and inhuman treatment of Russian prisoners. It was again the "responsiblity" which the army would now have to bear that was emphasized.[67]

That such violations of law gave the basic impetus to Beck's

[64] Von Hassell, *op. cit.*, p. 25.

[65] *Ibid.*, p. 59.

[66] *Ibid.*, p. 114.

[67] *Ibid.*, pp. 189, 199.

opposition to the regime which he now considered "vicious" and "pernicious" is evident from the address prepared for delivery by him if the *coup* of July 20, 1944 had been successful. In this "Appeal to the German People" Beck questioned the legality of the Hitler government; speaking of Hitler he was to have said:

> Not called to power by the German people, but becoming the Head of the Government by intrigues of the worst kind, he has spread confusion by his devilish arts and lies and by the tremendous extravagance which on the surface seemed to bring prosperity to all. . . . In order to remain in power, he added to this an unbridled reign of terror, destroyed law, outlawed decency, scorned the divine commands of pure humanity and destroyed the happiness of millions of human beings. . . . He enthroned lawlessness, oppression of conscience, crime and corruption in our Fatherland which had always been proud of its integrity and honesty.[68]

Unfortunately the man who had such a clear insight into the evils of the Nazi state apparently lacked some of the qualities needed in the leader who could overthrow it. He has been criticized for being too theoretical, for lacking will-power, for depending too much on others for political knowledge.[69] A serious operation in March 1943 incapacitated him for the rest of that year, weakening his influence on the conspirators. On May 31, 1944, von Hassell noted that Beck had spoken that day on Foch at the "Wednesday Club" and had been "his old self again," but meanwhile much valuable time had gone by. And even then von Hassell felt that in the long run "this 'old self' . . . has proved to be more of a pure 'Clausewitz' without a spark of 'Blücher' or 'Yorck.'"[70]

Yet when the final moment for action came it was Beck who was most determined to go along with the tyrannicide proposed by Stauffenberg. When the latter's first few attempts did not materialize, Goerdeler and Gisevius tried to convince Beck that a capitulation to the Western powers by Field Marshal von Kluge

[68] Wheeler-Bennett, *op. cit.*, p. 728. The entire text is given on pp. 727-730, based on the German text in Pechel, *op. cit.*, pp. 305-309.

[69] Von Hassell, *op. cit.*, pp. 230, 282.

[70] *Ibid.*, p. 347. Foerster takes issue with this statement, *op. cit.* p. 138.

would be more practicable than an assassination, but Beck was adamant; even if the *putsch* did not succeed, it must be attempted. Gisevius writes:

> An unsuccessful *Putsch* with a dead Hitler would be better than a partially successful uprising in which that master of the black arts would be alive to lead the other side in a civil war.
> Beck explained this decision with such gravity that I could not help realizing how much inner struggle it had cost him.[71]

To the end, Beck waited for the military leader, Colonel Count von Stauffenberg, to give the required signal. Only after the assassination had occurred would he, a civilian, take over the reins of government. But when it became known that Hitler had not been killed, and a wave of fear and confusion swept over the conspirators gathered at the Bendlerstrasse on the evening of July 20, it was Beck who quietly urged them to go ahead with their plans to seize the government. "Let us be strong for Germany," he counseled and encouraged them.[72]

When power had been reassumed by the Nazis and the conspirators had lost what was obviously their last chance to overthrow Hitler, Beck chose to commit suicide rather than submit to a disgraceful arrest and execution. Permitted by Colonel-General Fromm to shoot himself twice, he did not succeed in killing himself, for Schlabrendorff in relating these details, wrote that ". . . a little later Fromm had him released from his suffering." [73]

In the "Appeal to the German People" his concept of the army as the guardian of the people is quite clear. At a time when the *Wehrmacht* was in retreat on all fronts, he would still have assured the people that "Our brave *Wehrmacht* is a pledge of security and order." His trust was firmly established in this symbol of legitimate defense.

> Firmly relying on our incomparable *Wehrmacht* and in confident belief in the tasks assigned to man by God we will sacrifice everything to defend the Fatherland and to restore a

[71] Gisevius, *op. cit.*, p. 532.
[72] Wheeler-Bennett, *op. cit.*, p. 653.
[73] Schlabrendorff, *op. cit.*, pp. 118-119.

> lawful solemn state of order, to live once more for honour and peace with respect for the divine commandments, in purity and truth.

It is impossible to state definitively to what extent Beck was influenced in his resistance activity by his religious beliefs. In the evidence cited above there are several hints of a Calvinist mentality: reliance on an "institution"—the army—to check the tyranny of a ruler rather than upholding the individual's right to do so; denunciation of Hitler's "blasphemous delusion that he was the chosen and favored instrument of Providence"; strong emphasis on responsibility and duty; finally, the promise only of "hard work" to the Germans if they would cooperate with the new regime. The RSHA report states that according to Admiral Canaris, Beck had a "strongly Christian attitude," but nothing more specific than this has been located.[74]

It is suggested therefore that the motives which prompted Beck to lead the Resistance Movement against Hitler were rooted in: (1) a conviction of the unlawful character of the Nazi state; and (2) a firm belief in his personal responsibility as an army officer of high rank to defend the people against the criminal policies of such a government. These convictions sprang, no doubt, from an inherent rebellion against such flagrant violations of natural law, a rebellion amplified and intensified by his religious beliefs and his home and military training. Certainly a study of his ideas and activities demonstrates that his opposition to Hitler came not from any desire for personal gain but from deeply ethical convictions which bore fruit in his constant and energetic support of all the plans directed toward the overthrow of the Nazi regime.

While Colonel-General Beck has been described as the head of the Resistance, Carl Goerdeler has been repeatedly proclaimed its heart. His record of anti-Nazi activity antedates that of Beck and most of the other conspirators, and is one clearly stemming from a fundamental opposition to all that Hitler stood for. His biographer, Dr. Gerhard Ritter, writes unqualifiedly: "Goerdelers Motive waren ausgesprochen moralischer Natur. Er hielt Hitler

[74] RSHA report, Aug. 7, 1944, Dept. of the Army. MS, 105/22.

für einen Satan, auch wegen seiner Juden- und Christenverfolgungen."[75]

Goerdeler, a native of Schneidemühl, studied law at the University of Göttingen, served in the army during World War I, and then became a civil servant.[76] He was chosen as Mayor of Leipzig in 1930, and in 1932 and 1934-35 also served as Reich Commissar for Price Control in Prussia. Extremely capable as an administrator, trained as both a lawyer and a banker, he was re-elected as Mayor and continued to enjoy popularity despite his warning against the "braune Flut" as early as 1933.

In a speech at Leipzig in 1935 he made no effort to conceal his opposition to the regimentation enforced by the Nazi regime, and in 1936 when the anti-semitism of the Party demanded the removal of a statue of the composer Felix Mendelssohn-Bartholdy from a public center in the city, he refused to have it touched. The Nazi deputy-mayor had it removed while Goerdeler was out of town, and when he returned he immediately submitted his resignation, November 1936—to become effective not later than April 1, 1937.

The United States Consul General in Leipzig reported to the Department of State that Goerdeler was resigning in protest and "with a heavy heart."[77] In 1944 this same official testified that he had known Carl Goerdeler intimately, and that at a very early date he had been unalterably opposed to Hitlerism.

> I know that Doctor Goerdeler never faltered in the conscientious performance of his public duties, in his loyalty to democratic principles, and in his opposition to the Hitler regime, which he loathed on account of its racial and political persecutions, its propaganda against the Christian Churches, its educational perversion of the German youth, its aggressive militarism, its tyranny and reign of terror. He particularly denounced the Nazi persecution of the Jews and of others on account of their race, religion, or political beliefs. . . . He

[75] Letter to the writer, Dec. 29, 1953.

[76] Biographical information is taken from the introduction to Carl Goerdeler, *Goerdelers politisches Testament,* herausgeben F. Krause (N. Y.: F. Krause, 1945).

[77] Report of Amer. Consul General in Leipzig to Sec. of State, Jan. 11, 1937, State Dept. MS, 862.00/3640.

> often expressed to me and other friends the fear that Hitler's revival of German militarism, the chauvinistic propaganda, and the aggressive foreign policy of the Nazi regime, would eventually bring Germany into mortal conflict with the democratic countries.[78]

When Goerdeler visited the United States Department of State in November 1937, he impressed those with whom he spoke as being fully aware of the evils and dangers of the Hitler regime.[79] While in the United States at that time, he wrote his *Politisches Testament* in which he analyzed clearly the nature of the totalitarian state and urged in its place a new German state based on a return to the moral and social principles of Western Christendom. He left this document with a friend of his in this country, and it was published only after his execution in 1945.

It was not only the prospect of another world war which dismayed him, but the completely amoral and anti-Christian basis of Nazism. In his *Politisches Testament* he attacked with particular vehemence the annihilation of the reign of law in Germany, pointing out that judges had been instructed to lay aside the law if it conflicted with the interests of the party. He protested state action against the churches and the abandonment of an objective standard of right and wrong, for which the judgment of the party was being substituted. His concern for the preservation of the law is shown again in March 1941 when, despite the increasing danger for critics of the regime, he planned to present Colonel-General von Brauchitsch with a copy of the misgivings of the Reich Supreme Court members "with respect to the complete decay of justice" in Nazi Germany.[80]

In an article entitled "Der Grosse Irrtum," Goerdeler showed a penetrating awareness of the ultimate reasons for the Nazi rise to power.[81] Man had become completely materialistic and so con-

[78] Letter from the Former Amer. Consul General in Leipzig to Sec. of State, Aug. 5, 1944. State Dept. MS, 862.20200.

[79] Inter-departmental Memorandum, Jan. 13, 1943. State Dept. MS, 862.20200.

[80] Von Hassell, *op. cit.*, pp. 174-175.

[81] Carl Goerdeler, "Der grosse Irrtum," *Deutsche Rundschau*, April, 1938 as reprinted in *Goerdelers politisches Testament*, pp. 53-55.

cerned for his own security and economic well-being that such moral evils as birth-control were widespread. To fight such materialism, he wrote, requires great courage and "freedom of the individual and of the whole people is a necessary prerequisite for such splendid courage."

Criticized by many for his indiscretion and over-optimism, Goerdeler has been acclaimed by all as a man of sincerity and determination. Unafraid to take the consequences of his decision to work for the overthrow of the government and the arrest of Hitler, he was tireless in his efforts to win cooperation, especially from the generals whose support was absolutely necessary. Gisevius has testified:

> This Doctor Goerdeler, who had always been a fearless and untiring fighter, had in those days unequaled courage. Like Doctor Schacht he went from one ministry to another, from one general to the next, and he also believed that now the hour had come when we could achieve a united front of decent people led by the generals.[82]

When one of the generals demurred for fear of being discovered, while Goerdeler would be comparatively safe, this intrepid man reportedly wrote out a full indictment of the Nazis, signed it, and gave it to the general as security.[83] In November 1942 he made a dangerous excursion to see Field Marshal von Kluge in Smolensk and Field Marshal Küchler with the Northern Army Group in order to convince them of the need for immediate action.[84]

Under cover of a job for the industrialist, Robert Boesch, Goerdeler was able to travel a great deal abroad as well as at home. Before the war he was a frequent visitor to London, Paris, and Brussels. In 1937-38 he visted the United States, Canada, England, and France struggling to convince all whom he met of the real nature of Nazism.[84a] Sometime between December 1939 and March 1940 he spoke with the king of Belgium, seeking his help in arranging an early peace.[85] Many trips were made to Sweden

[82] *IMT*, XII, 203.

[83] Dulles, *op. cit.*, pp. 32-33.

[84] Von Hassell, *op. cit.*, p. 274.; Wheeler-Bennett, *op. cit.*, p. 530.

[84a] Cf. *Infra.*, pp. 81-82.

[85] Von Hassell, *op. cit.*, pp. 102, 120.

where his friends, Marcus and Jacob Wallenberg, acted as intercessors with the British.[86] In 1942-43 he frequently was in Switzerland seeking contact with the allies.[87] Usually his advances were met with polite but disinterested remarks; sometimes he was even suspected of working for the Nazi regime.

While Goerdeler deplored this lack of understanding on the part of the governments abroad, he never attempted to excuse the cowardice of the many Germans who refused to accept the responsibility of saving themselves from the lawlessness and moral decomposition of the Third Reich. To him it was not just a question of averting war, but of an essential need to rid the country of its tyrant. "Hitler is Germany's evil spirit," he said. "It is imperative that he be removed."[88]

Writing to Max Jordan shortly after the Allied landing in Sicily, Goerdeler discussed the guilt of the German nation.

> I know too well how much guilt we have to expiate as a nation. I know that the innocent must suffer with the guilty. But I wish I could at least have some hope for the future. . . . This time, when it is all over, we Germans who are left will have only one chance—to throw ourselves on the mercy of the victors. . . . I know that retribution cannot be avoided. . . . Can we hope that statesmen will rise above the hatreds engendered by years of battle, that they will think of future generations and sow the seeds of peace and good will, rather than the dragon teeth of new wars?[89]

Though he did not live to see the post war days, he contributed his share to a positive approach to the problems of reconstruction. He was convinced that once the terror and secrecy which enshrouded the German people were removed, they would recognize the guilt inherent in toleration of such evil. But to make this possible, a violent overthrow of the regime was necessary, and to this effort he gave his full energy.

[86] Dulles, *op. cit.*, pp. 142-146. A long memorandum by Jacob Wallenberg summarizes his contacts with Goerdeler 1940-44.

[87] Bern to Washington # 5665, Dec. 5, 1942. State Dept. MS, 862.20200; Bern to Washington # 100, Jan. 7, 1943. State Dept. MS, 862.20200; Bern to Washington # 9392, Sept. 29, 1944. State Dept. MS, 862.00/9-2944.

[88] Jordan, *op. cit.*, p. 267.

[89] *Ibid.*, pp. 322-324.

Goerdeler's great contribution to the Resistance Movement was the "single eye" with which he prescinded from the decisive factors among the various oppositional circles and concentrated on the common goal. He was in contact with all the different groups, but his main co-workers were Beck and von Hassell. There was never any doubt about the fact that Goerdeler wanted to *act* against the Hitler government. An entry in von Hassell's diary on August 14, 1939 says of him:

> Fresh, clear-headed, active. Perhaps a bit sanguine. One hears generally that he is imprudent and is being closely watched. It is a relief, though, to speak with a man who wants to act rather than grumble.[90]

Unfortunately, he was never in a position to take the decisive action himself, and, as Gisevius noted,[91] for a man of his temperament that was a particularly tragic circumstance.

In a letter written to General Olbricht on May 17, 1943, the man of action is most apparent. Goerdeler was impatient at the long delay in the execution of the plans for a *coup;* he was no longer willing to await what the generals had consistently referred to as the "proper psychological moment" for the revolt.

> If by this we mean the moment at which events cause us to take action then it will coincide with the beginning of the collapse; action would then be too late to be exploited politically. In the meantime irreplaceable cultural monuments and the most important industrial centres would be heaps of ruins and the responsibility for precious lives would fall on the military leaders. Therefore we must not wait for the 'psychologically right' moment to come, *we must bring it about.*[92]

Goerdeler's main thesis reappears in this letter: the abandonment of the reign of law in the public life of Germany is the root evil. He deplored the senseless waste of lives in the "unparalleled defeats" of Stalingrad and Tunis, and even more the unjustified murder of civilians in many nations as well as Russian prisoners

[90] Von Hassell, *op. cit.*, p. 58.

[91] Gisevius, *op. cit.*, p. 437.

[92] Wheeler-Bennett, *op. cit.*, pp. 567-569. Mr. Wheeler-Bennett gives the English translation of the letter which appeared in *Die Wandlung*, 1945-46, Heft 2. Italics are mine.

of war, a total which he estimates at over one million. Furthermore, " the manner of their deaths is monstrous and is far removed from chivalry, humanity and even from the most primitive ideas of decency among savage tribes."

How does he explain the passivity of his fellow-countrymen in the face of such a criminal government?

> In face of this the patience of the people is inexplicable. But this perversity is based only on the fact that terror fosters secrecy, lies and crime. It will disappear as soon as the people realize that terror is being attacked, corruption removed and that sincerity and truth are taking the place of secrecy and falsehood. At that time every German will pull himself together again, both the decent and the corrupt, each will reject and condemn the action which he tolerated yesterday or to which he took no exception, because it was secret, because the decent German will again see decency and the others will be faced with responsibility.[93]

That he had such an optimistic view is not difficult to understand in the light of his own high ethical and religious principles. Motivated by a love of truth and justice he apparently found it difficult to believe that his fellow countrymen might not all be as virtuous. Max Jordan described him thus:

> . . . utterly free of self-consciousness because he was sincere, honest, straightforward. He was a Christian, a Lutheran of high ethical convictions, tolerant of other faiths, a moderate conservative who loved his country deeply, but to whom the moral law and considerations of right and justice meant more than the flag-waving pseudo-patriotism of so many of his own social class.[94]

Nothing which has come to light regarding Goerdeler's part in the Resistance gives evidence of an inner conflict regarding the justification of active opposition to the government. Unlike many of the other conspirators, he seems never to have been in a dilemma about whether or not he should participate in the various plots to overthrow Hitler. His basic attitude is based on a presupposition of a duty for all decent and honorable men to refuse obedience and service to a government ruling by force and terror. Nowhere does

[93] *Ibid.*

[94] Jordan, *op. cit.*, p. 260.

he seem to be searching for reasons to fight against the Nazis; it seems to him to be the only logical and right thing to do. Although a strong Lutheran, he was not inhibited by Luther's condemnation of active resistance, nor does he seem to have felt that those who did not resist were motivated by religious scruples.

It is not so easy to define his attitude toward tyrannicide. Some of his statements indicate an opposition to the plan for assassination on the grounds that it would be a psychological error; others present it as a matter of conscience.[95] Although Mr. Wheeler-Bennett presumes that early in 1943 Beck and Goerdeler made the decision in favor of assassination,[96] the supporting evidence seems rather inadequate. On the other hand, as late as the end of 1943 von Hassell was still speaking of arresting Hitler.

> With him (Popitz) and Goerdeler I was also in agreement about the terribly difficult and fundamental decision as to whether it was not already too late, and whether it would not be better to let the catastrophe run its course. We believe that in spite of everything it is imperative, for moral reasons and for the future of Germany, that an attempt be made before the end if there is any opportunity or prospect at all. Above all, it is essential that through this effort immediate trials be started against the Party criminals.[97]

Possibly the growing chaos evident in 1944 led him to accept assassination as the only possibility which remained, but it is difficult to be sure. Back in 1939 he had said to Max Jordan: "But I am not in favor of aping his methods! If he were killed, he would only become a martyr."[98] Writing after the July 20, 1944 attempt had been made, Jordan concluded:

> Goerdeler, undoubtedly, could never have been a part of any terrorist scheme. He had expressed himself consistently against murderous nazi methods. He knew that two wrongs

---

[95] E. g., Prof. Konstantin von Dietze's statement that Goerdeler was opposed to tyrannicide because it was forbidden to a Christian. RSHA report Dec. 4, Dept. of the Army. MS, 105/28. Von Schlabrendorff maintains that Goerdeler opposed it because he feared a stab-in-the-back legend unless Hitler went on trial. Von Schlabrendorff, *op. cit.*, p. 49.

[96] Wheeler-Bennett, *op. cit.*, p. 542. He relies here on Gisevius.

[97] Von Hasssell, *op. cit.*, p. 322 (November, 1943).

[98] Jordan, *op. cit.*, p. 267.

> do not make a right, and he did not think killing Hitler would help the situation, because obviously it would only have made a martyr and hero of him in the eyes of the gullible masses, and might have provided the excuse for another stab-in-the-back legend to explain away the defeat. All along Goerdeler had felt that the German people had to empty the bitter cup of hitlerism to the last drop, that they had to go all the way in their misery if there was to be any hope of regeneration.[99]

Quotations could be added supporting both points of view, but, in any case the question is purely academic for by the time of the July 20 *attentat,* the leadership of the conspiracy had passed into the hands of Colonel-Count von Stauffenberg. Although Goerdeler was in touch with him, his influence could scarcely be considered decisive. He revealed that on July 18 he had met with Stauffenberg, but did not relate the details of their conversation.[100] Since a warrant for his own arrest had already been issued, it cannot be said with certainty whether Goerdeler's withdrawal from the scene of the active conspiracy in these final days was a measure of prudence or an indication of disapproval of the plans for assassination.

What were Goerdeler's relations with the Kreisau group? This is a question which is still in need of clarification, but it is obvious that they were in agreement as to their general objective—the establishment of a new Germany built on a foundation of Christian principles. Nevertheless, as is always possible among good Christians, they were not agreed as to what that meant in terms of specific political and economic goals. Dr. Gerhard Ritter, Goerdeler's biographer, has described his subject as an "entschieden liberaler Wirtschafts-politiker,"[101] but the relativity of the term "liberal" is well known. Goerdeler's thoughts on the relations between capital and labor are outlined briefly in his "Ein Weltfriedensprogram," written in 1938, and it demonstrates that he was strongly suspicious of any regimentation. Why?

---

[99] *Ibid.*, p. 337.

[100] Interrogation of Goerdeler, RSHA report Aug. 13, 1944, Dept of the Army. MS, 105/22.

[101] Letter to the writer, Dec. 29, 1953. Dr. Ritter has since published his fine work, *Carl Goerdeler und die Deutsche Widerstands Bewegung* (Stuttgart: Deutsche Verlags-Anstalt, 1954).

> The best achievement is only possible if the soul is satisfied. Man lives not by bread alone. His soul demands freedom and goodness. The state creates the foundation through correct laws and the protection of personal freedom.[102]

His concept of the role of the state in economic matters was, therefore, somewhat more conservative than that of the men of Kreisau, and a certain amount of conflict was inevitable. A few random notes from von Hassell will indicate the difficulties involved in reconciling Goerdeler's views with those who gathered around von Moltke. In September 1941 he recorded:

> We were rather concerned about Goerdeler, who is much too optimistic and too 'reactionary' . . . I was disturbed by his facile prophecies of an early breakdown of the regime. He also worries me with his somewhat childishly contrived plans.[103]

A few months later:

> Goerdeler . . . is too sanguine, always sees things as he wishes to see them, and in many ways is a true reactionary, though otherwise he has splendid qualities.[104]
>
> Goerdeler takes an almost completely unfavorable attitude toward the ideas of these young men (Yorck, Trott, Moltke, Guttenberg) who, on their part, disapprove of him.[105]

Yet, by the end of 1943 his perseverance and tireless efforts at argument had apparently convinced the Kreisau circle that their points of conflict could be resolved, and unified preparations for post war organization went ahead.[106] Despite Gisevius's insistence on the eastern-orientation of the Kreisau group,[107] their writings indicate, to this writer, a far greater affinity with the postwar Christian Social Democrats than with Communist Russia. Jakob Kaiser, a former leader of the Christian Trade Unionists and a cooperator with the Kreisau circle, states emphatically that Goerdeler was able to merge forces with the Social Democrats at Kreisau on the basis of their common belief—the perniciousness of the Hitler system—and their common goal, to overthrow it.[108]

[102] Goerdeler, "Ein Weltfriedensprogram" in his *Politisches Testament*, pp. 47 ff. Translation mine.

[103] Von Hassell, *op. cit.*, p. 214.

[104] *Ibid.*, p. 230.

[105] *Ibid.*, p. 231.

[106] *Ibid.*, p. 321.

[107] Gisevius, *op. cit.*, p. 486.

[108] Jakob Kaiser in *Das Parlament*, July 20, 1952.

Goerdeler, as we have indicated, watched the affair of July 20 from afar. He was now a man " with a price on his head "; after July 20 a reward of one million Reichmarks was offered for knowledge of his whereabouts.[109] The reward was paid to Helene Schwaerzel, a woman in East Prussia who recognized him, and Goerdeler was arrested August 13, 1944. Placed on trial with von Hassell, Leuschner, Wirmer, and Lejeune-Jung, he was condemned to death;[110] the sentence was executed February 2, 1945 at the same time as that of Popitz and Father Delp.[111]

Naturally, Carl Goerdeler was not free from human weakness; he was overoptimistic, indiscreet, and, perhaps, too anxious to have political details settled before the *coup* had actually occurred. It would not be true, however, to dismiss him as a politician seeking power for himself and a clique of friends. His opposition to Hitler and the Nazi Party rested on fundamental moral grounds. No better analysis of his motives can be found than his own statement, written at the end of 1943.

> Confidence must be based upon a regard for truth and the veneration of justice. Hitler rejected both truth and justice. In place of truth he set up propaganda; and in place of justice, violence. By means of propaganda, and of the Gestapo, he maintained his tyranny. For him there existed only one ultimate value, the State. Therefore he made it and called it the totalitarian State; it stood in the place of all other values, and to it everything led. The State was above and outside justice and morality. The individual and the community alike had to subordinate themselves to it completely. In the new formula, ' Right is that which is useful to the People ' the principle abhorred by all good men was openly proclaimed: ' The end justifies the means.' The idea of individual right peculiar to Christianity as well as to the Germanic peoples was denied by him. Man was no more than a part, a member, and a functionary of the State: he was to be remodeled as a collective being, and to forego any right to an independent personality.[112]

---

[109] Dulles, *op. cit.*, pp. 30, 175.

[110] Von Hassell, *op. cit.*, p. 362.

[111] *Ibid.*, p. 363.

[112] Schlabrendorff, *op. cit.*, p. 83.

3 The leader of the Kreisau group, Count Helmuth von Moltke, was a leader of the German Resistance in a sense somewhat different from that of the leaders already discussed.[113] Gifted with a keen intellect, strength of character, and a deeply ethical and religious spirit, von Moltke visualized his role in the movement as that of a long-term planner, one who would prepare the way for the new Germany to be built on the ruins of Nazi totalitarianism. Although he could have remained in London in 1938, he felt bound in conscience to return to Germany. He said that if he were to accept the hospitality of Great Britain he would feel obliged to serve the British Government and fight against his own country, and this he could never do. The Nazi regime, he argued, must inevitably disintegrate, and then only those who fought Hitler from within Germany would deserve to set up a new government there.[114]

Count von Moltke had strong ties with England. His mother was the daughter of a Chief Justice in South Africa, James Rose-Innes, and he himself was admitted to practice before the English bar. This gave him an opportunity to visit London frequently and may well have influenced his attitude toward National Socialism. Although both of his parents were Christian Scientists, Count von Moltke did not apparently adhere to the same religious belief.[115] He is counted among the Protestant participants in the Kreisau circle and was very much interested in working for greater cooperation among the various denominations, as well as closer union with Roman Catholics.[116]

The discussions held at Kreisau frequently centered on religious questions such as church-state relations, new liturgical developments, and the need for religious education. Von Moltke's last

[113] Biographical information on Count von Moltke is taken from the introduction to his *Letzte Briefe aus dem Gefängnis Tegel* (Berlin: K. H. Heussel, 1951).

[114] Dorothy Thompson, letter to the writer, Dec. 23, 1953. Miss Thompson was a personal friend of Helmuth von Moltke and broadcast a series of messages March 27-Sept. 4, 1942 designed to encourage him and his friends to revolt. These have been published as *Listen Hans* (Boston: Houghton Mifflin Co., 1942).

[115] *Ibid.*

[116] RSHA reports, Aug. 16, 1944, Dept. of Army. MS, 105/23; Sept. 15, 1944, MS, 105/25; and Oct. 4, 1944, MS, 105/26.

letters written to his wife and sons from prison reveal a thoroughly Christian spirit.[117] The chaplain at Tegel prison, Harald Poelchau, wrote to von Moltke's brother-in-law in August 1945, revealing to him that toward the end of his life, the prisoner had read only two books, his Bible and Hymnal.[118] He strove, according to the chaplain, to convince himself that the hand of God must be seen in all the misfortune brought on by the wickedness of men, and in this way maintained great peace of soul.

An analysis of the Kreisau leader's motives for opposition to Hitler is not difficult, for he has left us, in his letters, clear testimony of a resistance based on a deeply Christian conscience which rebelled at the Nazi denial of God and its devaluation of the human person. He had been deeply moved by the measures taken against the Jews, the persecution of the Christian churches, the denial of free speech and the abolition of legal procedures. Besides, he was thoroughly opposed to the foreign policy of the Fuehrer.

Despite the fact that he was not enthusiastic about the terms of the Treaty of Versailles, he believed that a government was obliged to keep the treaties which it had signed. "Though from a distinguished military family, he hated war."[119] He recognized the innate tendency toward excessive nationalism among his people and worked against it. In a letter to his sons from prison he wrote:

> I have fought during my entire life against the spirit of narrowness and force, of overbearing, of intolerance and of the Absolute and the pitiless attitude which accepts all consequences, which inheres in the German and has found its expression in the National Socialist state. Moreover, I have stood for having that spirit and its evil consequences vanquished, such as nationalism in excess, racial persecution, loss of faith, and materialism.[120]

---

[117] Von Moltke, *op. cit.*

[118] *Ibid.*, p. 20.

[119] Dorothy Thompson, letter to the writer, Dec. 23, 1953.

[120] Moltke, *op. cit.*, p. 9. "Ich habe mein ganzes Leben lang, . . . gegen einen Geist der Enge und der Gewalt, der Uberheblichkeit, der Intoleranz und des Absoluten, erbarmungslos Konsequenten angekämpft, der in den Deutschen stekt, und der seinen Ausdruck in dem nationalsozialistischen Staat gefunden hat. Ich habe mich auch dafür eingesetzt, dass dieser Geist mit seinen schlimmen Folgeerscheinungen, wie Nationalismus im Exzess, Rassenverfolgung, Glaubenslosigkeit, Materialismus, überwunden werde."

In view of this fundamental opposition to the Nazi state, what did Count von Moltke do to bring about its downfall? He himself exulted in the fact that the People's Court could condemn him and his co-workers only for "having thought" and for having worked toward the establishment of a fully Christian state only by means of discussions and writings.[121] They did not concern themselves with the problem of overthrowing the government; that they left to the military elements and the Beck-Goerdeler group. By July 20, 1944 some of them were in agreement with the plans of Count von Stauffenberg, but they could not be said to have participated actively in the plot.

Their determination from the days of their earliest meeting in 1940 was to have ready the plans for political, economic, and social rehabilitation when the moment of promise should arrive. In the spring of 1942, Count von Moltke needed a sociologist to help him draw up plans for the postwar social order which he wanted to build on Christian principles. This task was undertaken by the Rev. Alfred Delp S. J. with the permission and support of his Father Provincial, Rev. Father Roesch S. J.[122] Von Moltke's cooperation with the Jesuits was dwelt upon at length by Judge Roland Freisler during the trial before the People's Court.

Both Father Delp and Count von Moltke have recorded Freisler's view that a Jesuit was *a priori* an enemy of the state, and anyone who was in contact with one of them was unworthy of the name of "citizen" in the Third Reich. A touch of humor lightens von Moltke's account of his trial when he confides to his wife that the accusation that he was to die a martyr for St. Ignatius Loyola was a fine joke and would surely arouse the ire of his dead father who was so anti-Catholic.[123]

He was accused of treason on the grounds that defeatism is treason and postwar plans which did not include Hitler were surely a sign of defeatism. As Count von Moltke saw it, "Treason is whatever does not suit Herr Freisler." The power of thought was so feared by the Nazis that they were determined to root out

[121] *Ibid.*, p. 40. A letter to his wife written Jan. 10, 1945.

[122] P. Paul Bolkovac, S. J. "Introduction" to Alfred Delp, S. J., *Im Angesicht des Todes* (Frankfurt am Main: J. Knecht, 1947).

[123] Moltke, *op. cit.*, p. 39.

everything that had been infected by it. Freisler made it quite clear that it was not concrete plans or preparations but the "spirit" which should be persecuted, and von Moltke was happy to represent that spirit.[124]

Nevertheless he also had his concrete plans. It was in trying to provide for the future realization of those plans that the Kreisau group came into contact with the Beck-Goerdeler and military circles. Von Moltke was by no means a stranger to the other resistance groups. Having accepted a post in Canaris's office where he handled problems of international law for OKW (*Oberkommando der Wehrmacht*) he was naturally well known to the Oster circle. Furthermore, he was in touch with the group of resisters in the Foreign Office, and was introduced by one of them, Erich Kordt, to the "Uncle Emil" group.

Ruth Andreas-Friedrich has given us a note on her impression of him when he first appeared at one of their meetings in October 1942: "In one corner, leaning quietly back in an armchair, is a grave man. . . . He says little, and scarcely mingles in the excited discussions." He was identified for her as von Moltke ". . . our best mind . . . one who knows the road that will lead us back out of the darkness."[125] And in March 1943 she noted that preparations for a *coup d'état* were being made, after which the plans "on which Moltke has been working for five years" would be used in setting up a new government.[126]

That he had connections with the Solf circle is also clear. It was in attempting to warn Otto Kiep, a member of that group, of his impending arrest that Count von Moltke was himself imprisoned in January 1944.[127] At that time his group was already indirectly in touch with Colonel Count von Stauffenberg for he wrote later of a meeting between the latter and Peter Yorck von Wartenberg on January 19, 1944.[128] Joint meetings with the Beck-Goerdeler

[124] *Ibid.*, p. 40.

[125] Ruth Andreas-Friedrich, *op. cit.*, pp. 83-84.

[126] *Ibid.*, p. 93.

[127] Dulles, *op. cit.*, pp. 87-88.

[128] Although Prof. Rothfels, *op. cit.*, p. 127 considers this date to have been July 19, 1944 it was given by Yorck at his trial as Jan. 19, 1944. Cf. Max Braubach, *Der Weg zum 20, Juli 1944* (Koln: Westdeutscher Verlag, 1953), p. 32 n. 18.

circle had been begun as far back as 1941,[129] and integration of the workers' groups with the Kreisau movement had been accomplished through the cooperation of the Socialists in the group, Carl Mierendorff and Theodor Haubach, with Wilhelm Leuschner, Julius Leber, and Jakob Kaiser.[130] But in working with all these different elements in the Resistance Movement, Count von Moltke had primarily in view the need for a broad cooperative program for the future, not the plotting for an attack on Hitler's life.

Most writers agree that the Kreisau group was opposed to the use of violence. It is consistent with their deep religious spirit that they should hesitate to use physical force to overthrow what was technically a legal government. J. W. Wheeler-Bennett refers to them as the "conscientious objectors of the Resistance, deeply genuine in their Christianity yet failing to take cognizance of Christ militant. . . ."[131] However, as we have seen, the concept of "Christ militant" in the sense of upholding tyrannicide is not a clear-cut Christian teaching by any means.

Paulus van Husen, a survivor of the Kreisau circle, maintains that it was not easy to apply the scholastic teaching on resistance and tyrannicide to a situation which did not rest on royal power. To distinguish between the "tyrannus usurpationis" and the "tyrannus regiminis" was a difficult and complicated task. The only thing demanded of a Catholic citizen appeared to be non-obedience to the unjust laws.[132]

Count von Moltke was not alone in his thinking that to have agreed to the assassination of Hitler would have been a taint on his soul,[133] and he rejoiced that God had removed him from the midst of the conspirators just at the moment when he might have been drawn into the active preparations. Countess von Moltke has insisted that "her husband and his more radical friends never approved of Goerdeler's active plans and would have nothing to do

[129] Von Hassell, *op. cit.*, pp. 230-231.

[130] Wheeler-Bennett, *op. cit.*, p. 502.

[131] *Ibid.*, p. 545.

[132] Paulus van Husen, "The 20th July and German Catholics," *Dublin Review*, 219 (July, 1946), 1-9.

[133] Moltke, *op. cit.*, p. 54. Letter to his wife, Jan. 11, 1945.

with his hazardous conspiracy." [134] Moltke himself wrote just before his death:

> I have never wished for or promoted an act of violence like that of July 20, 1944, but on the contrary have fought against its preparation since I disapproved of such violence on many grounds and above all I believed that the fundamental spiritual evil would not thus be destroyed.[135]

An account of the joint meeting of January 1943 of the Kreisau and Beck-Goerdeler groups written by Eugen Gerstenmaier has given some the impression that von Moltke would have gone along with the final plans for July 20, 1944 if he had not been imprisoned.[136] Gerstenmaier wrote that at the end of this meeting all the participants agreed, "to arrange for the *coup d'état* as quickly as possible." Even if this report is accepted as accurate, does it prove that von Moltke would have agreed to assassination?

A *coup d'état* implied the removal of Hitler from power and probably his arrest, but not necessarily an assassination. As late as the summer of 1943, for example, the conspirators in Paris, grouped around Stülpnagel and in contact with Beck, were still in two definite groups: one considered the death of Hitler a necessary counterpart of any *coup*; the other did not.[137] The decision that there would be an *attentat* was probably not reached in Berlin until the spring of 1944,[138] so that presumption that talk of a *coup* early in 1943 as reported by Gerstenmaier implied assassination is hardly tenable.

The Reich Security Office in its exhaustive study of the July 20, 1944 plot concluded that there was a wide range of opinion among the conspirators. Some were utterly opposed to tyrannicide, others would go along if necessary, and some openly favored "a cold

[134] Moltke, *Round Table* (June, 1946), p. 229.

[135] Moltke, *Letzte Briefe*, p. 15. A letter written to his sons.

[136] Ulrich von Hassell, *Vom Andern Deutschland* (Zurich: Atlantis Verlag, 1946), Appendix, pp. 379-380. A letter of Gerstenmaier to Wolf-Ulrich von Hassell, June 25, 1946. This is not contained in the English translation of the book. Cf. Rothfels, *op. cit.*, p. 125.

[137] Wilhelm von Schram, *Der 20 Juli In Paris* (Badworishofen: Kindler und Schiermeyer Verlag, 1953), pp. 18-22.

[138] *Ibid.*, p. 21.

and brutal murder" of the Fuehrer. Those who opposed it had different reasons for doing so—religious, psychological, or technical.[139]

It would be a mistake, therefore, to seek unanimity among the members of the Resistance Movement on this question, and the attempts to prove that Moltke would have finally agreed to it appear unjustifiable and unnecessary. To be opposed to Hitler and to the Nazi regime did not demand agreement with the notion of tyrannicide. It required a refusal to bend one's neck to the yoke of the party, a consistently anti-Nazi political philosophy, and a participation, in some way, in the plans to overthrow the government.[140] Count von Moltke wanted the Allies to win the war; he trusted in their generosity toward the German people, and felt that the anti-Nazis among them would then have a chance to reconstruct their country and Europe on a solidly Christian basis.[141]

Wheeler-Bennett states correctly that, "To them (Moltke and Yorck) the conflict was not against a regime so much as against the perversion of the human spirit and of the dignity of man." But the conclusion that he draws: "Their remedy, however, was little more than an amalgam of Prussian mysticism and Prussian Christian Socialism" is questionable.[142] Their remedy, as can be seen from a close study of the Kreisau documents and the letters of von Moltke, was belief in God, religious education, social justice, development of political and economic democracy, and a satisfactory working basis for church-state relations. There is nothing particularly "Prussian"[143] about such a program; rather it is universal and Christian in the best sense of the term.

For having devised such a program, Moltke was, as he himself

[139] RSHA report, Dec. 4, 1944. Dept. of the Army. MS, 105/28.

[140] In this connection it is interesting to note that the "Prosecution Brief" in *U. S. vs. von Weizsäcker* (p. 12) sets three standards for genuine resistance: (1) A political philosophy opposed to Nazism; (2) The intention of removing Hitler from power . . . includes preparations for a policy to replace the one removed; (3) Prevention or sabotage of such measures and propaganda which made Nazism what it was.

[141] Dorothy Thompson, letter to the writer, Dec. 23, 1953.

[142] Wheeler-Bennett, *op. cit.*, p. 546.

[143] Cf. Jordan, *op. cit.*, Appendix III, "Prussians and Germans" for an interesting comment on the use of the term "Prussian."

noted, condemned by the People's Court "not as a Protestant, not as a great landowner, not as a noble, not as a Prussian, not as a German even. . . . No, I stood there as a Christian and nothing else."[144]

While Count von Moltke represented the predominently meditative and non-violent elements in the anti-Nazi movement, his natural complement was the dynamic Colonel Count Claus von Stauffenberg, the man whose name became famous when he placed the bomb on July 20, 1944 intended to kill Hitler. Unfortunately we have no record of their opinions of each other, but one imagines that the youthful Bavarian Catholic would have found von Moltke over-intellectual, too passive, and hopelessly idealistic. On the other hand, the owner of the Kreisau estate, indicated his awareness of the powerful personality of Claus von Stauffenberg when he expressed the fear that if he were not already in prison he might have been drawn into the plans for the *attentat*.

As early as 1941 on a visit to Fabian von Schlabrendorff and Major-General Henning von Tresckow on the eastern front, von Stauffenberg revealed to them his deep-rooted opposition to Hitler, and Schlabrendorff considered it as a direct result of his Christian faith and training.[145] Von Stauffenberg had been brought up as a Roman Catholic, but according to his brother's testimony he did not attend church regularly.[146] A young Captain Kaiser related, however, that he had been most impressed by the fact that Colonel Count von Stauffenberg always wore a gold cross around his neck.[147] Another report mentions that he had received the Sacraments of Penance and Holy Communion just before the *Attentat*.[148] All these are indications of faith and religion, but add up to nothing conclusive about the depth of his religious convictions.

Much has been made of his association with Stefan George, into whose intimate circle of friends he was admitted while still very young. It was George's *Anti-Christ* which the Count used to recite

[144] Moltke, *op. cit.*, p. 56. Letter to his wife, Jan. 11, 1945.

[145] Schlabrendorff, *op. cit.*, p. 66.

[146] RSHA report, Oct. 4, 1944. Dept. of the Army. MS, 105/26.

[147] RSHA report, Aug. 7, 1944. Dept. of the Army. MS, 105/22.

[148] Heinrich M. Waasen, "Hie Stauffenberg—Hie Remer," *Die Österreichische Furche*, Feb. 7, 1953.

with great feeling, giving his hearers the impression that it summed up his hatred for Hitler; Wheeler-Bennett describes such a scene in detail.

> He would recite it with fervour, his great frame striding up and down the room and his maimed claw of a left hand gesticulating fiercely; his one remaining eye gleaming a vivid blue, a black patch covering the empty socket of the other. The final verses would excite him to particular elation, since, in their fire and venom, they expressed with surpassing eloquence the hate which burned within him and the contempt which he could barely contain for those who would not act.[149]

The final verses, as translated into English, read:

> The Master of Vermin far stretches his realm;
> No treasure that fails him, no luck that forsakes . . .
> Destruction take all other rebels!
>
> You clamour, enticed by the devilish show,
> Lay waste what remains of the sap from the spring
> And feel your need first when the end comes.
>
> Then you hang out your tongues o'er the emptying trough
> Stray like herds without aim through the courtyard in flames,
> And fearfully rings out the trumpet.[150]

Unfortunately no competent study of von Stauffenberg has yet appeared, and it is difficult to reconcile the many remarks which have been made about his "religious spirit" with Gisevius's statements such as: "Stauffenberg was motivated by the impulsive passions of the disillusioned military man whose eyes had been opened by the defeat of German arms."[151] Again, Gisevius insists that von Stauffenberg was "fighting for the continuation of Nazi-militaristic 'legality'[152] and was strong in his opinion that all "political activity must be directed to the East."[153] Both Hans Rothfels and J. W. Wheeler-Bennett hold that Gisevius is wrong

[149] Wheeler-Bennett, *op. cit.*, p. 582. According to those familiar with George's circle, such a manner of recitation is not in the George manner. Unfortunately Wheeler-Bennett does not give the source of his description.

[150] *Ibid.*

[151] Gisevius, *op. cit.*, p. 510.

[152] *Ibid.*, p. 511.

[153] *Ibid.*, p. 509.

in his estimate of von Stauffenberg [154] and provide different reasons for the latter's desire to cooperate with the Left. Yet, little factual information is volunteered by either side.

The widow of Enoch von Guttenberg, a member of the Resistance to whom Count von Stauffenberg was related by marriage, wrote of the young leader of July 20: ". . . he became convinced that Hitler . . . was indeed controlled by a diabolic power. He was sure at last in his own mind that in the assassination of Hitler he would be removing a creature actually possessed, body and soul, by the devil." [155]

This is a conclusion which would certainly explain his decision to go ahead with a personal attempt to kill the Fuehrer. He felt that an oath to such a person could have no binding force, and he tried to convince his subordinate officers of that fact.[156] In the spring of 1944 he visited Bishop von Preysing, and one writer suggests that this meeting played an important part in his decision.[157] This, however, is pure conjecture, and it is just as likely that their conversation was concerned with possible church-state relations in the future.[158]

In any case, having made his decision, he threw himself wholeheartedly into the execution of the *coup d'état*, the only one of all those that had been planned which actually took place. The personal bravery which Colonel Count von Stauffenberg demonstrated certainly out-weighed, in any evaluation of his character, the evident inefficiency of the plans. Beck seems to have had great confidence in his sincerity and loyalty, and to have been willing to abide by his decisions in the military area, until the *coup* should have been achieved. Undoubtedly there would have been problems to settle among themselves if they had been able to overthrow the Nazis, but they were not insuperable ones.

[154] Wheeler-Bennett, *op. cit.*, p. 582; Rothfels, *op. cit.*, p. 128.

[155] Elizabeth von Guttenberg, *Holding the Stirrup* (N. Y.: Duell, Sloan and Pearce, 1952), p. 194.

[156] RSHA report, Oct. 4, 1944. Dept. of the Army. MS, 105/26.

[157] Waasen, "Hie Stauffenberg—Hie Remer."

[158] Von Stauffenberg, Goerdeler and von Moltke had all visited Catholic prelates, especially Bishops von Preysing and von Faulhaber for the purpose of discussing future church-state relations. Cf. RSHA report, Oct. 4, 1944. Dept. of the Army. MS, 105/26.

When the plot was foiled and Colonel-General Fromm recovered control of the Bendlerstrasse, Colonel Count von Stauffenberg was sentenced to death by a summary court-martial consisting, apparently, of just one man, Fromm. Without condescending to name von Stauffenberg, Fromm ordered that "the Colonel" be shot.[159] One of the potential leaders of postwar Germany thus died at the age of 37 with the words on his lips: "Long live the eternal Germany."[160] Again it is clear that the plot of July 20 was not the work of traitors or of anarchists, but of men who worked indefatigably and risked their lives in the hope that they could bring about a return of true life, life based on law, to their country. The statement prepared for publication on July 20 explaining the ideals and aims of the new Reich government is perhaps the best indication of von Stauffenberg's political thought, since his approval of it is implicit in its publication.[161] Some of the most interesting sections were:

1. The restoration of the full majesty of law. . . . No human society can exist without law. . . . In His ordering of the universe, in His creation and in His commandments God has given us the need of law. . . . Security of person and property will again be protected against arbitrary action. . . . The concentration camps will be abolished as soon as possible.
2. Restoration of principles of morality in all spheres of private and public life. . . . One of our noblest tasks is to restore the family as the nucleus of the community. For this we need the influence of the home, the power of religion, the co-operation of the Churches. . . . Immorality must be attacked if our children are not to be demoralized; for how can parents expect their children to be pure if they themselves do not exercise self-control and show their children the best example?
3. We declare war on falsehood. The sun of truth shall dispel the thick fog of untruth. . . . In his order of things God admits no double morality.

---

159 Wheeler-Bennett, *op. cit.*, p. 663.

160 Statement of Dr. Bauer at the Remer trial in 1952, cited in Weisenborn, *op. cit.*, p. 30.

161 Wheeler-Bennett, *op. cit.*, Appendix C, pp. 734-743. Translated from the version in Pechel, *op. cit.*, pp. 314-325.

4. The freedom of mind, conscience and faith which has been destroyed will be restored. The Churches will again have the right freely to work for their faith. In future they will be completely separated from the State, because only by being independent and by remaining aloof from all political activity can they fulfil their task. . . . The press will again be free.
5. Youth and education is one of our main cares. . . . First and foremost this education will be placed in the hands of the parents and the schools. . . . Education must again be placed deliberately on the Christian-religious basis.
6. Administration must be reorganized. . . . It is essential to restore at once clear responsibility. . . . The civil servant shall once again obey only the law and his conscience. Luxury is out of place in Government offices. . . .
7. The arrangement of the administration, the proper distribution and fulfilment of public duties are only possible on the basis of a Constitution. . . . Prussia will be dissolved. The Prussian provinces, as well as the other German *Länder* will be amalgamated into new *Reichsgaue*.
8. In war-time economy can only be conducted in the form of State control and control of prices . . . but . . . we will cancel all measures which have interfered too much with the freedom of the individual . . . autarchy is a cowardly denial of the possibility of participating in the goods and services of the whole world. . . . Property is the basis of all economic and cultural progress. . . . It will therefore be protected.
9. Social Security benefits for the sick, aged, etc. . . . but refusal to make promises of economic well-being. . . . This depends on industry and thrift.
10. Reorganization of taxation and public funds.
11. All possible resources must be given to the men fighting at the front. We . . . will carry on this war until we can obtain a just peace.
12. The importance of striving for an early peace and bringing to justice those who are responsible for the war . . . our highest duty is to . . . cleanse the much dishonored German name. God . . . demands that His order and His commandments are not violated. . . . Let us follow earnestly and in everything the commands of God which are engraved on our conscience even when they seem hard to us.

Such then was the program which evolved from the various discussions and inter-group planning which preceded the attempted *attentat.* It sets in bold relief the ideal which the conspirators hoped to see realized and thus constitutes an excellent source for a study of their motives, for it is the " final end " of von Stauffenberg's attempt to assassinate Hitler.

Section 6 of the above document discusses in detail the qualities of the "civil servant." He is entrusted with public power and must therefore be "worthy of his special position by special devotion to duty." To no one can these words be applied with more truth than to the fifth member of the Resistance whom we have chosen for our study, Ernst von Weizsäcker.[162]

Born into a family of university professors and clergymen, von Weizsäcker surprised everyone by wanting to go to sea; in 1900 he joined the Imperial Navy where he served until the destruction of the fleet in 1918. In 1920 he entered the Foreign Office, and worked through a succession of posts until in April 1938 he was appointed State Secretary. In 1943 he was removed from that position and sent as Ambassador to the Vatican; consequently he was not in Berlin at the time of the July 20, 1944 affair. In 1947 he was brought to Nuremberg as a "voluntary witness," only to find himself recalled there at the end of the year as a defendant. On April 14, 1949 he was condemned to seven years' imprisonment, but was released under an amnesty decree in 1950. He died August 4, 1951.[163]

It was indeed a strange end to a career of one whose only aspiration seems to have been "to be devoted to duty," yet in a totalitarian state the identification of one's duty is not simple. Very few writers on the Resistance Movement have accorded the German State Secretary a place in its ranks. In part this may be due to the fact that his case was still before the Nuremberg Tribunal when they published their books,[164] but in some instances it is simply that his story is not accepted.[165]

[162] Biographical information is taken from his *Memoirs* and from the transcript of his trial at Nuremberg. Cf. chapter I, n. 7.

[163] Wheeler-Bennett, *op. cit.*, p. 416 n. 1.

[164] E. g. those of Dulles, Rothfels and Gisevius. Mr. Dulles feels, however, that there is no reason to doubt von Weizsäcker's sincerity. Personal interview, March 6, 1954.

[165] E. g. Namier, and Wheeler-Bennett.

At his trial, however, hundreds of affidavits were submitted on his behalf by relatives of the other conspirators against Hitler, and they contain weighty evidence of his intimate connection with Beck, Canaris, von Hassell, and Halder as well as his leadership of the young men in his office: Adam Trott zu Solz, Albrecht von Kessel, Brucklemeier, and the Kordts. The oral and written testimony contained in the records of his trial convincingly tells the story.[166]

His greatest efforts to circumvent the policies of Hitler and Ribbentrop were made before the outbreak of World War II. As far back as 1932-33 he had been noticed for his efforts on behalf of disarmament agreements and had been recognized as an opponent of the incipient Nazi movement. In April 1934 the eminent churchman Karl Barth met von Weizsäcker in Berne, and received the impression that he was opposed to the Nazi attitude toward the churches and also:

> . . . that he was certainly having doubts and reservations with regard to the government which he had to represent in Berne. My impression of his personality at that time was that he was a gentleman of pure character, who for some reason or other had taken over a part and had to act it, but that this part troubled and worried him; that he did not only want to act personally as a gentleman but that, as far as his work was concerned, he also wanted to do his best under the given circumstances.[167]

Von Weizsäcker, more than any of the other conspirators, seems to personify the traditional Lutheran view of the proper relationship that man should have to the political world.

> My principle and also my political confession of faith has always been that I should not interfere with destiny any more than necessary; that is, that everything that is good and capable of life should be allowed to grow without interference and the way should be cleared for it. That is, obstacles should be removed, friction should be removed, and parasites should be removed, and woods should be uprooted, and then we should let everything look after itself.[168]

---

[166] See chapter I, n. 7.

[167] Affidavit of Karl Barth, April 25, 1948. Von Weizsäcker Defense Document Book 5.

[168] Testimony at Nuremberg, transcript of the trial, p. 7711.

But he apparently felt that the National Socialist regime was a part of the woods to be uprooted. In his *Memoirs* he wrote:

> On the question of whether those who suffer tyranny have the right to use force against the tyrant I had no moral doubts whatever. The more brutal and inhumane the regime is, the more justified one is in using corresponding methods against it. Nor could the oath of loyalty to Hitler, which Civil Servants had to take, make any difference; for Hitler had been the first to betray his trust.[169]

Here, of course, he clearly diverges from the Lutheran path. One would like to know whether his statement, "I had no moral doubts whatever" is an accurate remembrance. Actually those who were in almost daily contact with him at the Foreign Office felt that he was going through a serious inner conflict on the problem of his duty to the regime. The former Ambassador from France to Berlin, André François-Poncet wrote:

> My impression of Herr von Weizsäcker was that he was tormented by the conflict between his personal feelings, the judgment of his moral conscience and his conception of his duty as a servant of the State and a patriotic German. It seemed to me that he suffered as a result of this internal conflict. In this, he was not alone. He was, however, one of those in whom this suffering was the most apparent.[170]

Having made his decision that Hitler was a tyrant, von Weizsäcker did not draw any line between overthrowing the regime and assassinating the Fuehrer. The brother of Albrecht Haushofer, also one of the conspirators, testified: "The basic assumption of these discussions between my brother and Weizsäcker was that Hitler would have to be eliminated by any means whatsoever." [171]

Granting then that von Weizsäcker was an ideological opponent of Nazism, did he personally take sufficient action to justify being classified with the active Resistance Movement? Von Hassell, who

[169] Von Weizsäcker, *Memoirs*, p. 296.

[170] Statement in writing Sept. 5, 1947 submitted as von Weizsäcker Defense Document 199. M. François-Poncet had by then spent twenty-two months as a prisoner in Germany and could scarcely be considered prejudiced in favor of the defendant.

[171] Affidavit of Heinz Haushofer, May 7, 1948. Von Weizsäcker Defense Document Book 5.

had once been strongly reproved by von Weizsäcker for his "indiscretion," wrote in a rather peevish mood (December 1943) after von Kessel had remarked that von Weizsäcker was "pressing for action": "That is easy to do from the Vatican! Before that he certainly did not get very involved." [172] Was that really true?

On the contrary there is now sufficient evidence to prove that during 1938-39 State Secretary von Weizsäcker used every diplomatic channel available to work for the preservation of peace.[173] This was directly opposed to the policies of Hitler and Ribbentrop at that time and had to be done at grave personal risk. During the whole time that he was in office he kept Beck and Canaris informed on the state of foreign relations,[174] and allowed his position to be used as a cover for the activity of Trott zu Solz and the Kordts which will be described later.[175]

Frequently he received the Papal Nuncio Msgr. Cesare Orsenigo contrary to Ribbentrop's instructions, and intervened on behalf of the churches whenever possible. Msgr. Raphael Forni, formerly Secretary to the Papal Nuncio in Berlin, described von Weizsäcker as a "noble, quiet, peaceable, and benevolent person" who was a sincere friend of the Papal Nuncio.[176] He recognized in him a deep love for his country as well as a sad awareness that the unhappy fate of Germany was the logical consequence of the absence of reason and order. On one occasion the State Secretary spoke with Msgr. Forni of the need for a modern St. Francis of Assisi who would repair the damage wrought by the capitulation of the religious and cultural spirit. This view was, according to Msgr. Forni, typical of his deeply religious outlook.

After the war began, von Weizsäcker's personal ethical problem became more complex. He had been willing to use the full power

[172] Von Hassell, *op. cit.*, p. 332. They had been very friendly until May, 1942. Cf. von Hassell, *op. cit.*, pp. 256-257, and von Weizsäcker, *op. cit.*, p. 275.

[137] *Infra.* chapter III.

[174] Testimony of F. von Schlabrendorff at Nuremberg in *T. of W. C.*, XIII, 389. Von. Weizsäcker, *op. cit.*, pp. 142-3 and 182. Cf. also his testimony in the transcript of his trial, p. 7704.

[175] *Infra.* chapters III, IV, V.

[176] Affidavit of Msgr. Raphael Forni. Von Weizsäcker Defense Document Book 9.

of his office to work behind the backs of Hitler and Ribbentrop in order to prevent war, but to work for the military defeat of Germany appeared to him to be treason. From this position he did not retreat, even when on trial before the Nuremberg Tribunal.[177] He insisted repeatedly that his resistance consisted in holding on to his job as State Secretary, thereby retaining control over at least a small area of activity and preventing a radical Nazi from receiving that position.[178] Whether or not this was the best way of fighting Hitler will be discussed later but in von Weizsäcker's opinion it certainly was.

As a devoted civil servant, he saw his duty in serving not a particular regime or constitution but the fatherland; during his particular term of office that required working against the incumbent government. Therefore, he did so. He objected vehemently when Ribbentrop, at the time of the crisis before Munich, refused to listen to his estimate of the situation and told him to have "blind faith in Hitler."[179] To von Weizsäcker that was contrary to the conscience and sense of duty of a true civil servant. He would certainly have subscribed, one feels, to the statement in the "Appeal to the German People" which reads: "The civil servant shall once again obey only the law and his own conscience."[180]

Hans Speidel, a close friend of Colonel-General Beck, declared that Beck thought very highly of von Weizsäcker and depended on his continuation in office for the success of the Resistance Movement.

> Weizsäcker did not become an advocate of change of regime, the maintainance of peace, and the saving of his people when the catastrophe was unavoidable, but he held those views at a time when the later Allies were still countenancing Hitler's successes with his foreign policy.[181]

---

[177] Von Weizsäcker testimony, transcript of the trial, pp. 7888-7900. Cf. Erich Kordt, *op. cit.*, p. 437.

[178] Von Weizsäcker testimony *T. of W. C.*, XII, 920; speech of the defense counsel, pp. 234-41. Lord Halifax stated that his advisers had frequently reported to him that von Weizsäcker was using his position to hinder the policy of Ribbentrop. Halifax affidavit, Apr. 28, 1948, *T. of W. C.*, XII, 911.

[179] Von Weizsäcker testimony, *T. of W. C.*, XII, 798.

[180] *Supra*, pp. 71-72.

[181] Affidavit of Hans Speidel. Von Weizsäcker Defense Document Book 5.

In 1938 he deliberately tried to sabotage the Nazi plans to solve the problem of Czechoslovakia by force.[182] In his own opinion, the summer of 1938 was the decisive moment regarding the proper path of duty for him to follow.

> . . . it had become clear to me that if an official wanted to serve peace and his fatherland he had the choice between only two ways, that is, to promote his aims and ideas within the state, that is, to sabotage the course steered in the direction of war or else to remove the heads of government. With the means I had at my disposal, that is, politically to redirect the course towards peace, seemed to me my active and direct part.[183]

The case of Ernst von Weizsäcker is extremely significant because of the problem which it exemplifies. Should a person holding office under a tyrannical government resign in protest, or can he do more for the ultimate good of his country by remaining in office in the hope of sabotaging the policies of the government? It is an ethical problem, so wide in scope and so deep in meaning, that a separate chapter will be devoted to a consideration of it. The different conspirators had different answers to it, but von Weizsäcker certainly remained in office from a sense of "duty" to God and to his country. Regardless of the ultimate answer to the problem, his final plea at Nuremberg is of interest in explaining his action:

> I have only a few words to say in conclusion. I have been a member of two silent services; and here, too, I should have preferred to have remained silent. But I stand here not for myself alone.
>
> What does a sailor do when the weather and the captain have brought the ship into danger? Does he go below deck in order not to have any responsibility? Or does he set to and do all he can to help, with all his strength and all the means at his disposal?
>
> I did not attempt to leave the danger-spot but tried to stick it out and to fight. Such was my decision.
>
> My goal was peace—peace for my country and for the world I live in. . . . If I faced the same situation to-day, I should take the same decision.[184]

---

182 Infra. chapter III.

183 Von Weiszsäcker testimony, transcript, p. 7704.

184 Von Weizsäcker, *Memoirs*, pp. 310-311.

The recurring theme in our discussions of the motives of the leaders of the German Resistance Movement is this sense of duty, of responsibility to act according to one's conscience. To Beck the primary thing was his obligations as a military leader; to von Moltke, his responsibility to live and act as a Christian; to von Weizsäcker, his duty as a civil servant bound to serve his country faithfully. It seems reasonable to suppose that the men who gathered around these leaders and worked with them sympathized, in general, with their sincere opposition to a lawless, criminally irresponsible government.

Von Hassell, Gisevius, von Tresckow, von Schlabrendorff, Oster, and Olbricht have all indicated their agreement with the high ideals and basic principles of the leaders described above. The best synthesis of their reasons for fighting Hitler and the Nazis has probably been given in the terse statement of Peter Yorck von Wartenburg before the People's Court. When Judge Freisler accused him of disagreeing with the Nazi conception of justice, he replied:

> The decisive factor which brings together all these questions is the totalitarian claim of the state on the individual which forces him to renounce his moral and religious obligations to God.[185]

This renunciation the men of the German Resistance were not prepared to make.

[185] **Quoted in Dulles, *op. cit.*, p. 84.**

CHAPTER III

PATRIOTISM OR TREASON?

An analysis of the German Resistance Movement requires a description of the conspirators' activities in the field of foreign relations in order to label them as "patriots" or "traitors." Because of the international implications, the ethical problem of fighting against Hitler was particularly acute. It was one thing to work for the overthrow of a lawless government by a group of its loyal citizens; it was something quite different to seek cooperation from foreign powers in this attempt.

Yet the Nazi program, essentially nationalistic as it was, implied an aggressive and extra-legal policy toward the entire international community. To capitalize on this fact became, for the conspirators within Germany, a cornerstone of their own plans. From 1937 to September 1939 they worked steadily to sabotage the foreign policy of Hitler and von Ribbentrop; during World War II they made several attempts to negotiate a peace, the primary condition of which would be the overthrow of the Hitler regime.

The first phase of their conspiratorial activity held two goals: (1) the preservation of peace, and (2) the overthrow of the Nazis. Some of the men in the Resistance Movement emphasized the first, and considered the second chiefly as a means of accomplishing it; others sought primarily the end of the regime, and intended to utilize Hitler's embarkation on an aggressive war to conciliate popular opinion, in the hope of thus avoiding civil war. Nevertheless, these groups concerted their plans, and worked in unanimity for a two-point program: (1) to convince Hitler that the Western Powers would go to war if he attempted to settle Germany's "living space" problem by unilateral revision of the Treaty of Versailles, and (2) to secure a firm British attitude in the face of Hitler's demands.

Quite naturally, the group which figured most prominently in this aspect of resistance was the "younger set" in the Foreign

Office, who, under the protection and with the support of State Secretary von Weizsäcker, managed to keep open the channels of communication with the British. In constant touch with General Ludwig Beck and Carl Goerdeler, they were able to utilize their diplomatic posts and their acquaintance with important persons in England for the achievement of the work at hand.[1]

In 1937, 1938, and 1939 there were direct visits to London by Goerdeler, Ewald von Kleist-Schmentzien, Erich and Theo Kordt, Adam Trott zu Solz, Fabian von Schlabrendorff and others. In 1937 Goerdeler visited Washington, followed at the end of 1939 by Adam Trott zu Solz. During the war, efforts were made on several occasions to arouse Allied sympathy and to secure an opening for peace negotiations through Switzerland, Sweden, the Vatican, and other neutral spots. These efforts did not cease until the death of most of the conspirators after the abortive plot of July 20, 1944.

During the months prior to the Sudeten crisis, the decisive question in Germany was: "If Hitler moves against Czechoslovakia, what will England and France do?" The testimony at Nuremberg and the publication of the German Foreign Office documents show that von Ribbentrop's whole force was behind the conviction that England would do nothing. The conspirators realized very early that they must work hard to convince Hitler that the opposite was true.

An attempt to inform Hitler of the resurging economic and political strength of the Western countries may be seen in Carl Goerdeler's reports on his 1937-38 trips to Captain Wiedermann, Adjutant to Hitler.[2] Goerdeler had visited France, Belgium,

[1] On the membership and development of this group cf. Hans Rothfels, "International Aspects of German Opposition to Hitler," *Measure*, II, pp. 175-190.

[2] These reports are in the files of the Office of Strategic Services at the National Archives, under custody of the Department of State. They were received by the Office of the Coordinator of Information some time prior to 1942. It may have been the possession of these reports which inclined U. S. observers to question Goerdeler's opposition to the regime as late as 1944. While Goerdeler was in the United States in November 1937 he visited Sec. of State Hull to whom he gave the impression of a sincere awareness of the evils of the Nazi regime. Cf. chapter II, n. 79.

England, Canada, and the United States, and his observations, seen in retrospect, are very interesting. He emphasizes the steady recovery from the economic depression, the lack of government control of economy in the areas visited, and the political freedom enjoyed particularly by the citizens in the United States.

He noted that public opinion toward him, as a German, had changed considerably between his 1937 and his 1938 visits to London, and attributed it to the *Anschluss*. He also reported that it was the treatment of the Jews and the growing persecution of the churches, rather than the political and economic policies of the Reich, which had aroused resentment abroad against Germany.

A similar effort to counteract von Ribbentrop's predictions regarding England and France's lack of interest in the fate of Czechoslovakia was made by Colonel-General Beck in his memorandum of November 12, 1937. He asserted without qualification that action against Czechoslovakia would precipitate a world war.[3] This estimate of the situation became the basis of the political thinking of the Resistance Movement and, as late as August 30, 1938, State Secretary von Weizsäcker wrote in a memorandum for von Ribbentrop: ". . . if Germany invades Czechoslovakia, she will have the Western Powers as her enemies."[4] The capitulation of Great Britain and France at the time of the *Anschluss* did not, apparently, dim the hopes of the conspirators that, in the case of Czechoslovakia, things would be different.[4a]

Steps must be taken, they felt, to prevent war, but the prevention of war had to indicate a defeat for Hitler. How could this be done?

There is no doubt that many, if not most, of the men of the Resistance Movement believed that the Sudeten area should be incorporated into the Reich.[5] It would be erroneous to see in their

[3] Foerster, *op. cit.*, pp. 80-82.

[4] Memorandum for von Ribbentrop, *Doc. on Ger. For. Pol.*, II, 662.

[4a] The discussions in the House of Commons following the *Anschluss* should have revealed to them as well as to the rest of the world that the West would not defend the *status quo* in Central Europe. Cf. Sister M. Antonia Wathen, *The Policy of England and France Toward the "Anschluss" of 1938* (Washington: The Catholic University Press, 1954). Note especially pp. 186-188.

[5] As late as September 1943, Goerdeler, Beck, and Olbricht were agreed

efforts to strengthen British opposition to Hitler's demands at this time any desire for a strong independent Czechoslovakia. Their objection to Hitler's decision to solve the Czech question by unilateral action rested on their belief that such action would lead to a world war. As Theo Kordt expressed it quite bluntly at Nuremberg, ". . . we established contact with the British government not in order to be of use to the British policy, but in order to spare Germany and the entire occidental world from an unheard-of catastrophe." [6]

During the hot summer months of 1938 the conspirators began to act. Ewald von Kleist-Schmentzien, a Prussian Conservative who fought consistently against Hitler for twelve years and was executed in April 1945, was selected by the Beck-Goerdeler circle to visit London in August 1938. Equipped with a false passport by Admiral Canaris's office in ABWEHR, he visited England from the 18th to the 23rd of August, and there presented the case of the "moderate elements" in the General Staff to several prominent persons in or close to the government.[7]

It will be remembered that Colonel-General Beck resigned as Chief of the General Staff on August 18, 1938. He had already set in motion the von Kleist mission, for on that same day Herr von Kleist had a conversation with Sir Robert Vansittart, chief diplomatic adviser in the British Foreign Office. In view of Vansittart's later denial of the existence of a resistance movement within Germany, it is important to describe this conversation in some detail. On August 18, Vansittart reported to the Secretary of State: [8]

I spoke to you this morning about Herr von Kleist. In the

---

that one of the peace terms should be that the Sudeten territory would remain within the Reich. Interrogation of Goerdeler by RSHA, RSHA Report, Sept. 21, 1944. Dept. of the Army. MS, 105/25. Von Kessel testified at Nuremberg that if the Sudetan Germans could have been peacefully incorporated he would have favored it. Transcript of von Weizsäcker Trial, pp. 9459-60. Cf. von Weizsäcker, *Memoirs*, p. 145.

[6] Testimony of Theo Kordt, Transcript of von Weizsäcker trial, p. 12284.

[7] Ian Colvin, *Master Spy* (N. Y.: McGraw Hill Co., 1952), p. 67.

[8] *Documents on British Foreign Policy 1919-39*, Series III, II, 683-692. Here are collected all the various items related to the von Kleist mission Vansittart's letter is pp. 683-85.

> afternoon about 4 o'clock I received an application from him to see me. He said that I was one of the few people in this country with whom he wished to speak and would be able to speak freely. . . .
> Herr von Kleist at once opened up with the utmost frankness and gravity. He said (and this coincides with a great deal of other information which I have given you from entirely different sources) that war was now a certainty unless we stopped it. I said "Do you mean an extreme danger?" He answered: "No, I do not mean an extreme danger, I mean a complete certainty." I said "Do you mean to say that the extremists are now carrying Hitler with them?" He said: "No, I do not mean that. There is only one real extremist and that is Hitler himself. He is the great danger and he is doing this entirely on his own. He receives a great deal of encouragement from Herr von Ribbentrop who keeps telling him that when it comes to the showdown neither France nor England will do anything." (You will remember that I gave you the same information from an entirely different source this morning as to R's present attitude and influence.)

Lord Vansittart went on to say that Herr von Kleist had told him that all the generals were against war, but that unless something decisive were done before September 27, it would be too late. He added that Lord Lloyd had received the same tentative date from another informant. According to von Kleist, England and France must make Hitler realize that they were not bluffing; they should have one of their leading statesmen make a speech emphasizing the horrors of war and appealing to the "moderate" elements in Germany. He described himself to Lord Vansittart as "a Conservative, a Prussian, and a Christian," and added:

> . . . that there was no prospect whatever of any reasonable policy being followed by Germany so long as Hitler was at the head of affairs but that he believed that if war was avoided on this occasion as it had been in May, it would be the prelude to the end of the regime and a renascence of a Germany with whom the world could deal.

Obviously, von Kleist wanted not only to prevent war, but also to bring about a situation which would literally demand the removal of Hitler.

The report of Lord Vansittart on this conversation was in the hands of Prime Minister Chamberlain early on the 19th of August, and although Chamberlain acknowledged that the information was in agreement with that received from other sources, he was of the opinion that although von Kleist was, no doubt, "violently anti-Hitler," his group was analagous to ". . . the Jacobites at the Court of France in King William's time." He added, ". . . I think we must discount a good deal of what he says."[9]

Meanwhile, von Kleist met with Winston Churchill and reviewed the situation once more.[10] He stated that an attack on Czechoslovakia was imminent, and that it would probably occur between the Nuremberg *Parteitag* and the end of September. Hitler alone wanted war, and the generals would—if they received encouragement from abroad—refuse to march. It was a gesture of this sort which von Kleist sought, a gesture which would "crystallize the wide-spread and indeed, universal anti-war sentiment in Germany." If the generals could be brought to the point of insisting on peace, he said, there would be a new German government within forty-eight hours. To bring them to this point, the conspirators needed some written assurance from abroad that Hitler's demands would be met by force.[11]

Churchill complied with von Kleist's request, giving him a letter to bring back to the oppositional elements in Germany. In part, it read:

> I have welcomed you here as one who is ready to run risks to preserve the peace of Europe and to achieve a lasting friendship between the British, French, and German people for their mutual advantage.
>
> I am sure that the crossing of the frontier of Czechoslovakia by German armies or aviation in force will bring about a renewal of world war. . . .
>
> Do not, I pray you, be misled upon this point. Such a war, once started, would be fought out like the last to the bitter end, and one must consider not what might happen in the first few months, but where we should all be at the end of the third or fourth year. . . .
>
> As I felt you should have some definite message to take back to your friends in Germany who wish to see peace preserved

---

[9] *Ibid.*, p. 686.
[10] *Ibid.*, p. 687-88.
[11] Colvin, *op. cit.*, p. 67.

> and who look forward to a great Europe in which England, France, and Germany will be working together for the prosperity of the wage-earning masses, I communicated with Lord Halifax. His Lordship asks me to say on his behalf that the position of His Majesty's Government in relation to Czechoslovakia is defined by the Prime Minister's speech in the House of Commons on March 24, 1938.[12]

The speech of March 24 to which Churchill referred had been strongly indicative of support for Czechoslovakia in the event of German aggression, but did not provide the definite assurance which the conspirators were seeking. Nevertheless, as a result of these messages received from Germany, the British Prime Minister decided to recall the Ambassador from Berlin for consultations; on August 24 instructions were sent to Ambassador Henderson to return to London.[13]

It is very difficult to assess the role of Neville Henderson during these days of critical diplomatic tension. State Secretary von Weizsäcker has written warmly of the splendid cooperation he received from Ambassador Henderson and the Italian Ambassador, Bernado Attolico, in his efforts to preserve peace and to circumvent the Hitler-Ribbentrop policies.[14] However, Henderson seems to have discounted the efforts of the German Opposition on several occasions. His own record of the period, *Failure of a Mission,*[15] understandably omits any reference to the "resistance" element within the Foreign Office, because publication of the facts in 1940 would have been criminally foolish. But nothing has come to light since which would indicate an understanding on his part of the Resistance Movement.

On August 16, 1938 he cabled to London that Ewald von Kleist was on his way there as an emissary of the moderates of the

[12] *Documents on Brit. For. Pol.* III, II, p. 688.

[13] *Ibid.*, p. 148. Telegram London to Berlin No. 325, August 24, 1938. Henderson arrived in London August 28 and remained until the 31st.

[14] In his *Memoirs*, von Weizsäcker wrote: "The relationship of mutual confidence between Henderson and myself dates from this period [May, 1938], and lasted till the day when Henderson left after war broke out in 1939." p. 135.

[15] Neville Henderson *Failure of a Mission* (N. Y.: G. P. Putnam's Sons, 1940).

General Staff, and would seek British assurance of strength against Hitler as a guarantee against war. Henderson advised that it would be unwise to receive him in official circles.[16] While von Kleist was in London, word was received from Henderson on August 21st[17] that the information forwarded on August 17th could be confirmed. An "informant" [unnamed but identified as an "army officer who had supported National Socialism but was now hostile to Hitler"] had told the British Military Attaché that Hitler would take military action against Czechoslovakia that fall. The date was set for the end of September, with mobilization scheduled for September 15th.

To this report of the 17th the informant now added that ". . . the German General Staff are staggered by the fact that it is being taken so quietly abroad," and he urged that France and England force Hitler to renounce his present intentions. This, he concluded, ". . . would lead to his downfall." But any effect such a message might have had in London must certainly have been nullified by the opinion appended to it by Ambassador Henderson. He noted that the informant was well known to him and "his pronouncements are clearly biased and largely propaganda. There is, however, nothing illogical in the above information and in view of many other pointers it would be wise not to take it (other than?) seriously." If Henderson was in such close association with von Weizsäcker and von Hassell, why was he so unenthusiastic about the receipt of such information and how could he consider it as no more than propaganda?

Reportedly the Ambassador in his conversations with Prime Minister Chamberlain at the end of August 1938 gave the impression that there was little genuine opposition to Hitler within Germany.[18] That he was unaware of many things going on in Berlin is clear from his ignorance as late as September 19 of Colonel-General Beck's resignation as Chief of the General Staff.[19]

[16] *Documents on Brit. For. Pol.* III, II, 683.

[17] Henderson to Halifax, August 21, 1938. *Ibid.*, p. 125. The cable of Aug. 17 is not published.

[18] Colvin, *op. cit.*, p. 72.

[19] Henderson to Halifax, Sept. 19, 1938. *Doc. on Brit. For. Pol.* III, II, p. 408.

The Prime Minister instructed Henderson to convey a serious warning directly to the Fuehrer, and to arrange, if possible, for a private meeting between him and the Prime Minister.[20] The Ambassador succeeded in having the first part of the instruction cancelled, and it is difficult to follow his line of reasoning on this. Was not the friendly but firm warning to Hitler one of the key points in the desiderata of the conspirators? It was the main point urged by von Weizsäcker several times as the one means of keeping the peace; why then, did Henderson kill it? At any rate, the Ambassador's visit had the effect of negating completely the mission of von Kleist.

Meanwhile State Secretary von Weizsäcker utilized two other channels to the British. At the end of August, he invited to Berlin the League of Nations High Commissioner for Danzig, Carl J. Burkhardt.[21] They had first become friends in the 1920's when in Basle, and von Weizsäcker's personal esteem for Burkhardt now prompted him to entrust to him an urgent mission—one which, if discovered, would endanger not only his position but his life. For the State Secretary had decided that a direct attempt must be made to inform the British of the true state of affairs within Germany and to ask their cooperation in preventing an international conflict.

He told Burkhardt, therefore, of the impossibility of securing an opportunity to place the truth about England and France before Hitler. He described the details of Colonel-General Beck's resignation, and of Hitler's intention of attacking Czechoslovakia with such overwhelming force as to preclude any defensive action by England and France who will not then, according to Hitler, "dare to intervene." The only hope for peace, said von Weizsäcker, lay in a personal letter from the Prime Minister to Hitler ". . . beginning with remarks calculated to please him such as reference to his desire for a peaceful settlement but ending by saying that if

[20] Henderson, *op. cit.*, pp. 147 and 150.

[21] Excerpt from the diary of Carl Burkhardt submitted at Nuremberg as von Weizsäcker Defense Document 169 f. The message brought to Berne by Burkhardt was relayed to London by telegram from G. Warner to Halifax, Sept. 5, 1938. *Doc. on Brit. For. Pol.* III, II, p. 242. A more detailed account was given in a letter from Mr. Skrine Stevenson to Mr. Strang, Sept. 8, 1938. *Ibid.*, p. 689.

Czechoslovakia were attacked, England would support her with all forces at her command. . . ." The British ought to send an energetic military man to Hitler to impress on him the great danger of conflict.

It must not have been easy for a civil servant of von Weizsäcker's moral constitution to take such a drastic step. He admitted to Burkhardt that the decision had been a difficult one. "He had, however, thought it over very carefully, and in the conflict of loyalties had decided that his sense of patriotism overcame his loyalty to his chief [von Ribbentrop] whose influence on the Fuehrer he regarded as fatal." Burkhardt told the British Minister at Berne, George Warner, that he had known von Weizsäcker a long time, and that his absolute loyalty to his superiors had always been so evident that this decision of his to inform the British was very impressive. The realization of how seriously von Weizsäcker regarded the situation had prompted Burkhardt to drive the 900 kilometers to Berne in one day, and to work with Warner that same evening composing a message to Lord Halifax. The next morning he reenforced this message by a telephone call to Butler in the Foreign Office. In the affidavit in which Burkhardt tells this story, he adds to his description of the affair. . . . "Yet, Chamberlain made his trip."

The second channel selected by von Weizsäcker was even more dangerous because it utilized official diplomatic officers and might easily have ended at von Ribbentrop's front door. The Foreign Minister had a young aide, Erich Kordt, who had been assigned to him in 1934 when he was appointed Commissioner for Disarmamament. At the time State Secretary von Bülow, who made the appointment, said to Kordt: "At no time conceal or correct the incompetence and errors of the new special commissioner (for Disarmament). Then he will have enough rope to hang himself." [22] Kordt was First Secretary at the London Embassy 1936-38 while von Ribbentrop was Ambassador, and when the latter returned to Berlin in February 1938 as Foreign Minister he took Kordt as his assistant.

Consistently anti-Nazi, Kordt was nevertheless able to retain his

[22] E. A. Bayne, "Resistance in the German Foreign Office," *Human Events*, III (April 3, 1946), pp. 2-3.

position and use it as a "listening post" for von Weizsäcker and the opposition group.[23] His brother Theo was Councilor at the German Embassy in London in the pre-Munich days, and together they devised a plan of getting in touch with the British for von Weizsäcker and Beck.

Beck, Oster, Canaris, Halder, and von Weizsäcker all urged Erich Kordt to make a further appeal for assurances from His Majesty's Government that plans for overthrowing Hitler would be supported by a firm stand on the part of Britain. "All were agreed," he wrote, "that, without an open and unmistakable declaration of the British government on their attitude toward a German-Czech war, the German people would not see the flock of dangers in which Germany found herself, and would not understand the necessity of a *coup d'état.*"[24] Beck and his associates felt that it was extremely important that the British Government know their plans to use the international crisis to overthrow Hitler so that the British, in turn, would refuse concessions to Hitler and make it clear to the German people on whom responsibility for war or peace lay.

Oster told Kordt plainly at this time:

> If the British Government will give us, by means of an energetic declaration, an argument which will impress also the common man, then you can explain to the British Government that the military Fronde with Beck at its head will know how to hinder the outbreak of war. Then there will be no Hitler any more.[25]

This message was entrusted by Erich Kordt to his cousin, Susy Simonis, a young journalist possibly connected with the "Uncle

[23] Paul Schmidt, official translator for Hitler, often exchanged bits of "intelligence" with him so that the conspirators would know what Hitler was doing. Schmidt stated that Kordt had "his own very efficient intelligence service." Interrogation of Paul Schmidt, De Witt C. Poole Mission, Oct. 19, 1945. Dept. of State. MS.

Ruth Andreas-Friedrich, *op. cit.*, p. 5, refers to early Kordt's anti-Nazi activity. In 1941 he was sent as Minister to Tokyo and was therefore out of the conspiracy at the time of the July 1944 affair.

[24] Kordt, *op. cit.*, p. 244. Translation mine.

[25] *Ibid.*, p. 248. Translation mine.

Emil" group described above.[26] She committed it to memory, and departed for London. There she communicated it to Theo Kordt and he immediately requested a secret meeting with Lord Halifax. Kordt was instructed to come to the back door of No. 10 Downing Street on the night of September 5, and there in the garden of the Prime Minister's residence he delivered the message from the German Opposition.[27]

> Extraordinary times demand extraordinary means. Today I come to you not in my character as German *Geschäftträger,* but as a speaker for political and military circles in Berlin, which wish to prevent a war by every possible means. The message which I now deliver to you has been thought over very carefully, and it seems to us that it deserves the attention of the British Government.[28]

Kordt then described the plans of Hitler to attack Czechoslovakia, continuing: "We believe that if one gives way to Hitler's policy of force in this case, the way to a return to conceptions of decency and honor among European nations will be definitely blocked."[29] Therefore, he sought a determined and clear declaration that Great Britain would stand by France in her agreement with Czechoslovakia, and assured Lord Halifax that if Hitler persisted in his bellicose policy the circles for which he spoke would take up arms against him.

> If the desired declaration is given, the leaders of the army are prepared to move against Hitler's politics with arms. A diplomatic defeat would be a very serious political set-back for Hitler in Germany and would practically mean the end of the National Socialist regime.[30]

In an attempt to explain this most unusual action which he, as German Councilor at the London Embassy, had taken behind the Foreign Minister's back, Theo Kordt said to Halifax:

---

[26] Ruth Andreas-Friedrich, *op. cit.*, p. 5, identifies Erich Kordt as the cousin of her friend "Karla Simeon." Since pseudonyms are used throughout the book it is possible that this is Susy Simonis.

[27] The details of the Kordt mission are from Interrogation of Erich Kordt, De Witt C. Poole Mission, Jan. 7, 1945. Dept. of State. MS.

[28] Kordt, *op. cit.*, pp. 279-280. Translation mine.

[29] *Ibid.* Translation mine.

[30] *Ibid.* Translation mine.

> It is not easy for me to speak in this way with the British Foreign Minister . . . but the German patriots see no other way out of the dilemma but close cooperation with the British Government in order to avert war.[31]

Certainly it was a situation unique in history. While the Head of State and his Foreign Minister were pursuing a bold foreign policy designed to frighten all potential opponents into docile submission, the Chief of the General Staff and his predecessor in that office, the head of the Counter-Intelligence and his aides, and the State Secretary and his subordinate officers were working intensively to convince the opponents that a display of force on their part would cause a successful revolution within Germany.

How did they justify such unofficial use of their government positions and of the information received because of them? It was, according to von Weizsäcker, " a conspiracy with the potential enemy for the purpose of assuring peace." [32] To the State Secretary, peace was synonymous with the common good of the fatherland, and, as such, must be preserved at all costs.

Several other minor emissaries were also sent to the British at this time. Lieutenant-Colonel Hans Boehm-Tettelbach arrived in London September 2, under orders from Colonel-General Halder to establish contact with the British War Office and Military Intelligence. He was to tell them to remain firm and not to retreat before the demands of Hitler. Although Boehm-Tettelbach told General Oster upon his return that he had no doubt that Lord Vansittart had " put the facts in the record," nothing more substantial came of his trip.[33]

On August 31, as tension was mounting, Ambassador Henderson returned from London to Berlin and that night had dinner with State Secretary von Weizsäcker. He stated quite frankly that he brought back with him no threats from London, but that he had observed a growing unanimity of opinion among the Londoners with regard to Germany.[34] Von Weizsäcker, noted Henderson,

[31] *Ibid.* Translation mine.

[32] Von Weizsäcker, *Memoirs,* p. 145.

[33] Wheeler-Bennett, *op. cit.*, p. 417; Fritz Halder, *Gespräche mit Halder,* compiled by Peter Bor (Wiesbaden: Limes Verlag, 1950), p. 121; Colvin, *op. cit.*, p. 88.

[34] Berlin to London, No. 403, Sept. 1, 1938, *Brit. Doc. on For. Pol.* III, II, 203.

remarked somewhat ominously that if Great Britain had spoken in time in 1914, war might have been avoided.[35] On September 7, 9, and 10 von Weizsäcker felt it necessary to inform the Ambassador that Göring, von Ribbentrop and others had not yet received the impression from him that England would take part in a war in Central Europe.[36]

While these repeated requests for help and warnings of imminent danger were being given to the British, both in London and Berlin, were any similar steps taken in regard to the French? It was France, after all, which was specifically bound by treaty to come to the aid of Czechoslovakia; her case for standing firm against Hitler was stronger than that of England. Yet, traditional enmity and distrust formed a barrier against an approach to the French Government. The French Ambassador in Berlin, A. François-Poncet, does mention the receipt of some information at this time regarding Hitler's determination to invade Czechoslovakia at the end of the month unless he had received a satisfactory settlement of the problem. The date indicated was September 27 or 28, but the informant is identified only as ". . . an excellent source from amid Hitler's intimate circle." [37] None of the members of the Resistance Movement claims to have been this informant, and there is no ground for concluding that it was one of them.

The second piece of intelligence was given by the Kordts in London to Pierre Maillaud, deputy chief of HAVAS Agency in London. They urged him to use his influence on his government against any further concessions to Hitler. Erich Kordt claimed that the reason for not dealing more directly with the French was their known indiscretion which would have endangered the whole resistance movement.[38]

A young member of the German Foreign Office, Edwart von Selzam, approached the United States Ambassador in London, Mr. Joseph P. Kennedy, during the Sudeten crisis.[39] He urged a state-

[35] Berlin to London, No. 408, Sept. 3, 1938. *Ibid.*, p. 216.

[36] Von Weizsäcker, *Memoirs*, p. 146.

[37] André François-Poncet, *The Fateful Years: Memoirs of the French Ambassador in Berlin 1931-38.* (N. Y.: Harcourt Brace, 1949), p. 259.

[38] Kordt, Interrogation, Jan. 7, 1945.

[39] Letter from Mr. Joseph P. Kennedy to Mr. Edwart von Selzam for submission to Nuremberg tribunal, July 10, 1946. Von Weizsäcker Defense Document Book 10A.

ment by President Roosevelt that the United States would go to war if Hitler resorted to force to solve the Czech problem. There is no indication of any attempt to establish contact with the Czechs or Russians. Admiral Canaris is reported to have made a trip to Hungary in 1938 to urge Admiral Horthy, Hungarian Regent, not to follow Ribbentrop's advice to present demands coincidental with those of Hitler.[40]

Meanwhile, time was running out and with little assurance from abroad the conspirators went ahead with plans to arrest Hitler when he would return to Berlin on September 15.[41] September 12 was *Parteitag* at Nuremberg, and there were gathered all the leading public figures and foreign diplomats. The incendiary speech of Herr Hitler did nothing to relieve the tension, but for some unknown reason, Ambassador Henderson evidently believed that the danger of war had lessened. Once more, a member of the Resistance, Herr von Kessel, attempted to counteract Henderson's erroneous view. In conversation with the Second Secretary to the British Ambassador, von Kessel spent several hours that evening attempting to convince him of Hitler's real intentions and the tremendous dangers inherent in British appeasement. He insisted that the British should distinguish between the legitimate desires of the German people and the aggressive policy of the Nazis. All this was, as he notes, a task " not easy for a patriot." [42] But, we might ask, was it not patriotism in this case to reveal the plans of the government one was serving to the very power against whom they were directed? This was the heart of the problem always facing the members of the Resistance group.

Those who like to speculate on the " ifs " of history will find interesting material in the course of events from September 13 to 28, 1938. Still under the impression that Hitler's demands on Czechoslovakia, if backed by force, would be met by force, the conspirators went ahead with plans to arrest Hitler as described above. It is not surprising that they should have allowed themselves to hope that the Western Powers would stand firm against

[40] Colvin, *op. cit.*, p. 74.

[41] *Supra*, pp. 12-14.

[42] Albrecht von Kessel, testimony at Nuremberg. Von Weizsäcker Transcript, pp. 9459-60.

concessions to Hitler since every answer to their proposals had indicated such a decision.

Ambassador Henderson, according to his own testimony, had lunch with Herr von Hassell on September 14 and asked him to tell General Keitel (whom he was to see that afternoon) that "while nothing will be more distasteful to the British nation than to go to war with Germany again, it would be impossible for us to keep out of it if Germany acted in any way which would compel France to come to the aid of Czechoslovakia."[43] At the same time Henderson revealed that he had "induced the British cabinet to propose Chamberlain's visit to Hitler," and arrangements were now being made through Woermann and von Weizsäcker.

The Fuehrer had gone to Berchtesgaden from Nuremberg instead of returning to Berlin, so that the attempted *coup* had been postponed. Now came the announcement of Chamberlain's visit. At first, this did not disappoint the conspirators. They felt that the British Prime Minister was coming to impart a strong personal warning to Hitler.[44] The one who seems to have had the clearest perception of the real meaning of the visit was the State Secretary. He considered it an indication that the British and French were ready to recognize German claims regarding the Sudetens.[45]

The story of Chamberlain's visit to Berchtesgaden, and subsequently to Godesberg and Munich, is well known. Only von Ribbentrop had been right in his estimate of the British lack of interest in fighting a war to save Central Europe. The plans made by the conspirators to arrest Hitler as soon as a signal was given to invade Czechoslovakia collapsed when the phone call came from Mussolini on the 28th suggesting the Munich Conference.

This does not mean, as some have implied, that the whole conspiracy against Hitler was thwarted by the British Prime Minister's policy;[46] it would be wrong to impute to him the

[43] Henderson to Halifax, No. 886, Sept. 15, 1938, *Doc. on Brit. For. Pol.* III, II, 330.

[44] Gisevius notes that they believed it was a tactical gesture on the part of the British which would clearly place the blame on Hitler. *Op. cit.*, p. 321.

[45] Von Weizsäcker, *Memoirs*, p. 150.

[46] This would seem to be the assumption of Colonel-General Halder. Cf. Interrogation of Halder, Feb. 26, 1946. Cf. Wheeler-Bennett's refutation of this thesis, *op. cit.*, pp. 420-424.

blame for World War II just because he could not see the realism of a strong policy against Hitler at Munich. But it does mean that he made the decision not to defend Czechoslovakia in the light of full knowledge about the existence of the resistance group in Germany. On September 14, 1938 Lord Halifax had telegraphed to Ambassador Phipps in Paris that: ". . . we have had increasing evidence of growing discontent with the regime in Germany and with Herr Hitler's conduct of foreign policy. This plan which we now propose, or the bare proposal of it, might strengthen the moderates in Germany." [47]

The awareness by the British of the German opositional forces was further attested to by Mr. Duff Cooper in submitting his resignation on October 3, 1938 in the House of Commons. Speaking of the days before Munich, he called attention to the fact that His Majesty's Government had been urged to a display of strength before the *Parteitag* at Nuremberg.

> On all sides we were being urged to do so, by people in this country, by members in this house, by the heads of foreign states, even by Germans who were supporters of the regime and did not wish to see it plunged into a war which might destroy it.[48]

And in the debate in the House of Lords on October 4, 1938 Lord Lloyd refuted Halifax's claim that they had not known what a crisis was upon them in the days before Munich. He said:

> . . . he knows that I was able to inform him in the very early days of August of the whole German plan that worked out to the actual day. He knows too where that information came from and that there was counsel from that source that to save the situation there should be an immediate declaration.[49]

The reactions of the men of the German Resistance to the decisions reached at Munich were diversified. State Secretary von Weizsäcker, whose basic motive for resistance was to preserve peace,

[47] Halifax to Phipps, No. 875, Sept. 14, 1938. *Doc. on Brit. For. Pol.*, III, II, 323.

[48] *Parliamentary Debates, House of Commons, Official Report, Great Britain, Fifth Series*, 339: 30.

[49] *Parliamentary Debates, House of Lords, Official Report, Great Britain, Fifth Series*, 110:1420.

confessed later that Munich was "the last happy day of my life. War had been avoided." [50] Yet he admits that many of his friends considered it as only a second-best solution and were disappointed that the plans for Hitler's arrest had not succeeded.[51] To Beck and Goerdeler, who regarded Hitler as the Number One enemy and the crisis in world affairs as a means of getting rid of him, Munich was a tragedy. Beck's entire thesis had been demonstrated false; the Western Powers had not fought.

Goerdeler described his feelings in a letter of October 11, 1938 to a friend in America:

> The development of the last few weeks can only be designated as very dangerous. An excellent opportunity has been lost. . . . If England had shown a resolute attitude and openly announced to the German people: We are ready to satisfy all your well-founded claims, only not under the pressure of power . . . if England and France had only taken the risk of a war, Hitler would never have used force. . . . Hitler and Göring have bluffed the entire world. . . . But the world had been warned and instructed in good time. If the warning had been taken and used as a basis for action, then would Germany already today be free from its dictator and act against Mussolini. . . .[52]

Goerdeler's optimistic temperament believed that this position would have enabled Germany to join hands with France and England to solve the Spanish problem, and then with the United States to restore peace in the Far East. Indeed Goerdeler seemed to feel that Utopia had just been missed by a split second! Unhappily, he concluded, England and France had lost their prestige in Europe and were now only a potential prey for the Axis.

We may presume that the other members of the Resistance Movement held opinions somewhere in between these two extremes. Von Hassell reported the general feeing as one of relief that war had been averted.[53]

After Munich, what were the relations of these "patriots" with

[50] Von Weizsäcker, *Memoirs*, p. 158.

[51] *Ibid.* cf. Kordt Interrogation, and von Kessel testimony in von Weizsäcker Transcript, p. 9464.

[52] *Goerdelers Politisches Testament*, pp. 57-64. Translation mine.

[53] Von Hassell, *op. cit.*, p. 7.

foreign powers? Hitler's success in out-bluffing the Western Powers led to a feeling of hopelessness among those who had been searching for a crisis in international affairs which would make their *coup* feasible. The crisis had come and gone, but it had not been used to advantage. However, it soon became clear that it was not the last crisis. On October 4, 1938—before the ink was yet dry on Hitler's pledge to Chamberlain—von Weizsäcker told von Hassell that Hitler was now speaking of the necessity of liquidating the Czech problem within a few months.[54] And, von Hassell noted: "Weizsäcker was deeply depressed." The "happy day" of Munich had shown its hollowness, and now what could be done to forestall Hitler's next move toward territorial aggrandizement?

Apparently very little was undertaken by the conspirators between Munich and the seizure of Prague in March 1939. Goerdeler remained abroad until December 1938,[55] but little is known of his activities there on behalf of the Resistance Movement. Professor Rothfels states that Theo Kordt saw Lord Vansittart almost daily during this period,[56] but the content of their conversations is unknown. At home, General Halder took the position that since Hitler had been given free passage to Prague by the Western Powers there was only one thing to do—wait and see what happened next.[57] Colonel-General Beck felt that, on the contrary, it was most important to keep alive the Resistance Movement; he hoped to consolidate and strengthen the original group so that all would be in order for a *coup* as soon as the Generals would cooperate. But apparently no one sent messengers to London, nor saw any point in doing so; it was all too obvious that the answer would be as meaningless as before.

Nor was support for a revolution likely to be had at home. Asked at Nuremberg why there had been no *putsch* before the seizure of Prague in 1939, von Weizsäcker replied that the internal situation was "unready," the German people were unaware of

[54] *Ibid.*, p. 9.

[55] Letter from Dr. Ritter to the writer, Dec. 29, 1953.

[56] Hans Rothfels, "International Aspects of German Opposition to Hitler," p. 2.

[57] Testimony of Gisevius, *IMT*, XII, 221.

the imminent danger of war, and would not have upheld such a move on the part of the generals.[58]

Two incidents, however, indicate the State Secretary's continued interest in finding a solution short of war. The German Chargé at Prague from October 1938 to March 1939 submitted an affidavit at Nuremberg stating that von Weizsäcker had instructed him to strive in his reports to the Foreign Office to make clear the exaggerations being publicized regarding the Czech Government and to emphasize instead its good intentions.[59] In February 1939 von Weizsäcker instructed Albrecht von Kessel, who was about to make a trip to Switzerland, to find a channel there to the British and urge them once again to send a prominent person (preferably a General) to impress Hitler with the determination of Great Britain to withstand further Nazi aggression. Von Kessel sent the message through an Austrian, Erwin Schoeller, but there was no reply.[60]

The forcible seizure of Prague on March 15, 1939 finally rekindled the spark of resistance, and Schacht, Goerdeler, and Gisevius departed for Ouchy, Switzerland to meet with a "person with considerable influence in London and Paris political circles."[61] The conspirators sought once again for strong assurances of opposition to Hitler's next attempt to solve international problems unilaterally and by force. In the record of this meeting—presented only by Gisevius—a change in point of view may be recognized. Hope of a strong successful action by the German generals had given way to an awareness of their lack of dependability, and the conspirators no longer felt that they could promise the West that an open revolt would take place. They could only emphasize the necessity of preventing an international conflict.

Schacht and Goerdeler differed as to the best way of impressing the West with the urgency of the situation. Both were trained economists, but they saw the situation in two different ways. The former[62] wanted to emphasize to the Western Powers the fact that

[58] Transcript of von Weizsäcker trial, p. 9423.

[59] Affidavit of Andor Hencke, Chargé at Prague, Oct. '38-Mar. '39, von Weizsäcker Defense Document Book 9.

[60] Testimony of von Kessel, von Weizsäcker Transcript, p. 9466.

[61] Gisevius, *op. cit.*, pp. 344-348.

[62] Hjalmar Schacht had been Commissioner of Currency and President of the Reich Bank from 1923 to 1930, Minister of Economics in 1934, and

the Nazis had a strong grip on the whole financial structure of the nation and, despite unorthodox economic measures, would not easily be defeated. Goerdeler, on the other hand, claimed that if the West made one firm stand against the Nazis, the regime would collapse because of its lack of financial soundness. The files of Daladier found later by the ABWEHR reveal that it was Goerdeler's view which was reported to London and Paris, and that the realism of Schacht had been ignored.[63]

Schacht also met Montagu Norman, Governor of the Bank of England, that same important spring of 1939 in Basle.[64] To him he gave a detailed report of conditions inside Germany, including the atrocities being perpetrated in concentration camps. It was hoped that such information would move the Western Powers to act against a state which was so flagrantly violating human rights. But the only answer received from London was that Chamberlain would deal only with official representatives of the government and not with Schacht who was "without political influence." [65]

On March 29, 1939 Mr. Ian Colvin, a British journalist who had been living in Berlin for some time, arrived in London as an emissary of Beck and Oster. He spoke with Sir Alexander Cadogan, the Permanent Under Secretary, with Lord Halifax, and with the Prime Minister.[66] His warning of Hitler's aggressive intentions toward Poland may well have hastened the British guarantee offered to that country on March 31, although it is doubtful if that was the result that the conspirators were hoping to achieve.

Plenipotentiary General for War Economy 1935-37. He served as Pres. of the Reichsbank again 1937-39 and as Min. without Portfolio 1937-43. Apparently he worked closely with Gisevius and Goerdeler in the pre-war conspiracy, but his opposition to the Hitler regime was anything but consistent. As late as January 27, 1938 he praised Hitler to a member of the Amer. Embassy as "a man of sound principles on whom the German people should pin its entire faith." Berlin to Washington, Jan. 27, 1938, Dept. of State. MS, 862.002/320. Cf. Interview of Schacht in *IMT*, XXXIII, 1-32.

[63] Gisevius, *op. cit.*, p. 348.

[64] *Ibid.*, *pp.* 348-350.

[65] Although Schacht was still technically "Minister Without Portfolio" the Cabinet did not meet after February 1938. Interrogation of Hjalmar Schacht, De Witt C. Poole Mission, Sept. 23, 1945. Dept. of State. MS.

[66] Wheeler-Bennett, *op. cit.*, p. 437.

These communications to the British on the part of the Resistance Movement were followed by another period of inactivity, until the Nazi-Soviet pact appeared on the horizon in the late spring. Understandably, the conspirators thought that such a possibility, feared throughout European history, might well be decisive in their struggle to get support from the West. State Secretary von Weizsäcker was absolutely opposed to the pact and therefore informed the British through Erich Kordt that Ribbentrop was planning a trip to Moscow.[67] Admiral Canaris sent Colonel Boehm-Tettelbach once again to London, this time to confer with Sir James Grigg and the various British Service chiefs as to the probable English attitude if Poland were attacked.[68]

During the spring and summer of 1939 several of the conspirators presented their case anew in London: Goerdeler, Pechel, Trott, von Moltke, the Kordts, and Fabian von Schlabrendorff.[69] Presumably the burden of all these conversations was to ascertain the point at which appeasement would cease and military opposition would begin.

To State Secretary von Weizsäcker, June 1939 represented a turning point. Previously it had been his purpose to play down the critical state of German-Polish relations in order not to provoke a war. Now he decided to publicize it as much as possible, hoping thereby to alarm the Western Powers into a show of strength.[70] As late as June 13, 1939, for example, Henderson had reported to London that the State Secretary had assured him that Hitler had no warlike plans and that the best policy would be to "let things simmer." An Anglo-Russian agreement would only increase the tension, according to von Weizsäcker. Furthermore, he felt that the British interference on behalf of Poland had already made things impossible.[71] On the other hand, by the end of the month,

[67] Von Weizsäcker testimony, *T. of W. C.*, XII, 1098. Erich Kordt had five or six conversations beginning in June 1939 with Lord Vansittart. Kordt testimony, von Weizsäcker transcript, p. 7558.

[68] Colvin, *op. cit.*, p. 88.

[69] Wheeler-Bennett, *op. cit.*, p. 441; cf. Bayne, "Resistance in the German Foreign Office."

[70] Transcript of von Weizsäcker trial, p. 9017.

[71] Henderson to Halifax, June 13, 1938. *Doc. on Brit. For. Pol.* III, VI, 59.

von Weizsäcker hoped that by informing the British of von Ribbentrop's proposed trip to Moscow he could get them to increase pressure for an Anglo-Russian accord. The British replied that they would certainly not let Hitler " steal a march " on them.[72]

During the summer of 1939 von Weizsäcker had several conversations with Colonel-General Halder,[73] conversations which centered on the necessity of preserving peace. Often he insisted that this would require the elimination of Hitler at the moment when he confronted the German people with war, and Halder appeared in perfect agreement. Yet in April of 1939 Halder had told a member of the American Embassy staff in Berlin that ". . . the German army must support Hitler under all circumstances no matter what." [74] It was conflicting reports like these which made the Western Powers dubious about the value of giving support to a group of internal dissenters who were sometimes so inconsistent.

In August 1939 the efforts to maintain peace became frantic, but unfortunately rather disconnected and fruitless. Adam Trott zu Solz, a former Rhodes scholar with connections in England, visited Halifax and Chamberlain a few weeks before war broke out," [75] but the precise nature of the conversations remains undisclosed. The position taken by von Weizsäcker at this time was that open threats against Hitler should be discouraged, since he feared that this would only encourage his madness as it had during the May crisis. Time after time he insisted to the British and French Ambassadors, Henderson and Coulondre, that strong personal " diplomatic warnings " would be most effective.

On August 15 he told Henderson of the definite plans for von Ribbentrop's trip to Moscow, and Henderson reported it to London along with the remark that von Weizsäcker believed that Russia would take her share of " the Polish booty." [76] In agreement with Coulondre on the same day, von Weizsäcker reported to his superiors

[72] Weizsäcker, *Memoirs*, p. 190. Cf. *T. of W. C.*, XII, 1098.

[73] Affidavit of Halder, von Weizsäcker Defense Document Book 5. Cf. von Weizsäcker, *Memoirs*, p. 182.

[74] Berlin to Washington, No. 247, April 13, 1939. Dept. of State. MS. 740/00.794.

[75] Hopkinson, *op. cit.*

[76] Von Weizsäcker, *Memoirs*, p. 200.

that an isolated war with Poland would be impossible, while the French Ambassador reported to Paris that France must show firmness with Hitler. Coulondre suggested further, possibly under the influence of von Weizsäcker, that France urge the government at Warsaw to a policy of greater moderation and stronger control over provincial authorities "in whose hands lay the treatment of the German minority." [77]

On August 19, von Weizsäcker renewed his earlier instructions to the German Ambassador in Brussels, von Buelow-Schwandte, to report to von Ribbentrop that the Western Powers would not accept any more *coups* by Hitler.[78] Just before August 22, the State Secretary urged Henderson to have his government send an outstanding general—possibly General Ironside—to Berlin in von Ribbentrop's absence. Direct access could then be had to Hitler, and ". . . this general was to make it emphatically clear to Hitler that any armed measures against Poland would simultaneously mean a war with Britain, and make it clear to him that the German chances in the case of such armed conflict would be most unfavorable." [79]

Instead came the famous letter from Chamberlain to Hitler of August 22. In this, the Prime Minister expressed British determination to stand by Poland, her willingness to reach an understanding with Germany, and her availability as a mediator between Berlin and Warsaw. The State Secretary got permission for the British Ambassador to present the letter personally to Hitler. This meeting took place at the Berghof on August 23, 1939; unfortunately von Ribbentrop returned sooner than expected and soundly berated von Weizsäcker for his interference.[80]

The signing of the Soviet pact, representing as it did a diplomatic triumph for Hitler and von Ribbentrop, was a severe blow to the cause of the Resistance Movement. When the Fuehrer announced it to his assembled generals at Berchtesgaden on August 22, the result, according to Gisevius, was that: ". . . a good many

[77] *Ibid.*, p. 202.

[78] Testimony of Victor von Buelow-Schwandte, von Weizsäcker Transcript, p. 9800.

[79] Von Weizsäcker testimony, Transcript, p. 7860.

[80] Von Weizsäcker, *Memoirs*, pp. 202-203.

of them were quite pleased with the effect Hitler's surprise pact had produced." [81] Their resistance was further weakened, no doubt, by Hitler's criticism of the "weakness and indiscretion of some highly placed Germans in 1938." He let them know that he was not unaware of oppositional elements at the time of Munich.

> It has done much damage that many reluctant Germans said and wrote to Englishmen about the Czech question: 'The Fuehrer carried his point because you lost your nerve and capitulated too soon. . . .' [82]

During these tense days von Weizsäcker tried to put pressure on Hitler from every possible angle. He urged Ambassador Attolico to suggest that Mussolini was not desirous of war and would prefer a conference of Great Powers. But, adds von Weizsäcker, "Ribbentrop sabotaged this idea." [83] Then he asked Carl Burkhardt to speak personally with Hitler. He succeeded in convincing Hitler of the determination of the Poles to fight, and pleaded with him to say "a word to save the peace of Europe." Hitler's reaction to this is described graphically:

> At that, suddenly, he turned around, his face livid, grabbed the heavy window drapery with both hands and tore it to the floor with a violent gesture, shouting: "No!" Whereupon he turned his back on me and walked out of the room.[84]

Finally, on August 24, von Weizsäcker had the opportunity of speaking to Hitler himself. He sought to convince him that there would be a world conflict if Poland were attacked, that Italy would not help them, and that more could be gained by resuming conversations with the Poles.[85] Hitler, however, expected momentarily the British Parliament's loss of confidence in Chamberlain.[86] When no rejection of the Prime Minister was reported, Hitler made the

[81] Gisevius, *op. cit.*, p. 364.
[82] Telford Taylor, *op. cit.*, p. 293.
[83] Von Weizsäcker, *Memoirs*, p. 197.
[84] *Ibid.*, p. 193. The description of the meeting is from Jordan, *op. cit.*, pp. 230-231.
[85] Von Weizsäcker, *op. cit.*, p. 204.
[86] *Ibid.*, p. 203. As soon as Henderson left the room after his conversation with Hitler, the latter laughed and said: "Chamberlain won't survive that conversation: his Cabinet will fall this evening."

first stab at war on the 25th. The necessity of withdrawing this order to the troops gave new hope to the conspirators; now, they insisted, Hitler had suffered a grave psychological defeat from which he would not be able to recover.[87]

But nowhere is it made more clear that state policy is inexplicable and unpredictable when it depends on the whims and decisions of one man! Unable to discover from one moment to the next what the Fuehrer was planning to do, the attempt to forestall him by a *putsch* was bound to remain sterile. Not only had several of the reliable military participants in the pre-Munich plot, such as General Erwin von Witzleben, been assigned to new posts outside of Berlin, but the members of the Resistance Movement still there were hopelessly divided as to the proper moment for striking.

It was at this point that Colonel-General Beck tried unsuccessfully to incite Colonel-General Halder to action. While the Chief-of the General Staff agreed with all his former superior had to say against Hitler, he insisted that the moment was inopportune. They should await the actual orders to march; then public opinion would support their *coup*.[88] But when that moment came, he was to urge waiting for the first military defeat!

On August 31 von Weizsäcker sent for von Hassell who, as former Ambassador in Rome, had some influence with Attolico and, as a personal friend, was esteemed by Henderson. The State Secretary asked him to get Henderson to urge the Polish Ambassador Lipski to recommend to Warsaw that the plenipotentiary demanded by Hitler as a prerequisite to the reopening of conversations be sent at once. Von Hassell felt that the "one vital thing was to avoid world war." He went to Henderson who promised to do what he could, but said that he felt the Germans erred seriously in thinking that the British could "order the Poles around."

[87] *Ibid.*, p. 207. Von Weizsäcker did not agree with this opinion of Canaris, Hassell, and others. Canaris was particularly insistent on this point. Cf. Gisevius, *op. cit.*, p. 373.

[88] Gisevius, *op. cit.*, p. 359. It is clear from the arguments used here by Halder that the "revision" of Germany's eastern boundaries did not seem to him to be adequate cause for a *coup*. Gisevius says of Halder and Beck: "When they parted, they shook hands for the last time. Beck had found Halder wanting neither in understanding nor patriotism nor a sense of his class tradition. He simply lacked the will."

Meanwhile, von Ribbentrop had demanded that the State Secretary have no further contact with Ambassador Henderson.

Acting on the advice of Henderson, Lipski finally presented himself at the Foreign Office, but by then von Ribbentrop had decided not to receive him. The end of this exhausting and tense day found von Hassell urging Attolico to call Rome at once and ask Mussolini to intervene at the eleventh hour.[89]

Despite all their good intentions and their feverish activity, the conspirators were unsuccessful in preventing the outbreak of war. Poland was invaded on September 1; on the 2nd, von Weizsäcker made a last desperate effort to secure Italian mediation,[90] but on the 3rd, the case was closed. England and France, refusing to mediate while German troops remained in Poland, declared war on Germany. Hitler had finally succeeded in beginning the war which was to end in the downfall of his regime and the destruction of most of Europe. The German Opposition had failed to prevent the catastrophe.

In the efforts which were made by Beck, Goerdeler, von Weizsäcker, and their associates as described above should we recognize treason or patriotism? It would seem that, as Professor Rothfels has pointed out, there was required here on the part of the conspirators, a substitution of the ideal of international morality for that of narrow nationalism.[91] Von Kessel has testified that von Weizsäcker considered the sacrifice of the independent small states of Eastern Europe (which would be a natural result of the pact with Russia) as "immoral."[92] Erich Kordt considered the initiation of World War II as "the greatest crime that had ever been committed in human history,"[93] while Admiral Canaris once admitted to his aide, General Lahousen, that after this war there would be no difficulty in ascertaining who had been guilty of starting it.[94]

[89] Von Hassell, *op. cit.*, pp. 68-72; von Weizsäcker, *Memoirs*, p. 209.

[90] Von Weizsäcker, *Memoirs*, p. 210.

[91] Rothfels, "International Aspects of the German Opposition to Hitler," p. 190.

[92] Von Kessel testimony, von Weizsäcker transcript, p. 9478.

[93] Rothfels, "International Aspects of the German Opposition to Hitler," p. 181.

[94] Colvin, *op. cit.*, p. 193.

These various admissions, on the part of the conspirators, that Hitler's foreign policy embodied repeated violations of international law, as well as of fundamental moral law, should be added to what evidence we have already cited regarding their conviction that the Third Reich was a "lawless" state. Patriotism implies a love of and a devotion to one's country. But the loyalty which the patriotic citizen owes to his government is limited by the lawful quality of that government. Convinced, therefore, that they no longer owed loyalty to the Nazi regime, it was not far to the next step—namely, to utilize all means, even the cooperation of foreign powers, to end the regime and restore the "reign of law" in Germany.

The conspirators were in agreement that this was an act of highest patriotism. But with the advent of war, a total war in which the existence of the fatherland and the lives of thousands of German soldiers were at stake, the problem of true "patriotism" became more complex, and the group was no longer unanimous in their estimate of their duty. September 3, 1939, therefore, represents the end of one ethical problem and the beginning of a new and more difficult one.

CHAPTER IV

WAR AGAINST THE FATHERLAND?

The men of the German Resistance had fought a determined battle to prevent the outbreak of World War II. Having failed to achieve victory in that regard, they found themselves in a new dilemma. Should they continue to work for the downfall of the Hitler regime now that the country was at war? Should they even, perhaps, work for the defeat of Germany by the Allies, so that the Nazi terror would come to an end? Or was peace so important, that they should stand behind the government in an approach to the Western Powers for an early armistice?

Treason, in its most limited definition,[1] is the "act of levying war" against one's country, or "giving aid and comfort to the enemy." In its wider meaning, it includes all attempts to overthrow the legitimate government or to kill or injure the sovereign.[2] In German law, there had been traditionally a distinction between "*Hochverrat*" and "*Landesverrat*." The former term applied to the legal fact of conspiring against the government, while the latter implied a "selling-out" of one's country for pecuniary gain. In war time the two were included under "*Kriegsverrat*," and any opposition to the government became treason.[3]

This concept of treason, driven to its logical conclusion, was depicted in the trial of von Moltke to which we have referred above. From the statements and attitude of the presiding judge, von Moltke concluded: "Whatever does not please Herr Freisler is treason."

But such a subjective interpretation cannot be the criterion for

[1] The Constitution of the United States of America, Art. III, Sect. 3.

[2] Webster's New Collegiate Dictionary . . . 2nd ed. (Springfield, Mass.: G. & C. Merriam Co., 1949).

[3] Typescript of the von Witzleben discussions. Cf. their discussion of "Landesverrat," *Europäische Publikation*, No. 5 printed in *Aus Politik und Zeitgeschichte*, XX, 54 (May 26, 1954).

our judgment of the men of the German Resistance, since it is obviously a false one. If, rather, we use the older, more traditional explanations of "treason," we shall have to study the activities of the Resistance group during the war years with two questions in mind: (1) Did they conspire against the government, giving aid and comfort to the enemy? and (2) Did they do it for pecuniary gain?

The nature and extent of the contact which was developed between the conspirators within Germany and the Allied Powers cannot yet be appraised with certainty because many of the pertinent documents are not available to scholars. Nevertheless, there are several indications that the channels of communication were kept open, that several offers of peace were made, and that political and military "intelligence" was transmitted to Allied officers. Always fundamental to the proposals was the understanding that peace could be won only if Hitler were removed from office; consequently the offers to the West depended to a large extent on the opportunities at home for a *coup d'état*. But the conspirators were also insistent that any *coup* must be the work of Germans and must not show signs of foreign instigation; after it had been achieved, then cooperation would be welcome.

A few weeks after war was declared in September 1939, Adam Trott zu Solz left Germany to attend the Conference of the Institute of Pacific Relations to be held in November at Virginia Beach, Virginia. Trott had been in China at the time of Munich, and so had not been one of the participants in the preparations for that early plot. However, upon his return to Berlin he soon became one of the group in the Foreign Office engaged in "resisting" the policies of Hitler and Ribbentrop.[4]

In an analysis of the domestic situation in Germany as early as 1932 he had shown great insight into the troubles that lay ahead. Recognized by his friends as a Socialist, he was not in sympathy with the National Socialist program. He wrote:

---

[4] It is difficult to reconcile this data with Gisevius's statement: "When the war broke out, Trott was sent off to a diplomatic post in East Asia." Gisevius, *op. cit.*, p. 433. The reports on Trott zu Solz's visit to the United States are in Dept. of State. MS, 862.20211 von T./1-2-3-7-8.

> My chief worry is that Social Democracy will not take the right stand. If manoeuvered into a position of defending the present order, it will have lost what may have been the last chance of integrating the radical workers and forming the spearhead of a rational application of socialism. If the revolutionary forces break loose, an entirely new situation will be created—catastrophe for millions, and the country will be reduced to starting from a much more primitive level. It will then be no matter of approval or disapproval, but of an identification with whatever the state of the country is.[5]

During his visit to the United States, Adam Trott zu Solz tried to speak with influential persons in the hope of convincing them that "another Germany" than that of Hitler existed, and wished to get support in the fight against the Nazis. One of the men with whom he spoke was Felix Morley, then editor of *The Washington Post*. On November 20, 1939, Mr. Morley noted in his diary:

> Adam von Trott, who left Germany three weeks after the declaration of war, had tea with me yesterday, and today I arranged lunch for him with (Eugene) Meyer (publisher of *The Washington Post*) and me at the office. He is over as a Far Eastern expert, to attend the conference of the Institute of Pacific Relations at Virginia Beach, but is devoting most of his time to developing a receptive attitude here towards the big change which he thinks is coming in Germany. . . . It is a heroic work in which this noble and idealistic young German is engaged. . . . The chief problem is how to insure that a war of extermination against the Nazis will not force behind them all the elements beginning to cohere for Hitler's overthrow. And here von Trott confirms my feeling that if a Danzig formula would have been found there would have been no further aggression—because of the coalescing of anti-Hitler sentiment in Germany. Now it is far more difficult.[6]

On November 14, a representative of the Foreign Policy Association submitted a copy of a memorandum prepared by Trott zu Solz to the Secretary of State, Cordell Hull. This document urged an Allied statement of war aims which could serve as a basis for action by oppositional groups within Germany. Trott cautioned, however, against repeating the Versailles insistence on the "war guilt" of the German people.

---

[5] Hopkinson, *op. cit.*

[6] Maley, *op. cit.*

> If the theory is accepted that Germany is bound to remain a nefarious element in the European family of nations, any proclamation of war aims on this basis can only do harm. Such an act could only contribute to the prolongation of the war. Even though the German people are increasingly opposed to the National Socialist Government and embittered by its policies it is clear that only a negligible minority of Germans will deny their support to the present regime, if the preservation of the German nation is at stake.[7]

Both in his memorandum and in his subsequent visits with George Messersmith of the Department of State on November 20 and December 8, Trott zu Solz indicated clearly that the "moderates" whom he represented were convinced that the continuation of Hitler in power would be a "catastrophe" for Germany and the world.

The fact that Trott had left Germany with official permission and was in touch with persons in the United States closely connected with the German government caused Messersmith to refrain from taking any drastic action. However, he notified Ambassador Kirk in Berlin of Trott's suggestions, and advised Trott to speak freely to Kirk after his return to Germany if he wished to do so.

Meanwhile, the Resistance put several other irons in the fire. The rapid defeat of Poland, accomplished by September 27, followed by Hitler's questionable offer of peace to the Western Powers and their rejection of it, made it obvious that the offensive against France would now commence. On October 27 Hitler issued orders for the opening of the campaign in the West on November 12.[8] He had already, on October 10, informed the generals that this would demand the invasion of Belgium and Holland.[9] The conspirators learned of his plans, and were deeply dismayed at the possibility. Feeling that the German name had already been blackened beyond repair by the atrocities committed in Poland,

[7] Memorandum of Trott zu Solz, Department of State. MS, 862.20211 von T./1.

[8] Franz Halder, *Diary* (Aug. 14, 1939-Sept. 24, 1942) Washington: Infantry Journal, 1950). Entry for Oct. 27, 1939.

[9] Fuehrer Memorandum and Directive for Conduct of the War in the West, Oct. 9, 1939. *IMT* documents L-52, C-62. It was read by Hitler to his generals Oct. 10, 1939. Wheeler-Bennett, *op. cit.*, p. 464.

they were of the opinion that "the worst thing that could happen would be an invasion of the neutral countries." [10]

Goerdeler decided to go to Sweden and, through Wallenberg, approach the British once more. If terms of peace could be offered by them to Hitler, he held, and Hitler did not accept them, this would lead to his downfall.[11] He secured permission to make the trip for business reasons, and before leaving Berlin had a long talk with von Hassell on the economic, military, and political situation in Germany.

On an earlier occasion he had discussed with him the goals which he thought the conspirators should have in foreign policy:

(1) German parts of Poland to be retained; the rest to be independent.
(2) The restitution of the reign of law in Germany.
(3) General disarmament, with specific guarantees in the case of Germany.
(4) Restoration of world trade.[12]

On November 1, he left for Sweden; how much he intended to tell the British remains unknown.

Apparently General Beck was not too certain about the outcome of Goerdeler's mission, because at this same time he sent Dr. Josef Mueller to the Vatican to enlist the pope's aid in securing terms of peace from the West. Dr. Mueller, a Bavarian Catholic employed by ABWEHR, was on friendly terms with Pius XII's private secretary, Father Robert Leiber, S. J. During October and November 1939 they worked out a possible basis for peace, receiving the help of Monsignor Ludwig Kaas, former head of the German Center Party, and the cooperation of Francis D'Arcy Osborne, British Ambassador to the Holy See.

A full account of these conversations has not yet been published,[13]

[10] Von Hassell, *op. cit.*, p. 80 (Entry for Oct. 16, 1939).

[11] *Ibid.*, p. 77.

[12] *Ibid.*, p. 76. Naturally, "German parts of Poland" might be subject to different interpretations.

[13] This report is designated as the X-Report and there is apparently no copy of it available in the United States. Mr. Wheeler-Bennett maintains that although Beck instructed the conspirators to destroy all copies, one was found at Zossen after July 20, 1944 and two photostat copies are still

but various reports indicate that the following conditions were stipulated as a prerequisite for the undertaking of direct negotiations:

(1) The removal of Hitler and the Nazi regime.
(2) The formation of a new German Government and the return of the "reign of law" within Germany.
(3) No attack in the West by either side.
(4) The settlement of the Eastern Question in favor of Germany.

Furthermore, the Holy Father felt that the decisions regarding the future of Austria and Czechoslovakia should not be allowed to constitute "barriers" against a peace.

It is interesting to note here that Pope Pius XII, in his acceptance of the first point—requiring the overthrow of Hitler—at least implicitly recognized the right of the conspirators to active resistance. It is not clear whether the pope required this condition before he would act as mediator, or whether it was one of the demands of the British to which he merely acceded.[14]

The early reports from Mueller were utilized by Gisevius and Dohnanyi in drawing up a memorandum on November 1 for General Thomas to use as a basis for his contemplated approach to Halder.[15] The hopes of the conspirators were once more high regarding the Chief of the General Staff's willingness to stage a *coup*. The so-called *putsch* of Zossen was being planned at this time to take place as soon as the signal to invade the Lowlands was given, and it was believed that the British commitment through the Vatican would encourage the generals.

in existence. He does not indicate where they are located. Cf. Wheeler-Bennett, *op. cit.*, pp. 490-493 for his discussion of the Vatican negotiations. Dr. Mueller rewrote part of the details of the report from memory and these were included in the typescript of the Witzleben discussions, but the exact terms of the proposals were not included in the section of the typescript available to the present writer. Colvin also prints an account of Mueller's mission, but does not include the fourth point given below by Wheeler-Bennett. Cf. Colvin, *op. cit.*, p. 114.

[14] Wheeler-Bennett, *op. cit.*, p. 491 states: "It [the X-Report] stated that the Holy Father was prepared to act as intermediary for an understanding with Britain on the following terms. . . ."

[15] Gisevius, *op. cit.*, pp. 384-385.

Other attempts to secure mediation were made during this winter of 1939-1940. The German Ambassador in Brussels, Victor von Bülow, acting at the behest of State Secretary von Weizsäcker and Carl Goerdeler, encouraged the King of Belgium to make his proposals of peace jointly with the Queen of Holland on November 8, 1939.[16] Von Weizsäcker also worked in conjunction with Bishop Berggrav, Primate of the Norwegian Church and later an outstanding leader of the Norwegian Resistance.[17] In January 1940, at a church meeting in Holland, Bishop Berggrav drew up a list of war aims in agreement with his ecclesiastical confrères of various Protestant denominations who attended the meeting from England. With this statement of unofficial Allied views, he then went to Berlin to submit them to church leaders there, hoping they could push the matter with the government.

The church leaders refused to receive his proposals, but von Weizsäcker did so with words of appreciation and encouragement. Further, he urged the Bishop to make the program known to Lord Halifax. Berggrav thereupon returned to London, and the British Foreign Minister agreed to present the statement to the Cabinet. The distinctive point in these proposals was the provision for the full and restored independence of Poland and Czechoslovakia. The elimination of Hitler was, of course, a prerequisite.

One of the most significant and dangerous attempts to get official British assurances of willingness to negotiate with a new regime in Germany was made by Ulrich von Hassell in a series of meetings with Mr. J. Lonsdale Bryans between November 1939 and April 1940.[18] Bryans was an Englishman, unofficially connected with the British Foreign Office, who felt that there must

[16] Testimony of Victor von Bülow-Schwandte, von Weizsäcker transcript, pp. 9809-9811. Through the good offices of Count Capelle he was able to speak with King Leopold.

[17] Testimony of Bishop Eivind Berggrav, von Weizsäcker transcript, pp. 8522-8529. It is interesting to note that Berggrav volunteered to testify on behalf of von Weizsäcker because he was convinced that the German State Secretary was just as much opposed to the Nazis as he was, and it was a duty of justice for him to defend him.

[18] These meetings are recorded both in von Hassell, *op. cit.* and J. Lonsdale Bryans, *Blind Victory* (London: Skeffington and Son, 1951). Bryans was the "Mr. X" of the von Hassell record.

be some "good" Germans within the Reich who would be willing to make peace—without Hitler. Acting on this supposition he found his way, despite official red tape, to Rome.

There he met Detalmo Pirzio-Biroli who was engaged to von Hassell's daughter. After several visits together, they trusted one another sufficiently to explain their respective missions. Detalmo had been instructed by von Hassell to utilize any opportunity which might arise for conveying information to London about the organization and aims of the German Resistance. The terms of peace, presumably originating with von Hassell, which he now suggested to Bryans for communication to Lord Halifax were:

(1) Austria would remain a part of Germany.
(2) Czechoslovakia, except the Sudetenland, would be independently reconstructed.
(3) Poland, except for Danzig, the Corridor, Silesia, and a few frontier villages, would be reconstructed.
(4) Disarmament Conference would be held.
(5) There would be no demand for colonies.[19]

To this Detalmo added a written request for the British: could assurances be given that no advantage would be taken in the face of an inner crisis in the Reich?

This question, it may be suggested, indicates the "patriotism" behind the attempts of the conspirators to negotiate with the enemy. Obviously they did not contemplate betraying their country by creating an internal situation which would open wide the doors to a foreign power. Consistently they maintained that any *coup* would have to be a thoroughly German affair, and that it could not be undertaken unless they were sure it would be the means to an honorable peace.

At the end of December 1939, Mr. J. Lonsdale Bryans returned to London and presented Detalmo's document to Lord Halifax. The Foreign Minister approved of Bryans's efforts and permitted him to arrange for a meeting with von Hassell in Switzerland. On February 22, 1940 the two men met at Arosa, and von Hassell gave Bryans a list of proposals from the Opposition with a covering letter signed by himself as a testimony of good faith. This statement presented the following points:

---

[19] Bryans, *op. cit.*, p. 168.

I. All serious minded people in Germany consider it as of utmost importance to stop this mad war as soon as possible.

II. We consider this because the danger of a complete destruction and particularly a bolshevization of Europe is rapidly growing.

III. Europe does not mean for us a chess-board of political or military action or a base of power but it has "la valeur d'une patrie" in the frame of which a healthy Germany in sound conditions of life is an indispensable factor.

IV. The purpose of a peace treaty ought to be a permanent pacification and restablishment of Europe on a solid base and a security against a renewal of warlike tendencies.

V. Condition, necessary for this result, is to leave the union of Austria and the Sudeten with the Reich out of any discussion. In the same way there would be excluded a renewed discussion of occidental frontier-questions of the Reich. On the other hand, the German-Polish frontier will have to be more or less identical with the German frontier of 1914.

VI. The treaty of peace and the reconstruction of Europe ought to be based on certain principles which will have to be universally accepted.

VII. Such principles are the following:

1. The principle of nationality with certain modifications deriving from history. Therefore
2. Restablishment [sic] of an independent Poland and of a Czech Republic.
3. General reductions of armament.
4. Reestablishment of free international economical co-operation.
5. Recognition of certain leading ideas by all European states, such as:
    a. The principles of Christian ethics.
    b. Justice and law as fundamental elements of public life.
    c. Social welfare as *leitmotiv*.
    d. Effective control of the executive power of state by the people, adapted to the special character of every nation
    e. Liberty of thought, conscience, and intellectual activity.[20]

---

[20] *Ibid.*, pp. 68-69; von Hassell, *op. cit.*, pp. 117-118. The original text was written in English by von Hassell.

But this time when Bryans returned to the Foreign Office a very cold reception awaited him. The government was now in " official " contact with the same sort of people as von Hassell—they told Bryans—and so did not wish him to concern himself about the matter any longer. He might return to Arosa to inform von Hassell of the termination of their relationship; then he must retire from the scene. When he told this to von Hassell on April 15, the latter assumed that the " other channel " now being used by the Foreign Office was reaching the same group in Berlin.[21]

Apparently this other channel was Josef Mueller at the Vatican. In March of 1940 the complete report of Dr. Mueller was in Beck's hands and was known to Oster, Dohnanyi, and von Hassell. It was planned that von Hassell should use it to put pressure on Colonel-General Halder, but the latter refused to see him. Hence, without cooperation from the military sector, the conspirators were unable to fulfill the very first condition of any negotiated peace.

It was at this time that President Roosevelt decided to send representatives to Berlin to sound out the possibilities of a proposal of mediation being accepted. Contrary to the negotiations initiated by the German Opposition, the President of the United States still thought in terms of a peace *with* the Hitler regime.

The reports from the United States diplomatic and consular representatives in Berlin to the State Department in Washington as far back as 1935-36 had pictured graphically the conditions of the police state set up in Germany by Hitler.[22] Various visitors from abroad had reinforced those views with first-hand accounts of the racial and religious persecution, the farce of Nazi justice, and the imperialistic designs of the Hitler regime. Nevertheless, post-Versailles isolationism died hard, and the American public was not prepared to " interfere " in the domestic concerns of another nation. Yet, the desire to restore peace in Europe was very strong, and it was this aim, which Roosevelt apparently had in mind.

Late in February 1940 he sent instructions to Mr. James D. Mooney to go as his personal representative to Berlin and sound out the situation. There he had conversations with Hitler, Goering,

[21] Von Hassell, *op. cit.*, p. 133.

[22] See especially the reports of Dodd and Messersmith. Dept. of State. MS.

and von Ribbentrop during the first week of March. In the report which he sent to the President,[23] Mr. Mooney was extremely optimistic about the good faith of the German leaders who desired peace, he thought, if only it could be arranged justly and without a "loss of face." Mooney makes no mention of any oppositional group within Germany nor does he suggest any possibility of peace with a group other than that of Hitler.

Mooney's visits coincided with the more official conversations held in Berlin by Sumner Welles, Under Secretary of State. He spoke with Hitler, von Ribbentrop, Goering, von Weizsäcker, Hess, Schacht, and the Italian and Belgian Ambassadors.[24] His message, which he repeated to each one of his listeners, was that President Roosevelt said "unofficially" that a just and lasting peace could still be made, and then talks should begin concerning limitation of armaments and the establishment of sound international trade as a means of maintaining the peace. When von Hassell had spoken with Bryans in Arosa in February he had urged that Sumner Welles be urged to seek out unofficial as well as official circles while in Berlin.[25] The rules of diplomacy evidently decreed otherwise.

The only men with whom Welles spoke who could have told him of the oppositional activities were von Weizsäcker and Schacht. It is understandable but unfortunate that they were not more frank in their conversations with him. Yet, they both hinted at the truth. According to Welles's report, his visit with the State Secretary took a curious turn when the host suddenly moved both of their chairs to the center of the room (apparently, he thought, to avoid danger of recording devices) and urged him with a great show of agitation to tell Hitler that it was von Ribbentrop who stood in the way of peace. Would he also explain to the Fuehrer that Mussolini still felt there was a basis for peace?[26]

On March 3, 1940 Sumner Welles spoke with Hjalmar Schacht

[23] James D. Mooney report. Dept. of State. MS. No serial number.

[24] Sumner Welles report. Dept. of State. MS. No serial number.

[25] Von Hassell, *op. cit.*, p. 117.

[26] Although von Weizsäcker did not remember these details he said he could not deny that he may have acted in this manner. He felt, however, that Welles's publication of this account in 1944 was, at least, indiscreet. Von Weizsäcker, *Memoirs*, pp. 222-224.

at the house of the American Chargé, Alexander Kirk. In the preceding November Schacht had already asked Kirk if he could not be invited to the United States to make a "non-political speech." [27] Now, he renewed his request to Welles, adding that he wanted to get out of Germany in order to further the conspiracy which existed among the generals to supplant the Hitler regime. He told Welles that the atrocities in Poland were far worse than imagined, and that Hitler was "an amoral genius" and "the greatest liar of all time."

The one obstacle which prevented the generals from action, said Schacht, was the fear that Germany would be treated as in 1918. Schacht later said that at the time of Welles's visit he had been anxious to get to the United States in order to keep it from aiding Great Britain, thereby shortening the war.[28] But, in 1940, would that not have been to Hitler's advantage?

It was unfortunate, surely, that these were the only two representatives of the German Resistance whom Welles met. Schacht was too well known as an opportunist to be regarded with confidence, and von Weizsäcker was still thinking in terms of preventing war, or at least restricting the area of conflict, rather than in terms of a vigorous new order of things. Was he afraid to reveal too much to Welles, whose government was a potential ally of Great Britain? He had not been afraid in the pre-war days to reveal Hitler's plans to the British. Why, then, did he not tell the whole story to Welles?

He later wrote that he spoke to Welles on this occasion with "complete frankness," and that he was "quite pleased" with their meeting. Yet, neither he nor Welles, in their accounts of the conversation, mention any possibility of overthrowing Hitler or making peace without him. Was von Weizsäcker's reticence due, perhaps, to the fear that such a revelation might weaken Germany's bargaining position too severely?

[27] Cordell Hull, *The Memoirs of Cordell Hull* (N. Y.: Macmillan Co., 1948), p. 712. One cannot help wondering at the honesty of Schacht's report to Goerdeler in October 1939 that he "had been approached by someone from the American Embassy" who requested him to come to America. Cf. von Hassell, *op. cit.*, p. 77.

[28] Interrogation of Hjalmar Schacht by Lt. Col. Murray Gurfein, A. U. S., Oct. 17, 1945, submitted at Nuremberg. *IMT*, XXXIII, 1-32.

Anxious as von Weizsäcker was to get rid of the Nazis, he never considered it to be morally right to diminish Germany's political and military prestige. That he would have regarded as "unpatriotic." He wrote:

> I myself, before and during the war, always considered that I was morally justified, and even in duty bound, to go behind Hitler's and Ribbentrop's backs and let potential enemies have such information, whether secret or not, as might tend to stop war breaking out or prevent its extension. My aim was to prevent the potential enemy becoming an actual enemy. But however opposed I may have been to Hitler's aggressive actions, I could never have considered, either emotionally or intellectually, the possibility of attacking the German soldiers from behind. *I felt that Germany must be capable of negotiating and of inspiring respect, from a military as well as a political point of view.* Otherwise there could be no compromise peace and no stable conditions in Europe.[29]

The beginning of the war in September 1939 had changed things for von Weiszäcker, and activities which he would have undertaken in peace-time became, for him, now "treasonable." But it was not so for the others in the conspiracy.

The winter of 1939-40 had passed without the intended offensive in the West being realized. The Scandinavian countries would be subjugated first. On April 1, 1940 General Oster, deputy for Canaris in ABWEHR and hence presumably well informed, conveyed a message through Colonel J. C. Sas, Netherlands Military Attaché in Berlin, to the Danish Naval Attaché revealing Nazi plans for invasion of Scandinavia. On April 3 a similar report was sent to the Norwegian Embassy.[30] On this same day, Goerdeler informed Max Jordan that the attack was planned for that night.

He said that Hitler was acting contrary to the advice of Admiral Raeder and the top military men, but he would probably succeed "unless"—and here Jordan was left to conclude—"unless" there was a battle in Danish waters. Acting on this information, Jordan left at once for Copenhagen but, as a United States citizen, hesitated to act in a way that would be prejudicial to his status as a neutral. He alerted his New York office, "hoping that the

[29] Von Weizsäcker, *Memoirs*, p. 234. Italics are mine.

[30] Colvin, *op. cit.*, p. 125.

dateline of the radiogram would be a broad enough hint" of possible action.[31]

The views of the conspirators on the ethical problem involved in divulging such information is described by Gisevius in his account of the Norwegian attack.

> For the first time during the war, the question arose in our circle of friends of transmitting military information. The end of tyranny was within reach if—yes, if the other side knew what was to happen and what was at stake. Some of us laughed aloud at the suggestion that Hitler's preparations could possibly be unknown to the British. Others refused to accept personally the role of destiny. If the British muffed this unique chance they simply could not be helped, these friends maintained. Still others pointed out that British intervention based on our information would cost the lives of thousands of German sailors and soldiers. A minority in our circle took precisely the opposite view. Did we have the right to consider only the German casualties deriving from such an invasion? [32]

The Norwegian campaign was followed by warnings of invasion in the Lowlands. At the end of April, Beck dispatched Josef Mueller to Rome to warn the Allies of an impending attack scheduled for May 10.[33] On May 4 Colonel Sas reported to The Hague from Berlin that war was imminent. Two days later Queen Wilhelmina canceled all army leaves and decreed a state of siege. The exact hour of the operation—May 10 at dawn—was communicated to Sas by Oster and forwarded to the Foreign Minister, Dr. van Kleffens on the evening of May 9.[34] But all the efforts of the conspirators were in vain; no amount of advance information could have saved The Netherlands.

It is interesting to note that when von Weizsäcker was asked to support these statements about ABWEHR agents having sent ahead word of invasion, he would neither confirm nor deny them. How-

[31] Jordan, *op. cit.*, 269-272.

[32] Gisevius, *op. cit.*, p. 451.

[33] Colvin, *op. cit.*, p. 130.

[34] Wheeler-Bennett, *op. cit.*, p. 495-496. For confirmation of receipt of such a message cf. Eelco Nicolaas Van Kleffens, *Juggernaut over Holland* (New York: Columbia University Press, 1940), p. 79, and Berlin to Washington, 1264, May 10, 1940, Dept. of State. MS, 740.0011/2778.

ever, he was sure that if it had been done with Canaris's approval it must have been in the hope that such news would be published and cause a sensation, thus causing Hitler to call off his attack. Canaris, he maintained, would never have committed "treason." Unfortunately when he was asked what he meant by "treason," the question was ruled out as irrelevant.[35] Possibly we may gather what his reply would have been from the testimony of Erich Kordt. He said that von Weizsäcker would never have revealed X-day and hour of a planned attack since that would have meant sending innocent German soldiers to death.[36]

The rapid conquest of France and the withdrawal of British forces from the continent are adequate explanations for the dearth of Resistance efforts during the rest of 1940. Hitler's "most glorious victory of all history" made any plans for a *coup d'état* incredible. The generals were farther removed than ever before from cooperation in such a scheme, and as 1940 drew to a close, the conspirators were in dispositions of hopelessness.

In January 1941 Carl Burkhardt reported to von Hassell, whom he met in Geneva, that he believed that London was "unofficially" ready to conclude a reasonable peace: Holland and Belgium to be restored; some kind of Poland (minus former German provinces) to be reconstructed; Denmark within a German "sphere of influence"; and the former German colonies to be returned to Germany.[37] Since these terms were predicated, however, on the removal of Hitler from power, they amounted to nothing in the practical order.

In the spring of 1941, just before the spectacular arrival of Rudolf Hess in England, Albrecht Haushofer went on a mission for the conspirators to Switzerland. He left Germany with a formal order issued by Hess to get in touch with the Allies, but actually intended to use such contact for the purposes of the Resistance Movement.[38] Unfortunately the disappearance of Hess resulted in Haushofer's immediate arrest upon his return, and he

[35] Von Weizsäcker transcript, pp. 7888-7889.

[36] Kordt, *op. cit.*, p. 437.

[37] Von Hassell, *op. cit.*, p. 170.

[38] Affidavit of Reiner Hildebrandt, April 5, 1948. Von Weizsäcker Defense Document Book 5. Cf. von Hassell, *op. cit.*, p. 194.

was imprisoned until the summer of 1941. Von Hassell noted that Haushofer had frequently been used by Hess for various missions and that on March 16, 1941 he and von Hassell had discussed the possibility of his going to Switzerland and utilizing von Hassell's connections there. While there, Haushofer spoke with Burkhardt, an appointment was arranged by von Hassell's wife.[39]

About this time von Hassell had a series of conversations with an American business man named Stallforth.[40] He had come to Germany to press for peace, but, as late as April 20, 1941, had not yet been able to speak with any of the "leading people." In the middle of July, Stallforth attempted to convince von Ribbentrop that it would be wise to send von Hassell to Rome where he could speak with American Ambassador Phillips, an old friend of his, thereby finding "a common meeting ground for Berlin and Washington." This never materialized, and in September Stallforth again visited von Hassell after a visit to Hungary. At that time, von Hassell noted in his diary that Schacht and von Weizsäcker did not favor acting through Stallforth.

Stallforth told von Hassell that Roosevelt's policy was this: "his chief aim was to bring about the downfall of Hitler; if this succeeded, peace would be possible." This represents a sharp departure from the message of the Welles mission a year earlier. Then peace with Hitler had been the goal; now the implication was that peace was only possible after the removal of Hitler. Schacht was still angling for an invitation to the United States, and Mr. Stallforth considered him "fit" for such a possibility.

By October 1941 Stallforth had returned to New York and from there he sent word to von Hassell that the "proposition" had been well received, and asked if von Hassell would meet an "authorized person" in Lisbon. Von Hassell however, had some misgivings

[39] Von Hassell, *op. cit.*, pp. 174, 194.

[40] According to the index in von Hassell, *op. cit.*, "Stallforth" was a pseudonym for an American business man. However, this was not a pseudonym but the real name of von Hassell's contact, a New York business man, Federico Stallforth. For references to Stallforth cf. von Hassell, *op. cit.*, pp. 190, 202, 213-215, 217, and 218. For Stallforth's previous relations with the Dept. of State. Cf. MS, 840.00/390 and 740.0011/6061. Mr. Stallforth was kind enough to confirm this information for the writer, in a personal interview, Jan. 19, 1954.

about the whole affair, and there are no more references to Stallforth in his diary. Mr. Stallforth, in a personal interview with the writer, said that von Hassell had been seeking assurance of economic as well as political support in the event of a *coup*.

Another American in Berlin who was approached by the Resistance leaders was Mr. Louis P. Lochner, head of the Associated Press Bureau in Berlin.[41] In November 1941 he was invited to attend a meeting at the home of Joseph Wirmer, and was asked to inform President Roosevelt about the anti-Hitler movement within Germany. They wished Lochner to find out from the President what form of government in Germany would be most acceptable to the United States, if their *coup* succeeded.

Because Germany declared war on the United States in December 1941, Mr. Lochner was interned and did not reach the United States until June 1942. When he attempted to present his request to the White House, he was told that such an interest was "most embarrassing." Mr. Lochner received the impression that the administration had no desire to find out the extent of the German opposition nor in any way to be connected with it.

The year 1941 had seen not only the addition of the United States, but also that of Russia to the list of Germany's enemies. But the victories continued to lie with the Axis. The conspirators felt it necessary to arrange a *modus vivendi* with the Western Powers before the whole of Europe was engulfed in disaster. They therefore, in May 1942, utilized the services of one of the leading churchmen in Germany, Pastor Dietrich Bonhoeffer, who had had close relations with both the Oster and Beck-Goerdeler groups. He went to Stockholm to meet the English Bishop of Chichester, Dr. George Bell, and the latter has left a detailed record of the conversations.[42]

Dr. Bell had come to Sweden on behalf of the British Ministry of Information to renew the Swedish-British union of ministers.

[41] Rothfels, *op. cit.*, pp. 130-40; Wheeler-Bennett, *op. cit.*, pp. 551-52. Rothfels, "International Aspects of German Opposition to Hitler," pp. 182-183.

[42] [George Bell], Bishop of Chichester, "The Background of the Hitler Plot," *Contemporary Review*, 168 (Oct. 1945), pp. 203-208; Rothfels, *op. cit.*, 140-43.

On May 26 he was surprised by a visit from Dr. Hans Schönfeld who was working for the World Council of Christian Churches and was in touch with the Bureau of the Evangelical Church in Berlin. Despite his connection with this Government-sponsored sector of the German Church he had sympathy with the Confessing Church to which many of the "resisters" had been drawn.

Schönfeld outlined to Doctor Bell the three groups which comprised the German Resistance: members of state administration (or former members), former trade union officials and leaders, and high officers in army and state police. Apparently he knew of both the Beck-Goerdeler and the Kreisau groups. On May 29 the two men met again, and Schönfeld described the role of the churches in the Resistance Movement.

This was excellent preparation for the arrival of Pastor Bonhoeffer on May 31 in the little town of Sigtuna where Dr. Bell was staying. He was an old friend of Dr. Bell's, and now he came as an emissary for the Beck-Goerdeler group to ask cooperation in establishing contact with the British. It was the old request made anew: would the British assure the conspirators of a friendly reception if Hitler were overthrown?

In Pastor Bonhoeffer we have represented the most radical of the men of the Resistance. His anti-Nazi position was of long duration, and he considered opposition to the government of Hitler a moral necessity. When he left the United States, after the war had already begun in Europe, he explained his reasons for returning to Germany.

> I must live through this difficult period of our national history with the Christian people of my own country. . . . Christians in Germany will face the terrible alternative of either willing the defeat of their nation in order that Christian civilization may survive, or willing the victory of their nation and thereby destroying our civilization. I know which of these alternatives I must choose; but I cannot make that choice in security.[43]

At a meeting of clergymen in Geneva in 1941 he had expressed the logical conclusion of such a view. "I pray," he said, "for the

[43] George Bell, *The Church and Humanity* (N Y.: Longmans Green and Co., 1946), p. 187.

defeat of my nation. Only in defeat can we atone for the terrible crimes we have committed against Europe and the World." [44]

Faced with the moral problem of working to overthrow their government in time of war, the men of the Resistance could not have found a more solid basis for their decision than that expressed by Bonhoeffer. We do not wish to suggest that all of them would have subscribed to his ideal; most of them did not go so far as to "pray for the defeat" of their country. But is it not significant that at this moment when the German forces were still riding the crest of military victories, they selected Dietrich Bonhoeffer as their spokesman? They must have been aware of his sentiments and must have known that the terms of peace to which he would be a party would represent international justice rather than German hegemony.

It seems strange, then, that Mr. Wheeler-Bennett should maintain that for the British to have given the desired encouragement to the request sent by the Resistance through Pastor Bonhoeffer would have been interpreted as a sign of weakness. "The attitude of His Majesty's Government was entirely sound and justified." [45] What was that attitude? A completely negative one.

When Dr. Bell presented Foreign Minister Eden with the terms suggested by Bonhoeffer and Schönfeld, the result was not spectacular. Eden said that the information confirmed that which he had received from other sources, but that he must be careful not to act independently of Moscow and Washington. On July 17, 1942 the Foreign Minister simply informed Dr. Bell that no action would be taken.[46]

During 1942 unofficial American support was given to the German Underground by the broadcasts of Dorothy Thompson entitled "Listen Hans." Permitted, but not sponsored, by the Office of War Information, these broadcasts were directed to Helmuth von Moltke, urging him and his friends to show the world by some overt action that "another Germany" still existed.

[44] Dulles, *op. cit.*, p. 116.

[45] Wheeler-Bennett, *op. cit.*, p. 558.

[46] *Ibid.*, p. 557, n. 2. Mr. Wheeler-Bennett states that Bell gave a copy of Schönfeld's Memorandum to Mr. John Winant, Amer. Ambassador in London. Whether this represents the extent of the "consultation" with Moscow and London is unknown.

Moltke wrote twice to Miss Thompson during the war, once through a Swedish woman and once through a mutual friend in Switzerland, assuring her that what they wanted was peace.[47] When Miss Thompson heard that the resistance group was restrained by fear of an unreasonable peace, she urged Moltke and his friends to do whatever they could to repudiate the regime, and then there would be hope of a just peace.

On two occasions von Moltke tried to establish contact with representatives of the West stationed in Istanbul, but failed both times.[48] From Turkey in 1942 he wrote to Mr. Curtis, a friend in England, and made it clear what the oppositionists were hoping for. "We hope," he wrote, "that you are clear about the point that we are prepared to help you win the war and the peace." [49] Was this not "giving aid and comfort to the enemy"?

In November 1942 Mr. Allen Dulles was sent on a special mission to Switzerland under the auspices of the Office of Strategic Services, and a new chapter opened in the history of the relationship of the Underground in Germany with the Allied Powers. He has written his story in some detail,[50] and has confirmed the claims of the Resistance concerning their efforts to shorten the war by helping the Allies defeat Germany.

In the foreword to his book, Mr. Dulles writes:

> From Switzerland I was able to establish contact with the German Underground, and for many months before the culmination of the plot on July 20 [1944] I had kept in touch with those who were conspiring to rid Germany of the Nazis and the Nazi State. Couriers, risking their lives, went back and forth between Switzerland and Germany with reports of the conspirators' progress, and these reports reached me through secret channels I had developed. . . . On July 13 I radioed from Bern to Washington that the plotters had sent me word "the next few weeks will be our last chance to demonstrate the determination of the Germans themselves to rid Germany of Hitler and his gang and establish a decent regime."

---

[47] Dorothy Thompson, Letter to the writer, Dec. 23, 1953.

[48] *Ibid.*

[49] Moltke, *op. cit.*, p. 22.

[50] Dulles, *op. cit.* In a personal interview March 6, 1954, Mr. Dulles reaffirmed the story and said he had had no reason to change his mind about any of the persons involved since publishing his book.

This type of information—concerning resistance activity within Germany—reached Dulles through several channels. Gottfried von Nostiz (liaison man for von Weizsäcker with Burkhardt, Dr. W. A. Vissert 'Hooft, and Dr. Hans Schönfeld) testified that he had kept them informed about the Resistance Movement. They, in turn, passed it on to Mr. Livingston, the British Consul in Geneva, and Mr. Allen Dulles. This was the type of "intelligence" which von Weizsäcker could give the Allies without scruple.

Another one of the State Secretary's subordinates, von Etzdorff, discussed the difference between his work and the passing of "intelligence" which he would have considered treason. In his testimony at Nuremberg, he said:

> What we did in the opposition, and what we tried to do, was motivated first of all through the inclinations of a revolutionary conscience; therefore, the means which we employed in doing this stopped at certain limits, and those limits were the same which makes a patriot into a traitor. It is true that all of us were considered to be guilty of high treason according to the letter of the law; however, we did not sell out Germany to foreign countries. It would have been easy for me to sell my military information in Lisbon, in Stockholm, and in Madrid. By doing this, one could not stop the large fly wheel of military happenings. Hitler and his regiment were to be removed and could be removed only from inside.[51]

Other couriers gave Mr. Dulles even more specific information designed to help the United Nations defeat Germany. One of these was particularly noteworthy because he has explained his reasons for doing so. Fritz Kolbe, a member of the Foreign Office, had contact with the members of the Resistance Movement in Berlin but lacked confidence in their methods and thought that the only way to insure Hitler's downfall was by an Allied defeat of the Third Reich.

Under the official protection given him by his job, he was able to make about one trip every three months to Berne, where he turned over to Dulles microfilmed copies of Foreign Office telegrams, information concerning German war production, raw materials, and targets for Allied bombing.

[51] Testimony of Hesse von Etzdorf, Weizsäcker transcript, p. 9612.

On one occasion Kolbe warned the British that a German agent was working close to Churchill and was sending information to Berlin via Stockholm. To carry on his underground work, Kolbe had about twenty assistants, including members of the military, clerical, and industrial ranks. He had been an early opponent of the Nazis and had openly refused to join the party. At one time he had contemplated emigrating but had been urged by Father Schreiber, head of the monastery at Ottobeuern, to remain in his country and do what he could in his position to fight the Nazis.

That is what he did. When asked why he had wished for the military defeat of Germany by the Allies, he said that he saw it as the only means of ousting the Nazis and the key to his conduct lay in the maxim: "What profit a man if he conquer the whole world and lose his own soul?"[52]

Either through Kolbe or some similar source—possibly Waetjen, Strünk, or Kocherthaler[53]—the OSS received during eighteen months (1943-44) more than 1600 copies of secret and top secret German diplomatic correspondence.[54] There can be no doubt that the Opposition was conspiring with the enemy for the purpose of defeating Germany.

The main link connecting Allen Dulles with the German Resistance Movement was Hans Bernd Gisevius whose account furnishes one of the most complete pictures of the entire movement.[55] In his introduction to Gisevius's book, Mr. Dulles pointed out the motives which influenced the cooperation of the conspirators with Allied officials, showing them to be, not traitors to their country, but true patriots:

---

[52] Interrogation of Fritz Kolbe, De Witt C. Poole Mission, Sept. 23-24, 1945. Dept. of State. MS. Kolbe's connections with OSS were confirmed by Mr. Dulles, Personal Interview, March 6, 1954.

[53] *Ibid.*; cf. Affidavit of Eduard Waetjen, June 2, 1948 submitted as Defense Document 127 for Baron Steengracht von Moyland. Waetjen was permanent liaison man for Dulles with the Kreisau group. On Strünk, cf. Dulles, *op. cit.*, pp. 134, 139.

[54] Stewart Alsop and Thomas Braden, *Sub Rosa* (N. Y.: Reynal and Hitchcock, 1946), p. 227.

[55] Gisevius, *op. cit.* While it is true that Gisevius's account suffers from a lack of historical perspective and is colored by strong personal reactions, it constitutes one of the primary sources of information on the activities of the Resistance.

> Gisevius's philosophy can be summed up in a few words. To him, a victory for Hitler meant the end of Christian civilization, and of Western culture in Europe and possibly in the world. He proposed to do his bit to prevent it, and felt that in doing so he was only carrying out his duty as a German. Quite rightly he did not consider that he was working against his country; he felt he was working for it. But he wanted the Allies to hurry, to destroy Hitler before all the foundations on which a better Germany could be built had been demolished. He wanted to prevent Hitler from carrying on the fight "to the bitter end."

Since the notion of treason, or *Landesverrat,* implies the "selling-out" of one's country for pecuniary gain, it is significant to notice the testimony of Gisevius on this point. During the trials at Nuremberg, Dr. Seidl, counsel for Hess and Frank, attempted to disprove the credibility of Gisevius as a witness.

Dr. Seidl: "Witness, during the war were you at any time active in the service of a foreign power?"

Gisevius: "At no time. . . . I have said that I was never in the service of a foreign power. I was in the service of a good Germany."

S: "During the war did any power at war with Germany give you funds?"

G: "No."

S: "Do you know what the three letters OSS mean?"

G: "Yes."

S: "What do they stand for?"

G: "They stand for an American organization."

S: "And you were not connected with that organization?"

G: "I was in contact on a friendly and political basis with the members of that organization."

And Dulles comments on this:

> Gisevius had answered truthfully. He always conducted himself as the independent representative of a movement to free Germany of Hitler. Neither he nor his associates served as the agents of a foreign power or asked or received any promise of future consideration for service in what was viewed as a common cause.[56]

---

[56] Dulles, *op. cit.*, pp. 127-128.

Meanwhile contact with the Allies continued on other fronts. Goerdeler frequently met the Wallenbergs in Sweden and transmitted messages through them to the British Government. In April 1942 he asked them to secure Churchill's assurance of peace terms in the event of a successful *coup,* but they explained to him that advance commitments were not possible. In May 1943 Goerdeler gave them a memorandum for Churchill covering the plans of the "new" regime concerning punishment of war criminals, war damages, disarmament, and other problems. If the *coup* took place, the conspirators requested the Allies to curtail bombings in order to show the German people that the new Government would be treated favorably. There was no response from the British.

All during 1943 and 1944 Goerdeler kept them informed of the plans of the conspirators, and they remained alert for the opportunity to establish contact between a new regime and the Allied Powers. July 20, 1944 put an end to this arrangement as well as to all the others.[57]

There are scattered hints of proposals and negotiations through Ankara, Lisbon, Madrid, and the Vatican from 1943 to 1945 but little of an authoritative nature is available. Colvin claims that the conspirators tried to get American support through George Earle, then in Ankara.[58] Von Weizsäcker mentions a letter which he entrusted to Msgr. Kaas at the Vatican in 1944 for Cardinal Spellman. It was hoped that the Cardinal would present it to President Roosevelt, but no reply was ever received.[59]

In June 1944 Adam Trott zu Solz was sent to Sweden to seek contact with both the Western and Soviet representatives. This was one of a number of trips made by Trott to Sweden during the war—as well as other trips to Ankara, Lisbon, and Stockholm. On this occasion he tried to meet Mme. Kollontay, the Soviet Ambassador in Stockholm, but was unsuccessful.

[57] Cf. Wallenberg Memorandum in Dulles, *op. cit.*, pp. 142-146. The relations of Goerdeler with the Wallenbergs were uncovered in some detail by the RSHA in its investigation after July 20, 1944. RSHA report, Aug. 17, 1944, Dept. of the Army. MS, 105/23.

[58] Colvin, *op. cit.*, p. 214.

[59] Weizsäcker transcript, p. 8607.

The conditions which Trott proposed on behalf of the conspirators indicate the changed condition of German military power as well as the continued hope of the conspirators that a change of regime would be a " German " affair:

(1) Demobilization of the German Army in orderly fashion by the anti-Nazi government rather than by the occupation forces.
(2) The Anti-Nazi government should be allowed time to get started before occupation, so as not to seem like a Quisling government.
(3) No territory which was German before 1936 should be taken from Germany.
(4) The German war criminals apprehended in Germany would be tried in Germany.[60]

Two other " contact men " who continued to seek an understanding with the Allies were Josef Mueller whose activities at the Vatican were pursued regularly until early 1943 when he was arrested,[61] and Otto John who frequently used his position as a Director of the *Lufthansa* to visit Spain and meet British and American representatives there.[62]

There are two final considerations to be made regarding all these efforts of the German Underground to establish and keep contact

[60] Stockholm to Washington, No. 2309, June 26, 1944. 103.918/6-2644; No. 3631, Sept. 12, 1944. 740.00119 EW .9-1244; No. 3661, Sept. 14, 1944. 862.01/9-1444; No. 4140, Sept. 21, 1944. 811.91258/9-2144.

Although Dulles, *op. cit.*, p. 172, says that Trott was " reported " to have seen Mme. Kollontay, the information in the reports from Stockholm said he did not. One of the ironies of history can be seen in the BBC report at the time of Trott's visit to Stockholm that he had gone there as the representative of a clique of reactionaries and generals, thereby exposing his mission to the Nazis. Cf. Ritter, " Address at the Royal Institute of International Affairs," p. 341.

[61] In April 1943 he was arrested together with Dietrich Bonhoeffer, and Hans von Dohnanyi. Oster was retired at the same time, and the usefulness of ABWEHR to the Resistance came to an end. Otto John, *Das Parlament*, July 20, 1952.

[62] *Ibid.* At the time of the Normandy invasion, Otto John flew to Madrid to be on hand to propose an armistice to General Eisenhower if a *coup* were achieved in Berlin. He returned to Berlin on July 19 and left again on the 24th for Madrid. On Madrid connections cf. von Schlabrendorff, *op. cit.*, p. 44.

with the Allies during the war: (1) the importance of the ABWEHR in this connection, and (2) the effect of the Casablanca declaration demanding "unconditional surrender" from Germany.

Although the chief of the ABWEHR, the inscrutable Admiral Canaris, never gave himself completely to the Resistance Movement, he deliberately let his intelligence organization be used as a cover for all these contacts abroad. His two closest associates, General Oster and Colonel Lahousen, were deeply involved in all the plans of the conspiracy, and, as Gisevius writes: "Canaris tolerated the seditious activities of the Oster circle by deliberately refusing to take cognizance of them."[63]

Canaris's greatest gift was, apparently, that of cunning and dissimulation. He was able to continue working for Hitler and, at the same time, be working hard against him. It was the brutality of the Nazi regime to which he was particularly opposed, and his personal intervention was usually exercised in refusing to carry out orders such as those given him for the murder of Generals Giraud and Weygand. Colonel Lahousen said of his chief:

> Canaris was a pure intellect, an interesting, highly individual, and complicated personality, who hated violence as such and therefore hated and abominated war, Hitler, his system, and particularly his methods.[64]

Consequently, while he himself left no traces of direct transmission of military information to the enemy, he could not have been unaware of the activities of Oster, Gisevius, Mueller, Goerdeler, and Trott which we have described. Their frequent trips abroad were made possible only by the protection given them against the Gestapo by Canaris's organization.

What was the effect of the Casablanca declaration in January 1943 on the conspiracy within Germany? What may seem at this date to be a purely historical question is actually of perennial importance in the field of psychological warfare. One of the problems which constantly concerned the members of the Resistance Movement was that, after the war—if the Allies were victorious—there would be a vacuum in Central Europe which

[63] Gisevius, *op. cit.*, p. 443.

[64] Testimony of Lahousen at Nuremberg, *IMT*, II, 443.

might easily be filled by Soviet Russia. This fear was intensified by the demand for "unconditional surrender" because it meant that Hitler would fight to the last German.

The conspirators had been trying since before the war, as we have seen, to secure some kind of assurance that the aftermath of a *coup d'état* would be better and not worse conditions within Germany. The insistence at Casablanca that all reconstruction of Germany would depend on Allied good will took from the conspirators one of their main talking points with both the generals and the common people.

Von Weizsäcker felt that the statement at Casablanca meant that any attempt to use political means to end the war would not be acceptable to the Allies.[65] The generals, he said, now felt that it was "stand by Hitler" or lose everything. The German people, according to von Kessel, considered it a threat of "slavery" after the war, and they feared to imagine all that the term might imply. Von Kessel said that the announcement caused a quick withdrawal of many from the Resistance Movement, because capitulation to "unconditional surrender" was regarded by them as synonymous with treason.[66]

Trott zu Solz, in his conversations in Sweden in 1944, repeatedly stressed the fact that the Casablanca declaration had been a great blow for the German Opposition.[67] Canaris told Lahousen that it shattered hopes of a military *coup*. He said:

> You know, my dear Lahousen, the students of history will not need to trouble their heads after this war, as they did after the last, to determine who was guilty of starting it. The case is however different when we consider guilt for prolonging the war. I believe that the other side have now disarmed us of the last weapon with which we could have ended it. Unconditional surrender, no, our generals will not swallow that. Now I cannot see any solution.[68]

One of the arguments used against an *attentat* as late as March 1944 was that the blame for accepting "unconditional surrender"

[65] Weizsäcker transcript, p. 7916.

[66] Von Kessel, unpublished diary, p. 25.

[67] Stockholm to Washington, No. 2309, June 26, 1944. Dept. of State. MS, 103.918/6-2644; No. 4140, Sept. 21, 1944. 811.91258/9-2144.

[68] Colvin, *op. cit.*, p. 193.

should fall on Hitler and not on the new anti-Nazi regime.[69] It was argued, therefore, that it would be better to let things follow their own course. Many other opinions on the psychological effect of this hastily contrived slogan are cited by Professor Rothfels in his analysis of the problem.[70] Mr. Dulles hints that it was a great handicap in his subsequent dealings with the men of the Resistance, for what new government would want to accept the onus of such an unqualified defeat?

The contrast between the Casablanca declaration and the contemporary Moscow propaganda would make an interesting separate study, but it cannot be denied that the East's presentation was calculated to encourage dissident elements within Germany, while the West, to whom those elements had consistently turned, provided only grist for the mill of Hitler and Goebbels.[71]

With the future painted in such dark outlines, it must have taken tremendous conviction and courage to continue working with the Allies for the defeat of Hitler. Erich Kordt has indicated the unique problem faced by the German Resistance:

> At all times there have been revolutionary movements and conspiracies against hated regimes. But it is somewhat different to approach a foreign government about a destruction of the power within one's own land. Every normal sentiment must be restrained if one is to seek an alliance with an enemy country against a hated regime in one's own country.[72]

As the war progressed, and it became evident what destruction and chaos were to be the lot of Germany, only a strong belief in the moral rightness of what they were doing could have persuaded them to continue cooperating with the Allies. Because they fol-

[69] Stockholm to Washington, No. 3996, Oct. 2, 1944. Dept. of State. MS, 103.918/10-244. The report concerned the sentiment of the group around Wilhelm Leuschner, leader of the workers' group which was affiliated with the Kreisau circle.

[70] Rothfels, *op. cit.*, pp. 149-157.

[71] This significant difference was noted by Dulles, *op. cit.*, pp. 171-73. He wrote in a rather disappointed tone: "Both Washington and London were fully advised beforehand on all the conspirators were attempting to do, but it sometimes seemed that those who determined policy in America and England were making the military task as difficult as possible by uniting all Germans to resist to the bitter end." Pp. 172-3.

[72] Kordt, *op. cit.*, p. 245. Translation mine.

lowed their consciences in this regard, they have been denounced as traitors.

The Brunswick Court in trying the Remer case in 1952—Major Remer had branded the men of July 20, 1944 as "traitors"—decided in favor of the men of the Resistance Movement. They were not traitors to Germany, but had undertaken a patriotic struggle against the real enemy of their compatriots—Hitler.

A patriot, it was pointed out at the trial, is one who works for the common good of his country; a traitor is one who works against it. In giving help to the enemy and in working to overthrow the Nazis, these men were motivated by a sincere desire to support and defend the common good; they were indeed the true patriots of the fatherland.[73]

[73] Wiesenborn, *op. cit.*, p. 26 ff.

CHAPTER V

The Case for Conscience

In a revealing letter of April 22, 1947 to Count Bernadotte, Mr. H. R. Trevor-Roper admitted that his estimate of Admiral Canaris in *The Last Days of Hitler* had been a little " too rough." He maintained that he had not intended to judge the actions of the former head of ABWEHR or " of anyone who was honestly perplexed by the problem of overthrowing the Nazis." He confided that he himself would have been very perplexed, " and often ask myself what in fact a man should have done—without knowing the answer." [1]

These words of the noted English historian, usually critical rather than sympathetic toward Germany, sound the essential note in a consideration of the ethical problem at the core of the German Resistance. Granted that individuals were opposed to the Nazi ideology and felt justified in undermining the totalitarian regime, what should they have done?

As we have seen, several of them organized cells of active resistance, promoted plans for a *coup d'état,* and conspired for the military defeat of Germany. But what means did they deem best to achieve these ends, and what problems of conscience did the choice of such means involve?

For those who held office in the Hitler government the major question was: " Shall I protest against the Nazi excesses by resigning from office, or shall I remain in office in order to restrain and frustrate the policies being pursued? " For those in military service it was: "Am I not bound by oath to serve Hitler until death? " or "As a soldier, is not my only responsibility that of obedience to commands of my higher superiors? "

Reflection on these questions led the men of the German Opposition to different conclusions. Colonel-General Ludwig Beck re-

[1] Schellenberg Defense Document # 72. MS, Dept. of the Army.

signed from his office as Chief of the General Staff in protest against Hitler's schemes for war. State Secretary von Weizsäcker remained in office rather than abandon it to the von Ribbentrop forces within the Foreign Office. Admiral Canaris used his position as Chief of ABWEHR to furnish useful information to those working against Hitler, but, at the same time had to gather military intelligence for the Nazi war machine.

In 1937 Goerdeler resigned in protest from the office of Mayor of Leipzig whereas Helmuth von Moltke, Oster, Dohnanyi and others remained in their jobs at ABWEHR as long as possible.

When the war was over, what was the judgment of the victorious nations concerning those who had held office under the Nazis? In no other matter is the issue more obscure and confused. Although Hjalmar Schacht was president of the Reichsbank until his dismissal on January 20, 1939 and Minister without Portfolio until January 22, 1943, he was acquitted by the International Military Tribunal on the grounds that his promotion of rearmament was not criminal because not specifically directed toward aggressive war.[2] The court pointed out, in explaining its decision, that Schacht had resigned as Minister of Economics and Plenipotentiary General for War Economy on November 16, 1937.

Nevertheless it is quite clear from the evidence submitted at his trial that his reason for resigning was not based on ethical objections to Nazi policy but was simply the result of disagreement on financial policy. In 1939 it was Hitler who took the initiative and dismissed Schacht from the presidency of the Reichsbank; again, the issue was that of financial reforms.[3] It is true that Schacht had some connections with the Resistance group, but we have already noted his ambiguous position.[4]

On the other hand, Ernst von Weizsäcker, who played a far more important role than Schacht in the fight against Hitler, was found "guilty" of war crimes in that he cooperated in aggressive warfare against Czechoslovakia and initialed certain decrees regarding the deportation of Jews.[5] This contrast in the judgments of

[2] Judgment in the case of Schacht, *IMT*, I, 307.

[3] Von Hassell, *op. cit.*, pp. 32-33; cf. Gisevius, *op. cit.*, p. 281.

[4] Cf. *Supra*, p. 99, n. 62.

[5] Judgment in the case of von Weizsäcker, *T. of W. C.*, XIV, 340-385 and 475-509. Cf. dissent of Judge Powers, pp. 890-894 and 910-913.

Schacht and von Weizsäcker is pointed out because it highlights the issue of this chapter: how does one determine the guilt or innocence of those who remain in office when the government is pursuing an immoral and tyrannical course?

What should be made very clear at the beginning of our discussion is that, in the last analysis, each man must act according to his conscience and each case must be solved on its individual merits. Ethics gives us the principles, but the application of the principles is usually a sensitive and difficult operation. Since it is the work primarily of moralists, and especially of moral theologians, we cannot attempt to solve the problem in all its ramifications; here we are interested only in indicating the extent to which the political actions of the men of the German Resistance involved such ethical and moral problems.

If a man were convinced that he should work for the collapse of the Hitler regime, to what extent was it permissible to collaborate with the government in order to masque his real designs? Furthermore, if he had taken an oath of personal loyalty to Hitler, was he now free to violate it?

Great emphasis has been placed by some writers on the significance of the oath in the refusal of the German military leadership to overthrow Hitler. Fidelity to an oath of personal loyalty is generally considered an innate characteristic of the German personality. To what extent is it true that the oath was an obstacle to the success of the German Resistance Movement?

In writing about Colonel-General Franz Halder, who became Chief of the General Staff after Beck's resignation, Goerlitz states: "Halder's way was bound to be hard, precisely because he was a Christian and a descendant of an old officers' family, for whom the military oath had for generations been almost a sacrament."[6] Halder's rather scrupulous attitude toward oaths was indicated by his reply at Nuremberg when he was asked to take the customary oath before being interviewed: "Do you swear that the testimony which you are about to give will be the truth, the whole truth, and nothing but the truth, so help you God?" He answered: "I can only swear that what I am going to say I will feel is true. Only God alone knows what really is true."[7]

[6] Goerlitz, *op. cit.*, p. 317.

[7] Halder Interrogation, Oct. 27, 1945.

But was Halder's attitude typical? The oath, in the Judaic-Christian tradition, has been a sacred thing. It is a calling upon God to witness to the truth of what one is stating or to the promise that one is making.[8] Because we are calling upon God as a witness, the swearing of a false oath is a serious sin. In the case of a promissory oath there can be no mental reservation, and a dispensation from it is possible only under extraordinary circumstances.

This Judaic-Christian belief, intensified and strengthened by the feudal heritage of the German Empire, left a decisive mark on the German mind. It would probably not be an exaggeration to say that a passionate devotion to the concept of *Treue* has been one of the deepest formative influences on German youth. It is therefore not surprising that Hitler capitalized on this trait so deeply ingrained in the people whom he ruled.

Gradually all the employees of the Nazi government, civilian as well as military, were made to take an oath to uphold the government and serve the Fuehrer. In what did these promises consist? For the soldiers of the armed forces the oath read as follows:

> I swear by God this sacred oath, that I will render unconditional obedience to Adolf Hitler, the Fuehrer of the German Reich and people, supreme commander of the armed forces, and will be ready as a brave soldier to risk my life at any time for this oath.[9]

All public officials had to swear to the following oath:

> I swear: I shall be loyal and obedient to Adolf Hitler, the Fuehrer of the German Reich and people; respect the laws, and fulfill my official duties conscientiously, so help me God.[10]

According to a law of October 16, 1934 the Reichministers and the members of the *Landes Governments* were obliged to state:

> I take an oath to be loyal and obedient to the Fuehrer of the German "Reich' and people and to dedicate my ability and endeavors in the interest of the German people, to uphold the laws, to execute my duties consciencicusly [*sic*] and to

---

[8] Webster's Dictionary, 2nd ed. Cf. *Summa theologica*, IIa, 2ae, q. 89.

[9] Nuremberg Document #2061-PS, Oct. 24, 1945, MS, Dept. of the Army.

[10] *Ibid.*

> carry on my endeavors in an impartial and just manner in connection with everybody, so help me God.[11]

Special oaths were also devised for pastors, teachers, and the Hitler Youth. All of them included the promise of special fealty to their leader, Hitler. Indeed, so numerous were the occasions on which an oath was demanded that the German pastors in their *Memorial of the Confessing Church* deplored the consequent lessening of its value in the eyes of men. Furthermore there is a hint given that the binding force of such oaths is questionable.

> In the discharge of our Christian duties we hear ever more frequently of persons declaring that they did not feel bound by an oath which it would have threatened their very existence to refuse. The Evangelical Church would be able to combat more easily such a manner of thinking among its members that runs counter to the Christian requirement, if it were permitted to the Christian to give the explanation that no oath can cover proceedings that are contrary to God's commandment.[12]

The final portion of the statement—" no oath can cover proceedings that are contrary to God's commandment "—is in complete accord with Thomistic teaching. In his discussion of the binding force of oaths Saint Thomas makes several enlightening remarks which we shall merely summarize.

1. For a man is bound to make true what he has sworn, else his oath lacks truth. Now, if this thing be such as not to be in his power, his oath is lacking in judgment of discretion; unless perchance what was possible when he swore become impossible to him through some mishap. . . . If, on the other hand, it be something that he can do, but ought not to, either because it is essentially evil, or because it is a hindrance to a good then his oath is lacking in justice: *wherefore an oath must not be kept when it involves a sin or a hindrance to good.*
2. An oath taken under compulsion is not binding.
3. The thing sworn to may not be evil at the time the oath is sworn but may become evil through some new and unforeseen emergency.

---

[11] Nuremberg Document # 2757-PS, MS, Dept. of the Army.

[12] James F. Pollack, " Documents on the Nazi Government of Germany (1937)" in Rappard, Sharp et al. (ed.), *Source Book on European Governments* (New York: D. Van Nostrand Co., 1937), p. 153.

4. A man is bound in accordance with his own intention in taking the oath and not with the intention of the one to whom he swore it. Divine judgement is in accordance with the inward intention and not with the exterior expression.[13]

To sum up, Saint Thomas states: "Anything morally evil or hurtful is incompatible with the matter of an oath."

These criteria seem at first to answer all problems, but that would be an oversimplification. As we have already seen, the evils of the Nazi system were not immediately evident, nor for many individual Germans did they ever become evident to the extent that the persons concerned felt justified in breaking their oaths.

Instances of this attitude are found in the evidence collected at Nuremberg. General Jodl, in denouncing the "revolutionists" among the Germans, indicated his own intransigent position toward the oath he had sworn.

> If today people who co-operated actively to bring Hitler to power, who had a part in the laws which *we soldiers with our oath of allegiance to Adolf Hitler were bound to support,* if these people demanded revolution and mutiny of the Wehrmacht when they no longer liked the man, or when reverses occurred, then I can only call that wicked.[14]

Admiral Karl Doenitz gave expression to the same thought in defending his actions.

> The second pillar of my relationship to Adolf Hitler and the most essential and offering the strongest support was *my oath as a soldier*. The oath of the German soldiers was sworn to the person of Adolf Hitler binding their unconditional obedience.
>
> The oath of any decent man is sacred. Whoever breaks his oath is a rotter and a traitor before God. The fulfillment of contracts is quite rightly demanded. But then it is essential that every human being keeps his contracts and his faith in his word. No "reservatio mentalis" is here permissible. One must not be half-hearted with his oath but must resolutely hold to it.[15]

---

[13] Thomas Aquinas, *Summa theologica*, IIa, 2ae, q. 89. Italics are mine.

[14] *IMT*, XV, 299. Italics are mine.

[15] Interrogation of Admiral Doenitz, Oct. 7, 1945. MS, Dept. of the Army.

Even so unscrupulous a man as Himmler leaned upon the oath as his reason for not negotiating for peace through Schellenberg and Count Bernadotte in the spring of 1945. He said to the latter:

> You may think it sentimental, even absurd, but I have sworn an oath of loyalty to Adolf Hitler and, as a soldier and a German, I cannot go back on my oath.[16]

These statements express what is often designated as the "typical" German militaristic view. Yet, there were other military leaders who came to the conclusion that to continue in the loyal service of Hitler would be an evil thing, to which they could not be bound in truth by their oaths. Several of the conspirators in the July 20, 1944 attempt on Hitler's life advanced as an argument for assassination the psychological necessity of killing Hitler so that the soldiers would no longer feel bound by their oath.[17]

The men of the Resistance were indeed conscious of the mystical quality in the soldier's devotion to his oath, but they themselves—although they left little in writing about their thought on the matter—acted in such a way that one can only conclude that they no longer felt bound by the oath.

Their military leader, Colonel-General Beck, often mentioned his dismay at having taken the prescribed oath when it was presented to the army on August 2, 1934, and wondered aloud if he should not have refused to take it. That very evening he confided to a comrade: "This has been one of the most fateful moments of my life."[18] Gisevius said that Beck brooded over this incident up to the last hours of his life. Beck's brother has made the same remark: "Ihm selbst sind später daraus die schwersten Gewissenskonflikte erwachsen."[19]

An incident which illuminates Beck's position regarding the binding force of this oath occurred on the fateful night of July 20, 1944. General Kortzfleisch had refused to cooperate in the

[16] Colvin, *op. cit.*, p. 245.

[17] E. g., Von Kessel wrote in his diary that it would be important to kill Hitler so that the soldiers would be freed from their oath "dem viele immer noch Bedeutung zumassen." MS, p. 199.

[18] Gisevius, *op, cit.*, p. 278.

[19] Foerster, *op. cit.*, p. 27.

putsch, on the grounds of his oath to Hitler. Beck indignantly lectured him: " How dare you talk of oaths? Hitler has broken his oath to the constitution and his vows to the people a hundred times over. How dare you refer to your oath of loyalty to such a perjurer! " [20]

For many other military leaders—von Witzleben, von Tresckow, von Stauffenberg, Canaris, Olbricht, Oster—the problem was probably resolved in similar fashion. They had taken an oath to Adolf Hitler, but to him as the leader of the German people, entrusted with the common good. As time went on and the police terror could no longer be blamed on an intangible " Party " but had to be laid squarely at Hitler's door, these men saw the incompatability of a sacred oath and complicity in such murderous activities.

In one case, however, the oath proved to be a stumbling block over which the Resistance Movement was to fall several times—Colonel-General Halder. In a key position needed by the conspiracy and apparently non-Nazi in ideology, Halder should have played one of the major roles in the execution of a *coup.* When Colonel-General Beck turned over the office of Chief of the General Staff to Halder it was with the understanding that he would cooperate in the plans then being drawn up to overthrow Hitler if the Sudeten crisis evolved into war.[21]

But there was a serious deficiency in Halder's intention to cooperate. He made it clear, he has stated, to the Commander in Chief, General von Brauchitsch, that he was an enemy of Hitler and " as far as my oath as a soldier permitted, I would do everything possible against this man." [22] When the moment for action came, the conspirators realized that this was indeed a significant self-limitation; Halder always stopped short of decisive action.

At one time Halder said that it was impossible to justify breaking his oath when Germany's military position was so endangered by the Russian conflict.[23] Several of those who sought to influence him in favor of a *coup* have mentioned his preoccupation with his

[20] Gisevius, *op. cit.,* p. 552.
[21] *Ibid.,* pp. 282-286.
[22] Halder Interrogation, Oct. 27, 1945 p. m. MS, Dept. of the Army.
[23] Otto John, article in *Das Parlament,* July 20, 1952.

oath.[24] Despite numerous promising conversations in which he took part, Halder would never initiate action but insisted that orders must come from above.

Halder's devotion to his oath was interwoven with his concept of military obedience. How far this concept led him is pointed out by von Hassell in strongly critical words.

> On April 8 [1941] I conferred with Oster at Beck's. It makes one's hair stand on end to learn about and receive proof of orders signed by Halder and distributed to the troops as to measures to be taken in Russia, and about the systematic transformation of military law concerning the conquered population into uncontrolled despotism—indeed a caricature of all law . . .

And of the Commander-in-Chief, he adds:

> Brauchitsch has sacrificed the honor of the German Army in submitting to these orders of Hitler.[25]

Halder was not alone in this rigid interpretation of military obedience and the duty of living up to his oath, no matter what the circumstances. General Georg Thomas, although not a Nazi and strongly opposed to Hitler's war plans, would never consent to assassination of the Fuehrer because, he maintained, his religious beliefs made it impossible for him to break his oath.[26] General Thomas, it should be noted, was a Protestant.[27]

General Otto von Stülpnagel, Military Commander in France 1940-42, justified his action in shooting hostages on the ground that he was obeying "express orders of the Fuehrer." When his staff implored him to resign rather than carry out these orders he maintained that he must remain "to prevent worse things happening." [28]

The International Military Tribunal refused to accept such "blind obedience" as a defense offered by those accused of shooting

[24] E.g., Schacht Interrogation, Sept. 17, 1946, MS, Dept. of the Army. Schacht said that Halder would "never act against military tradition and the oath to the Fuehrer."

[25] Von Hassell, *op. cit.*, p. 189.

[26] Georg Thomas, "Gedanken und Ereignisse," p. 548.

[27] Letter from General von Witzleben to the writer, July 13, 1954.

[28] Von Hassell, *op. cit.*, p. 238.

hostages or of other similar crimes. Nevertheless, it has not offered a definitive answer to the problem of military obedience. If every soldier felt that he had the liberty—or even the duty—to question all orders of his superior officers and to execute only those of which he approved, military discipline would disintegrate rapidly. On the other hand, he is certainly not free to commit crimes in the name of obedience.[29]

It would seem that the " common good " should be the deciding factor. Ordinarily the common good would profit from unquestioning obedience to commands from a responsible officer. But in a particular instance it may be evident that the leader's intention is an evil one and the thing commanded is immoral; then, the soldier must realize that he has reached the limits of his obedience.

Nevertheless, many responsible German officers clung to their concept of " duty " in defending themselves for having obeyed the orders of Hitler. Field Marshal von Rundstedt, for example, stated: " We did our duty because Hitler had legally been made Chancellor by Hindenburg, and, because, after his death, he appeared as the Fuehrer on the basis of the testament." [30]

It becomes evident, as we go more deeply into this problem, that the validity of the oath was inextricably connected with the question of the legality of the Hitler state. Certainly if it had been proved that power had been usurped by the Nazi leader rather than transferred legally to him it would have been far easier to justify the breaking of the oath.

All agree that Hitler showed remarkable acumen in this regard; the cloak of legality was never shed—even in the final trials before the People's Courts. The deliberate intent of the Nazis to utilize the German weakness for " legality " is explained in a statement by Richard Heydrich, Assistant Chief of the Gestapo, in April 1936.

We destroyed the system (of the Weimar Republic) with its

---

[29] There is an interesting discussion of this problem, with special reference to contemporary life and literature in Hanson Baldwin's " The *Caine Mutiny* Issue," the *New York Times Magazine*, March 21, 1954.

[30] Testimony at Nuremberg, *IMT*, XXI, 38. The legality of the " Testament " has been called into question. Cf. Nuremberg Document, 2234-PS.

> own means. We placed ourselves under its own rules, we were "legal," just as the constitution stated, and we destroyed with constitutional means in a legal manner a system which, lacking inner substance, was prepared at any time to give itself up, if it only occurred in a legal manner.[31]

Recent opinions and court decisions—e. g., the Remer decision in 1952—maintain that the German Reich, through its abuse of power, had become an *Unrechtsstaat*, no oath to which was binding. This, however, must be recognized as a retrospective evaluation. The moral theologian, Dr. Ruppert Angermair, was asked to give an opinion during the trial of Major Remer, and he held that the oath to Hitler was implicitly an oath to uphold the common good of the German people. Hence, if Hitler misused his authority and broke his trust with the people, the oath to him was no longer binding because of the essential change in conditions.[32]

Dr. Bauer, at the same trial, insisted that historically the Roman-Germanic law had always held that the king or prince is bound by the law, and if he rules unjustly, the oath made to him no longer binds. He quoted the statement Lampert made in 1073: "Wenn er [the king] die aber übertritt, sind wir durch unsere Eidespflicht nicht mehr gebunden." [33] Why, then, we may ask, was it so difficult for the German of the 1930's to justify breaking his oath?

The post-war discussions held in Munich by the *Europäische Publikation* group, under the direction of Major General von Witzleben, considered this problem very thoroughly. Commenting on the Remer decision, one of the participants cautioned against a narrow legalistic view of the *Unrechtsstaat*. One cannot maintain that such a state exists simply because the government enacts an unjust law. In such a case, one may refuse to obey the particular law but may not deny complete obedience to the state. An *Unrechtsstaat,* they concluded, was one that abandons fundamental principles in so decisive a way that it has forfeited the obedience of its citizens.[34]

[31] *Deutsche Rechtwissenschaft,* April, 1936 quoted in the Office of Strategic Services, *Handbook on National Socialist Germany,* OSS, R. & A. # 376, n. d. Dept. of State Library.

[32] Wiesenborn, *op. cit.*, p. 27.

[33] *Ibid.*, p. 35.

[34] Witzleben typescript, "Observations," p. 4. It is implied that such a situation had arisen in Germany.

At the end of this particular discussion, Professor Kinder, a Lutheran theologian, was asked: "Were the members of the Opposition oath-breakers or not?" He answered: "No, because they had sworn by God, and in this case their obedience to God was higher than obedience to man."

The concept of an *Unrechtsstant* was apparently what Colonel Count von Stauffenberg had in mind when he tried to convince Major Leonrod of the necessity for assassinating Hitler. Leonrod, a young officer on von Stauffenberg's staff, objected to the plans on the grounds that as an officer he was bound to Hitler by oath. Von Stauffenberg, on the contrary, felt that in such a "distressed condition," one could no longer consider the oath as holy. "As a believing Catholic," Leonrod said (apparently quoting von Stauffenberg), "I was bound in duty . . . to act against this oath."[35]

It is impossible to decide with certainty whether the military leaders, such as Jodl, Keitel, Halder, and von Brauchitsch, sincerely believed themselves bound by the oath they had taken to Hitler, or whether they considered it simply a good excuse. It does not seem unlikely, however, that for many ordinary Germans the obligation of the oath posed a very real problem. Especially difficult was the position of those who took the oath after the terror methods of the Nazi head of state had become evident.

A lay Lutheran chaplain remarked to the writer that it had been his sad experience to receive frequent visits from both military and civilian personnel who were seeking a solution to the problem which would both calm their consciences and permit them to retain some sort of position so as to support their families. To refuse to take the oath was tantamount to a declaration of enmity to the regime, and the consequences of such an action are well known.

The first consequence was loss of position, and this seemed not only a personal loss but a surrender of one more opening to the Nazis. Many of the men of the Resistance, both military and civilian, felt that the best way of fighting Hitler was to hold on to their positions and do what they could to stem the tide of Nazi aggression and brutality. Among the high German officers the only one to resign was Beck. As we have seen, he had hoped for a collective resignation, but instead was forced to resign alone and

[35] RSHA report, Oct. 4, 1944. MS, 105/26. Dept. of the Army.

in an unostentatious manner. The intended force of the move was gravely weakened.

Once out of office, Beck—although the leader of the Opposition—no longer had the means necessary to bring about a successful *coup.* Nevertheless he felt strongly that resignation had been his only course of action, for what man of honor could submit to the capricious war plans of a Hitler? To Beck, the limits of military obedience were set at that point when "knowledge, conscience, and responsibility forbid the execution of an order." [36]

The higher the officer, the more responsible he is, for his is a coresponsibility with the head of the state. Beck believed this sincerely and felt that even a simple soldier must not allow his life to be spent for a lawless state.[37]

This is an attitude in sharp contrast to that of the Commander-in-Chief. When the members of the Resistance tried to secure his cooperation and were unsuccessful, von Hassell noted indignantly: "Brauchitsch hitches his collar a notch higher and says: 'I am a soldier; it is my duty to obey.' " [38]

Von Hassell himself agreed with Beck in this matter. He mentions that on November 1, 1939 he spent the evening with Brauchitsch's cousins and tried to show them "the tremendous responsibility the general now bears."

> A commander in chief is not just a divisional commander who does nothing but obey. He must also consider the political ramifications of strategy, to say nothing of the military question whether or not a certain move promises sufficient success to warrant the risk and sacrifice involved.[39]

Of further interest are his remarks of January 28, 1940:

> Prussian discipline is no longer really dependable where it is absolutely indispensable, namely, among the troops and in the officers' corps. But *at the upper levels, where obedience should be supplemented by judgment and political responsi-*

[36] Foerster, *op. cit.*, p. 122. "Ihr soldatischer Gehorsam hat dort eine Grenze, wo ihr Wissen, ihr Gewissen, und ihre Verantwortung die Ausführung eines Befehls verbietet."

[37] Max Pribilla, S. J., "Ein grosser Gegenspieller Hitlers," p. 260.

[38] Von Hassell, *op. cit.*, p. 6.

[39] *Ibid.*, p. 87.

> *bility,* it is applied all the more slavishly and against better knowledge.[40]

Because General Beck supplemented his obedience with judgment and a sense of political responsibility, he resigned. Some of his co-conspirators later questioned the wisdom of this decision since it removed a valuable position from their control, but all agreed that Beck could do nothing else since it was what his conscience dictated.

Learning perhaps from Beck's example and disillusioned by the failure of his successor to carry out his policies, the other army leaders who belonged to the Resistance remained in their posts, playing a double role until the moment when they were either dismissed by Hitler or were executed after July 20, 1944. One can only imagine the inner conflict that went on during those years in the German officers such as von Witzleben, von Tresckow, Olbricht, Canaris, and Oster.

Colonel Lahousen testified to the difficulty which confronted his chief, Admiral Canaris:

> Canaris merely had the choice of giving up the fight and resigning or of holding out consciously, as long as there was even the slightest hope of counteracting Hitler and his clique. Canaris decided to "hang on."

In making this decision he was motivated by two decisive factors.

> These were his profound religious tendency which was rooted in metaphysical and anthroposophic ideas and his determination not to let the ABWEHR which was entrusted to him become an instrument of evil; on the contrary to make it a clearing house for all efforts directed against Hitler.

And Colonel Lahousen concluded:

> The tremendous moral burden, the danger, and the inner tragedy of Canaris' underground struggle were inherent in the very difficult delimitation of this "apparent playing along."[41]

By retaining his position Canaris was able to circumvent many

[40] *Ibid.*, p. 108. Italics are mine.

[41] Affidavit of Colonel Erwin Lahousen, von Weizsäcker Defense Document Book #5, p. 40. MS, Dept. of the Army.

of the SS plans, and to enable many victims of racial and political persecution to escape from Germany. He intervened repeatedly in the Nazi treatment of war prisoners.[42] It was his office which furnished the "intelligence" transmitted to the Allies. On occasion he requested prisoners for use in ABWEHR so as to remove them from Himmler's jurisdiction. Another example of his service to the Resistance was the arrangement of a meeting of Intelligence Officers at Smolensk early in 1943 so that Hitler would come there —an arrangement desired by those plotting to assassinate him.[43]

Such opportunities for using an official position as a means of promoting the Resistance Movement inspired most of the men concerned to remain in office for the duration. Their motivation was well expressed by Fabian von Schlabrendorff in his testimony at Nuremberg.

> Resistance, not in a democracy but in a dictatorship, is according to our experience, possible only when some members of the resistance movement are in official posts because success for a resistance movement in a dictatorship is possible only by collaboration between those who attack the dictatorship from outside and those who work secretly in important posts within the dictatorship.[44]

In the very first entry in his diary, September 17, 1938, von Hassell indicated his awareness of the problem:

> During the past weeks I have asked myself repeatedly whether it is right to serve such an immoral system. However, "on the outside," the slight chance of successful opposition would be even smaller.[45]

Again, on November 2, 1939, he noted:

---

[42] E. g., His "Memorandum on the Directive of 8 September 1941 on treatment of Russian prisoners of war," dated September 15, 1941 in which he discusses the legality of the prescribed measures and states that the ABWEHR has grave "misgivings" about it. English translation in Margaret Carlyle (ed.), *Documents on International Affairs 1939-1946*, Vol. II (New York: Oxford University Press, 1954), pp. 78-81.

[43] Schlabrendorff, *op. cit.*, p. 52. Cf. Lahousen statement, von Weizsäcker Defense Document Book # 5, p. 93. MS, Dept. of the Army.

[44] Testimony of von Schlabrendorff, *T. of W. C.*, XIII, 399.

[45] Von Hassell, *op. cit.*, p. 1.

> All of us who are without government posts lack power of leverage and are without influence.[46]

The best illustration of the argument for remaining in office is the case of Ernst von Weizsäcker. The fact that he retained his office of State Secretary in the Foreign Office under the Hitler government was a key point in his trial at Nuremberg. Consequently a quantity of first-hand material is available on his reasons for having done so.[47]

Heinrich Brüning, former Chancellor of the German Republic, told von Schlabrendorff after three or four years of Nazi rule: "Now a man must choose between the Swastika and the Cross of Christ; the decision cannot be avoided." [48] Yet he felt that the members of the Foreign Office who were opposed to the Swastika should not resign but stay at their posts. He testified in 1947 that when Foreign Minister von Buelow had told him that many in the Foreign Office were considering resignation, he had urged them not to do so.[49] Why?

> . . . because after the dissolution of the political parties and the slow deterioration of Hindenburg's mental faculties they alone, with the moderate leaders in the Army, would be in a position to block an aggressive foreign and armament policy of Hitler's successfully. In my last meeting with Herr von Bülow at night a few days before my flight from Germany, I warned him that this task would be increasingly difficult in view of the unexpected acceptance of Nazi policy by the great powers, and that the gentlemen involved must not only work very cleverly from within, but must recognize that even under the best disguise their efforts might under some circumstances cost them their lives.

Brüning mentioned that one of those best qualified for such a task was von Weizsäcker.

Many friends, both at home and abroad, counseled von Weizsäcker to follow such a course of action. In 1937 when he was offered the

[46] *Ibid.*, p. 87.

[47] Complete transcript of the trial and documents submitted in evidence are available in manuscript, Dept. of the Army. Cf. *Supra*, p. 3, n. 7.

[48] Schlabrendorff, *op. cit.*, p. 13.

[49] Statement made by Brüning under oath, Dec. 22, 1947. Von Weizsäcker Defense Document # 1, MS, Dept. of the Army.

opportunity of moving from Berne to the Foreign Office in Berlin —with the probability of soon becoming State Secretary—he asked the advice of Mr. Ferdinand Lathrop Mayer, United States Counsellor at the Embassy in Berlin. Mr. Mayer has testified of the incident:

> In the circumstances, Weizsäcker wondered whether, as a patriotic German he should accept such an appointment, asking himself the question whether he could do anything to stem the tide as director or *Staats-Sekretaer* in the Foreign Office, or whether it would not be better to remain at Berne.

Mayer advised him to take the appointment in order to exert a moderating influence on German Foreign policy.[50]

In 1942 Winston Churchill asked Carl Burkhardt about von Weizsäcker's position and seemed glad to learn that he was still in the office of State Secretary.[51] Even Colonel-General Beck, although he had resigned himself, urged von Weizsäcker to remain at his post, thereby having the opportunity of directing matters into a peaceful channel. It is interesting to note that when Beck resigned, von Weizsäcker sent him a gift which expressed their oneness of purpose despite their divergent courses of action—a copy of Plutarch's *Lives*.[52]

The various other opponents of Hitler often discussed the question of von Weizsäcker's ambivalent position. Yet, it was always with the hope that he would succeed in avoiding dismissal, for they considered his position indispensable to the work of the group.[53] He gave vital political information to Beck and Canaris, covered up the work of the Kordts and von Kessel, shifted departmental personnel around thereby keeping useful men in key spots, helped von Dohnanyi in relieving extreme conditions of some Jewish families, and fought against every inroad made by von Ribbentrop into the Foreign Office.

[50] Von Weizsäcker Defense Document # 288. The statement was made Nov. 4, 1947.

[51] Testimony of von Kessel, transcript of von Weizsäcker's trial, p. 9491.

[52] *Ibid.*, p. 9524.

[53] E.g., Affidavit of Klothilde Bruecklmaier, von Weizsäcker Defense Document Book # 5, p. 58; of Hans Gisevius, p. 31; and of Werner Jentsch, Director of Religious affairs for YMCA, Document Book 9.

The noted German doctor, Ferdinand Sauerbruch (a colleague of Beck and von Hassell), wrote of State Secretary von Weizsäcker:

> I know that he suffered enormously from orders and assignments which were unworthy of him. Nevertheless he remained in his office, in order to prevent worse things, which he did at the cost of difficult struggles, and to preserve a nucleus in the Foreign Office which, after the elimination of the National Socialist regime, would be ready to take over.[54]

Herr Ernst Brandenburg, a close friend of Dr. Goerdeler, testified that the leading men of the Opposition considered it most fortunate that a man like von Weizsäcker "made the great sacrifice to remain in his position as State Secretary." He stated:

> When under the national socialist regime Herr von Weizsäcker took over the political department of the Foreign Office and soon afterwards became State Secretary, his appointment was received with great satisfaction by all political circles opposed to National Socialism. Dr. Goerdeler came to me and he was full of joy that it was possible to bring about this appointment because it meant a victory of the good elements at the Foreign Office.[55]

There are numerous affidavits testifying to the same opinion; the other conspirators were definitely in favor of von Weizsäcker's remaining in office. The former Ambassador to Belgium, von Bülow-Schwandte, resigned in 1942 because he lacked the "endurance and temperament needed to put up with the difficult position," but he went on record as admiring profoundly von Weizsäcker's "patience, sacrifice, and strength of will in the performance of his duty." [56]

The Italian Ambassador Attolico spoke of von Weizsäcker to Burkhardt early in the summer of 1939 and commended his efforts to prevent war. He felt that any other course would be easier than the one von Weizsäcker had chosen to follow.

---

[54] Affidavit of Ferdinand Sauerbruch, von Weizsäcker Defense Document Book # 5, p. 105.

[55] Affidavit of Ernst Brandenburg. *Ibid.*, p. 8. Brandenburg had been removed from office by the Nazis because he defended Niemoeller at his trial.

[56] Testimony of von Bülow-Schwandte, transcript of von Weizsäcker trial, pp. 9831-32.

> The easiest way is to emigrate and to protest, but even to plot uprisings, to conspire, needs less strength and courage than to wrest the impossible from hard reality day by day without much ado, defeated, yet starting anew time and again, apparently approving all that one abhors, tenaciously, completely unselfish, cleverly and with constant extreme alertness and intensity.[57]

How did von Weizsäcker himself regard his position? The main charge against him at Nuremberg was that he had worked as a "front" for Ribbentrop and had signed documents relative to the deportation of the Jews, thereby cooperating in the crimes of the Nazis.[58] His response was that the ultimate solution of the Jewish question depended on the removal of Hitler, and his own continuation in office was an integral part of the plan to remove him.[59] His testimony at Nuremberg on this point is revealing:

> Question: . . . what attitude did you take to these atrocious incidents as a whole?
>
> Answer: As far as the ethical side of these incidents is considered, it is unnecessary for me to say a word on that but I knew that the awful development and the course that was taken in the Jewish problem could be stopped by only one means—peace—that is, a peace eliminating Hitler, and it was this objective that I centered on. In order to retain that sphere of activity, in order to gain that final and ultimate objective, I had to permit documents to pass my desk which in normal times I would have hesitated to touch with my own hands. You would not even touch them with a pair of pliers.
>
> Question: You will understand that an outsider might raise the question why you continued to hold an office in which such documents even came to your perusal, even though you took no active part in the incidents reported in these documents.
>
> Answer: I can very well understand that question, only too well, but this was the infernal thing of that time. In the interest of resistance, I retained my office and in remaining in office, it was not possible for

---

[57] Affidavit of Carl Burkhardt, von Weizsäcker Defense Document # 499.

[58] Opening statement of the Prosecution, *T. of W. C.*, XII, 229.

[59] Von Weizsäcker transcript, pp. 8588-8590.

me to prevent such documents passing over my desk under such a state of government—I mean documents involving deportations, labor camps, seizures, and so on. I had to accept this and bear it for the very reason that I proposed to put an end to these measures and because it could only be brought about by these means, to put an end to these measures. Very often I was compelled to disguise my own attitude to the outside world and I was also driven to put on another face than would have been mine under the situation. I think whoever has not gone through these experiences personally, whoever cannot know personally what they signify, he is perhaps incapable of understanding these things. It is necessary to have lived under a dictatorship to understand this.

Question: There is a German proverb " Whoever touches dirt is apt to become dirty himself " or in other words " Who eats with the devil needs a long spoon." Didn't you have that feeling yourself in connection with these incidents?

Answer: Your question is a different one. The actual question is which of the two sullies his conscience more, that person who endeavors to do away with evil, or that person who resigns into his private life and just discusses these matters in the circle of his own family, in the hope and expectation that this phantom of dictatorship, this phantom of racial persecution might perhaps disappear of its own accord, spontaneously. But the question is only the following: There is no other way. How was it possible to achieve my objective—by resigning or retaining my position? It was not a question of how it was possible for me to prevent my hands being sullied, of avoiding a stain on my waistcoat to which other people might subsequently point.

Question: Now, this stain that you speak of—this is the very thing you are being charged with here, particularly in the Jewish question.

Answer: I don't want to be misunderstood here. I don't condemn those people who saw it to be a clearer and better and cleaner course to avoid being stained themselves but we learned under a dictatorship that whoever restrains himself may perhaps not visibly sully himself but I, in any case, saw the only chance to serve my objectives by retaining my office and the only chance of doing anything at all—unfortunately sometimes it was little enough—of doing anything at all against dictatorship. Perhaps you might be able to rephrase it as follows: In order to be more specific, I had to sit down at a desk and documents came across this desk. It was my desire to establish a chance for us, for Germany under the totalitarian regime, in order to reach a state which would make these types of documents impossible.

Question: Therefore you did not resign from office?

Answer: Yes, that is true. I didn't resign from office because I desired to act, and I do not regret it.

That von Weizsäcker was able to act in various ways to help the Jews is testified to by hundreds of affidavits submitted at his trial. As Ambassador to the Vatican in 1943-45 he was noted for his protection of them.[60]

In August of 1941 when the Nazi Party radicals were pressing for the arrest of Bishop von Galen, von Weizsäcker was asked to intervene. He indicated the problems he was facing in speaking to von Bülow-Schwandte.

> How long can one serve in that regime? . . . Believe me, every day I have to check my conscience as to what my task is here on earth as a human being. Fate has put me in this position and has given me the cross to bear to work together with Hitler and Ribbentrop and to serve them. As a true patriot I have to fight for Germany with them. I know that if I leave, a radical change will take place, or else the actual professional officials in the Foreign Office who hold a peaceful opinion now will no longer be in office. A higher authority has put me in this position. I can stop many things here and avoid many things. By filling out this position in my opinion, I am doing my moral duty.[61]

---

[60] Among these are affidavits by Thomas J. Kiernan, Irish Chargé at the Vatican; Rev. E. Gehrmann, Rector of Casa Missionaria in Riva, Italy, who had been in the Apostolic Nunciature in Berlin; Rev. Robert Leiber, S. J., of the Gregorian; the rectors of the Pontifical Bible Institute, Pontifical Institute of Oriental Studies, Irish Franciscan College, Stella Matutina in the Black Forest.

[61] Testimony of von Bülow-Schwandte, von Weizsäcker transcript, p. 9835.

At Nuremberg when von Weizsäcker was asked if the warnings he had sent to London prior to Munich were not unusual for a man of his character, he explained his justification of the dual role he was forced to play.

> Well, I did turn into a potential enemy in order to prevent the potential enemy from turning into a world conflagration, and in my opinion that is an adequate reason for such an unusual step. And, it was necessary, because, according to my observations at the time, the official world in London was not ready to act as it should have been. It may have been a little different in non-official, political circles, but since you ask me, I will put it like this, *that the end justified the means, namely, peace.* I can imagine that some people misunderstood me, and still misunderstand me today, especially people who generally share my opinions and who normally understand me. Some of them may say that I should not have served Hitler. Some may say, "Well, if you did serve Hitler at all, you should have served him loyally." However, *if the man at the top has thrown away the claim and the right to loyalty, then other fundamental rules apply;* and as far as schematism and primitive loyalty go, well, there are higher duties which have precedence.[62]

To von Weizsäcker then as to Beck, the failure of Hitler to live up to his obligations to the German people released his subjects from the oath of loyalty which had been demanded. Yet he felt that the best way he could work against Hitler was by remaining in office as long as possible. A fellow conspirator said that:

> . . . in spite of the identical inner attitude [of Beck and von Weizsäcker] Herr von Weizsäcker took it upon himself to remain in office, because he thought along lines of realistic politics and that he was well aware of the fact that only a person who was near to Hitler could do something decisive in order to remove him.[63]

Gisevius pointed out that the necessity of holding on to key positions often involved the performance of onerous duties such as signing decrees against the Jews. Canaris and von Weizsäcker,

[62] Testimony of von Weizsäcker, transcript, p. 7757. Italics are mine.

[63] Albrecht Haushofer said this to Reiner Hildebrandt. Affidavit of Reiner Hildebrandt, von Weizsäcker Defense Document Book # 5, p. 14.

he said, were both concerned about the problem, yet they knew that Hitler would not be overthrown by emigrants, deactivated persons, or prisoners in concentration camps.

> The same happened to them as to Field Marshal von Witzleben who, since 1938 was firmly decided to start a revolt. Since, however, as a single person, he could not do anything he had to stay in his position for six hard years; he even had to issue orders, which could mean death for innumerable people on both sides—only in order to be at hand for the decisive hour for which he had longed for years.[64]

The leaders of both Catholic and Protestant Church groups in Germany attested to the value of von Weizsäcker's protection which they received. In Rome numerous religious superiors acknowledged that his sympathy and help were never lacking under very trying circumstances,[65] and Field Marshal Albert Kesselring claimed that von Weizsäcker had a large share in the responsibility for declaring Rome an open city and saving it from destruction.[66]

But will a list of the positive gains resulting from his presence in the Foreign Office eliminate moral responsibility for signing questionable decrees? When the question was raised at von Weizsäcker's trial, Fabian von Schlabrendorff maintained that there was no way of avoiding such disagreeable tasks and that to refuse one's signature would have no effect. Signing such decrees was not a matter of making policy but merely of taking notice of what had already been decided upon by others. He stated:

> There was no one in Germany who could have evaded contact with national socialism. It was only a question of degree. . . . I knew the work of many other persons in similar positions and above all I knew that during a war a person in the Foreign Office could make no decisions in these things. In most cases it was just a matter of taking notice.

When he was asked further: " Did not the leaders of the German

[64] Affidavit of Gisevius, *Ibid.*, p. 31.

[65] Cf. Document Books # 3, 5, and 6, and Affidavit of Msgr. Raphael Forni, Secretary to the Papal Nuncio in Berlin 1939-42. Document Book # 9, p. 46. Msgr. Forni was very sympathetic toward von Weizsäcker's reasons for staying in office.

[66] Affidavit of Kesselring, von Weizsäcker Defense Document Book # 3.

Resistance Movement and yourself believe that as an enemy of national socialism one should keep aloof from such things?" von Schlabrendorff replied:

> Fundamentally we did believe that. I, personally because of my temperament and my somewhat uncompromising basic convictions, would not have signed or initialed such matters, but that probably would have been wrong. Keeping in mind the goal, the overthrow of Hitler, it was necessary in our opinion to do such things, no matter how much they might weigh upon one's conscience.

Finally, von Schlabrendorff was asked:

> As an expert on the resistance movement I shall now ask you in conclusion, how many Jews is it permissible to murder if one's final goal is to do away with Hitler—how many million?

The witness answered: "I would say nobody." [67]

While the cleverness of the implication is immediately obvious, one must bear in mind that von Weizsäcker had not "murdered" Jews. According to the evidence of the court, he had initialed documents bearing orders for the deportation of Jews, but the defense maintained that this initialing constituted "taking cognizance" of such a policy, not an initiation or execution of murder. It is, to be sure, a very fine line of distinction and possibly open to refutation, but it appears to this writer to be a fair estimate of the way that von Weizsäcker and his friends regarded the problem.

In speaking of the role von Weizsäcker played, Gisevius said:

> Dictatorships cannot be removed by press publications. Whoever wants to liberate his people and mankind from such evil must pay the price, namely, his outward deeds will be misunderstood by his contemporaries, and that he will even be condemned.[68]

It was put in similar words by the lawyer defending von Weizsäcker at Nuremberg: "Resistance through forced cooperation is the tragic task of a qualified person under a dictatorship." [69] How can we justify such "feigned cooperation"?

[67] T. of W. C., XIII, 395-402.

[68] Affidavit of Gisevius. Document Book # 5, p. 31.

[69] T. of W. C., XII, 241.

The fundamental ethical principle involved here is the concept of the "double effect." If an action, not evil in itself, has two effects—one good and one evil—the action can only be taken under certain conditions:

1. If the evil effect will not precede the good effect, for if it does then it is a means and, as such, is directly willed. But an evil can never be directly willed, whether as means or end. "We cannot do evil that good may come of it. The end does not justify the means."
2. There must be a sufficiently grave reason for desiring the good effect.
3. The intention of the agent must sincerely be concerned with the good effect.[70]

To apply this principle to the case of von Weizsäcker and others who followed the same course of action would be the work of a moral theologian. One would have to know with certainty the intention of the agent and the extent to which the evil effect as "means" was intended and directly willed.[71] A recent opinion of considerable weight holds that to be culpable in such a situation one must have the power of impeding the action considered evil. One may not will it; one merely tolerates it. The criterion for judging such actions must be the ultimate effect on the common good of society.[72]

From a negative point of view, one of the reasons often advanced for remaining in office was that a more radical person would be named as one's successor. Baron Gustav Adolf von Steengracht von Moyland, State Secretary 1943-45, described the consequences feared by those faced with the question of resignation.

> In consequence of the change to dictatorial government and the completely different concept of the State which the change of government involved, the individual suddenly found that he was no longer allowed to take a position of his own concerning this regime. The notorious reign of terror began. . . . Fear

---

[70] Paul J. Glenn, *Ethics* (St. Louis, Mo.; B. Herder & Co., 1930), p. 22.

[71] For a detailed study of this problem see Herbert G. Kramer, *The Indirect Voluntary* (Washington, D. C.: Catholic Univ. Press, 1935), chapter VI.

[72] *DTC*, XV, 3300-3309.

> of being reported. . . . Some would still have withdrawn if they felt it would improve things. . . . But it became obvious that such persons merely sacrificed themselves and especially their families unavailingly, because cases of the kind were painstakingly withheld from publicity and therefore had no effect. Worst of all was the fact that the appointment was filled by an especially radical man. Many people realized this and remained at their posts in order to prevent the development that I have just described.[73]

According to one witness, if von Weizsäcker had resigned, ". . . this would have been equivalent to a voluntary surrender of the entire diplomatic apparatus to the Nazis, that is, equivalent to a renunciation of every attempt to avert the disaster." [74]

Bishop Berggrav, leader of the Norwegian Resistance, in discussing a visit to von Weizsäcker in March 1940 related the latter's reasons for staying on as State Secretary. Von Weiszäcker was in despair but felt that it would be wrong for him to escape, thereby leaving things to their fate while saving himself. Asked by Berggrav why he remained, he replied: "If I go, there will be nobody here to act as a brake. This is my only hope now—to prevent the worst, wherever I may." [75]

The necessity of the Resistance Movement's having access to confidential information, the desire to prevent further Nazi control, to sabotage as many orders of the SS as possible, to plead the cause of prisoners of war and international conventions, to secure false passports for those being persecuted—these are the reasons given over and over by the participators in and defenders of the German Resistance Movement.

By way of contrast, what was the contribution to resistance of those who did resign? We have already discussed the case of General Beck and have seen that although he became the center of the movement, he was always hampered by his lack of command over troops. The inspiration which his moral courage gave to others was no doubt an important factor but one which it is impossible to measure.

[73] T. of W. C., X, 111-112.

[74] Affidavit of Ernst Eisenlohr, German Minister to Czechoslovakia, 1936-38, April 15, 1948, Weizsäcker Defense Document # 280.

[75] Affidavit of Bishop Berggrav, *T. of W. C.*, XII, 1171.

Two Cabinet members also resigned rather than accept responsibility for the Hitler program. Herbert von Bismark, State Secretary in the Prussian Ministry of Interior, resigned even when von Papen, von Blomberg, and Göring refused to go with him. According to von Schlabrendorff, he ". . . could not bear the thought that while he held public office and bore responsibility, men should be persecuted because of their race or convictions.[76]

In January 1937 Baron von Eltz-Ruebenach, Minister of Transport and Postal Affairs, declined membership in NSDAP. He wrote to Hitler:

> My conscience forbids me to accept this offer. I believe in the principles of positive Christianity and must remain faithful to my Lord and to myself. Party membership however would mean that I should have to face without contradiction the steadily aggravating attacks by party offices on the Christian confessions and those who want to remain faithful to their religious convictions.[77]

Thereupon, he asked permission to resign.

Courageous as was the action of these two men, it is significant that neither of their names is connected with the Resistance Movement as such. Did not the very bold statement of their position make them too "suspect" for useful work later on?

Such then is the very heart of the problem. How can there be a successful resistance movement if people openly commit themselves to an anti-government position by early resignation from power? Yet if they postpone resignation it soon becomes impossible (unless one accepts the fate of a concentration camp as inevitable), or it becomes useless since it receives no publicity and results only in the surrender of another position to the tyrannical party.

If one does not resign, how can he justify all the things he must do in order to remain in office? This is a problem which has reached a new complexity with the rise of the bureaucratic totalitarian state, for the possibility of escaping detection if one refuses to conform even in minor details has been sharply reduced. "Col-

[76] Schlabrendorff, *op. cit.*, p. 12.

[77] Document submitted in evidence No. 1534-PS. Translation in English, MS, Dept. of the Army.

laboration" is a most unpleasant word, and yet it is hard to condemn men who "collaborated" exteriorly with their own government for the purpose of overthrowing it at the first possible opportunity.

Not content to rest on Hamlet's "Conscience doth make cowards of us all," the men of the German Resistance risked being labeled "cowards" because they had the courage to act according to the voice of conscience. Day by day they attempted to resolve the problems presented to those retaining official status in a government dominated by one whom they considered "mad," "diabolical," or "criminal."

While not pretending to give a definitive answer to this problem which has so many ramifications in each individual case, the writer would suggest that the answer must rest on the belief in a right of resistance to a tyrannical regime and the conviction that an oath of loyalty to such a state would not be binding in conscience. Given those two premises, the conclusion, it is suggested, would be that men who utilized their positions to overthrow such a government are more to be praised than blamed. The evil which they "permitted"—but did not will—in order to retain their positions certainly appears less significant than the good effect which they were seeking, and came so close to realizing.

CHAPTER VI

Kreuz und Hakenkreuz

At the conclusion of World War II the Allies were faced with the serious and difficult problem of building a "new" Germany. For this task the churches were considered "one of the most important instruments for the reorientation of German society." In justifying its decision to use the churches for this purpose, the Office of the U. S. High Commissioner for Germany stated that the record of the churches in resisting the Nazis was, on the whole, "a very good one." [1]

The former German State Secretary in the Foreign Ministry, Ernst von Weizsäcker, testified at Nuremberg that: "The churches were the most reliable and unmovable pillars of the Resistance Movement." [2] Father Max Pribilla, S. J., a thoughtful student of the Hitler era, has echoed this opinion. He writes:

> Nevertheless it remains true that believing Christianity was the single power over which the National Socialists did not become Master and which . . . was still standing firm when it collapsed.[3]

In our study of the German Resistance Movement, it seems advisable to analyze the role of the churches from two points of view: (1) What was the official policy of the Roman Catholic and Evangelical churches toward Hitler and the Nazis? and (2) To what extent did Church leaders have contact with, and influence on, the members of the active Resistance Movement?

[1] Beryl R. McClasky, *The History of United States Policy and Program in the Field of Religious Affairs Under the Office of the U. S. High Commissioner for Germany.* U. S. High Commissioner for Germany, Office of the Executive Secretary: Historical Division. Research Project # 104, 1951. Introduction, p. i.

[2] Transcript of the von Weizsäcker trial, p. 8287.

[3] Max Pribilla, S. J., *Deutsche Schicksalsfragen* (Frankfurt am Main: Josef Knecht, 1950), p. 56. Translation mine.

In 1933, when the Nazis came into power, the ecclesiastical statistics read: 62% Evangelicals and 32.5% Catholics. But since every German is presumed to belong to the same church of which his parents are members—unless he specifically withdraws from church membership [5]—these figures are probably high with regard to actual "practicing" Christians. Nevertheless, the majority of the German people were apparently churchgoers, and, as such, might be expected to come into conflict with the Nazi movement.

The incompatibility of National Socialism and Roman Catholicism had already been formally stated before the Nazi ascent to power. On September 30, 1930 a parish priest in Kirschhausen in Hesse, Father Weber, gave a sermon in which he stated unequivocally:

1. Every Catholic is forbidden to be a member of the Nazi Party.
2. No members of the Hitler Party are allowed to attend funerals or other church services in group formation.
3. As long as a Catholic is a member of the Hitler Party, he cannot be admitted to the Sacraments.[6]

Quick to seize such an opportunity, the Gauleiter of Hesse asked for an explanation or repudiation of this sermon from the Bishop of Mainz. In return he received what was the first official statement of opposition on the part of the Catholic Church to the fundamental principles of Nazism.[7] His Excellency said that the parish priest had been acting on instructions from him, and that the reason for his opposition could be found in Article 24 of the Nazi program.

The article in question stated:

> We demand the freedom of all religious beliefs in the State insofar as they are no danger to the public weal and do not offend against the ethical and moral sense of the German race.[8]

---

[4] *Statistisches Jahrbuch Für Das Deutsche Reich* (Berlin: 1935), p. 14. Quoted in McClasky, *op. cit.*, p. 8.

[5] *Ibid.*, p. i.

[6] John Brown Mason, *Hitler's First Foes* (Minneapolis, Minn.: Burgess, 1936), p. 92.

[7] *Ibid.*, pp. 93-94.

[8] Quoted in Joseph F. Thorning, S. J., "The German Bishops and Hitlerism," *America*, 46 (Jan. 9, 1932), 333-334.

The Bishop held that such phraseology was, at best, ambiguous, and denied that the "ethical and moral sense of the German race" could be the criterion for religious beliefs. Furthermore, the Ordinary of Mainz denounced the "positive Christianity" of the Nazis, a concept which was intimately bound up with the racial propaganda of the Party.

The Bishop continued:

> Through this conception of religion the National Socialists fall into a position inimical to the Catholic Church. It is for that reason that National Socialist speakers have repeatedly expressed the idea in public meetings: "Our fight is against Judaism and Rome." Hitler, to be sure, has written in his book *Mein Kampf,* some words of acknowledgment about the Christian religion and Catholic institutions, but that does not deceive us about the fact that the cultural policies of National Socialism are in contradiction to Catholic Christianity.
>
> The above statements answer the questions: Can a Catholic be a member of the Hitler party? Can a Catholic rector permit members of this party to attend Church funerals and other church services in group formation? Can a Catholic who professes the principles of this party be admitted to the holy sacraments? We must answer these questions in the negative.[9]

This straightforward teaching was reiterated and strengthened in the various pastoral letters of the German hierarchy during the next two years. A particularly firm message was that of the Bavarian bishops on February 12, 1931. They condemned five doctrines taught by National Socialism:

1. Racialism puts race before religion.
2. It rejects Old Testament revelations, even the Ten Commandments.
3. It denies the primacy of the Pope because he represents an authority outside Germany.
4. It cherishes the plan of an undogmatic National German Church.

---

[9] Mason, *op cit.*, p. 94.

5. In Article 24 of its programme it sets up the moral feeling of the German race as the criterion of Christian morality which is essentially universal.[10]

To this statement by the Bavarian bishops, Cardinal Bertram of Breslau, Archbishop Schulte of Cologne, and the Bishops of the Upper Rhine added the weight of their authority.[11] At this early date, there was apparently unanimity among the bishops as to the incompatibility of Catholicism and National Socialism, and they were courageous in their denunciation of the errors inherent in the philosophy on which the latter was based.

But the Nazis were not yet in power. National Socialism was but a political party, and, as such, could be repudiated openly. The formation of the Hitler government on January 30, 1933 created a new situation. The perpetrators of the Rosenberg myth were no longer just a Party with an anti-Christian tone, but a legal government determined to effect a complete coordination—*Gleichschaltung*—of the German people.

In the elections on March 5, 1933 the Catholic voters failed to hold together; the figures indicate that many of them voted for Hitler. Only five and one-half million out of twelve and one-half million voted for the Center Party despite the pleas of their bishops.[12] This known hostility on the part of the hierarchy was soon punished by the new masters of the Reich.

Hitler and Goebbels—both nominal Catholics—refused to attend the High Mass offered in celebration of the opening of the Reichstag on March 21. They made the reason for their absence quite clear:

> The German Catholic Bishops have quite recently in a series of public declarations on which the clergy have not hesitated to act, stigmatized the leaders of the National Socialist Party as traitors who should be refused the sacraments. These instructions have not been withdrawn and are still being carried out. In these circumstances the Chancellor is reluctantly compelled to remain away from the Catholic service at Potsdam.[13]

---

[10] Robert D'Harcourt, *The German Catholics*, trans. Reginald J. Dingle (London: Burns, Oates, and Washbourne, 1939), pp. 11-12.

[11] Thorning, "The German Bishops and Hitlerism."

[12] D'Harcourt, *op. cit.*, p. 70.

[13] *Ibid.*, p. 72.

Yet, within the Reichstag Hitler's tone was conciliatory. On March 23, in his speech before that assembly, he pledged governmental support for religion:

> While the Government is determined to carry through the political and moral purging of our public life, it is creating and insuring prerequisites for a truly religious life. The Government sees in both Christian confessions the most important factors for the maintenance of our folkdom. It will respect agreements concluded between them and the States. However, it expects that its work will meet with a similar appreciation. The Government will treat all other denominations with equal objective justice. It can never condone, though, that belonging to a certain denomination or to a certain race might be regarded as a license to commit or tolerate crimes. The Government will devote its care to the sincere living together of Church and State.[14]

Presumably drawing friendly inferences from this speech, the Bishops on March 29 declared that they hoped the prohibitions of the past would not be necessary in the future.[15] Without retracting their condemnation of the errors implicit in Nazism, they took a more lenient attitude toward membership in the Party. Since they gave no reason for the change in their attitude, it can only be recorded; it cannot be explained. Should we see in this apparent about-face a desire to placate, if possible, the new government? Or, at least, to give it a chance to prove itself friendly to religion? On the other hand, might it not be simply an indication of their traditional respect for authority and their unwillingness to oppose the legal government of the State?

In any case, their hope of governmental protection of religious freedom was short-lived. Suppression of many organs of the Catholic press, the subtle purging of those who had been connected with the Weimar government, lively demonstrations against Catholic youth groups—all indicated in the spring of 1933 that the war between the Cross and the Swastika was just beginning.

[14] Nuremberg Document No. 3387-PS. Translation of the speech as quoted in *Völkischer Beobachter*, March 24, 1933.

[15] Mason, *op. cit.*, p. 96. In this same document the bishops admonish Catholics to be loyal citizens and to reject "on principle all illegal or subversive actions."

The hope of securing protection for the spiritual rights of Catholics led the Holy See to conclude a concordat with the Third Reich on July 20, 1933. The guarantees the Church received were summed up in Article I:

> The German Reich guarantees the freedom of the profession and the public exercise of the Catholic Religion. It recognizes the right of the Catholic Church, within the limits of the general laws in force, to regulate and to administer freely her own affairs and to proclaim in the field of her competence, laws and ordinances binding upon her members.[16]

On the whole, the terms were favorable to the Church and seemed to indicate a willingness on the part of the government to live in harmony with the Church.

But even while the Concordat was being born, violations of its spirit were observable. As a result of government-patronized Hitler Youth attacks on Catholic Action groups, the German bishops, assembled at Fulda, felt it expedient to caution the State against antagonizing the religious forces of the nation. They "welcomed" the goals of national honor and freedom proclaimed by the new regime, but insisted that they must be realized only through the application of sound moral principles. They requested protection of Catholic schools, youth organizations, and charitable enterprises and deplored interference with the freedom of press.

> . . .we trust that so much that has happened during the last months, which from the Catholic standpoint has appeared strange and incomprehensible, will prove to be only a process of fermentation, and that during the clarification of conditions it will sink to the bottom like dregs.[17]

While some of the members of the hierarchy, such as Cardinal Bertram, Archbishop Gröber, and Bishop Berning, attempted to discover a hint of improving relations with the State, others, such as Cardinal von Faulhaber and Bishop Count von Galen, were not deceived. In November 1933 the Bishops of Bavaria spoke publicly of the "events and decrees of recent months which have filled us

[16] NCWC Text of Concordat reprinted in Walter Consuelo Langsam (ed.) *Documents and Readings in the History of Europe Since 1918* (N. Y.: Lippincott Co., 1951), pp. 722-728.

[17] Mason, *op. cit.*, pp. 97-103.

with anxiety and sorrows." They indicated the points on which the State had already violated the Concordat, and pleaded for an "end to the oppressions of the Catholic conscience." [18]

The malicious Nazi anti-Semitism was answered by the Bishop of Munich in his intrepid sermons of Advent 1933. Speaking to his people of the beauties of the Old Testament and its intrinsic relationship with the New, Cardinal von Faulhaber exposed the Nazi errors with regard to Scriptures. He developed the ethical teaching of the Old Testament in such a way that the immorality of "German" neopaganism became evident, and the charges against Jewish morality were shown to be hollow.

In his sermon on "Christianity and Germany" all the contributions of Christianity to German life were reviewed and praised, and it was demonstrated that Germany would find its needed strength in a renewal of true Christian life rather than in the primitive German paganism which the Nazis were glorifying.

> What is the relation of Christianity to the German race? Race and Christianity are not mutually opposed but they do belong to different orders. Race is of the natural order; Christianity is a revealed religion and therefore of the supernatural order. Race means union with the nation; Christianity means primarily union with God.
> There is no need to turn our backs upon Christianity and to set up a Nordic or Germanic religion, in order to profess our nationality. But we must never forget: we are not redeemed with German blood. We are redeemed with the Precious Blood of our crucified Lord.[19]

Such words, thrown into the face of growing popular delight in the race theory, testify eloquently to the fortitude of this Prince of the Church. Error, no matter what its source, called for resistance.

The years of 1934 and 1935 gave irrefutable evidence that the Reich had no intention of abiding by the terms of the Concordat. Gestapo frequently interferred with Church services; children and their parents were intimidated and openly threatened if they con-

[18] D'Harcourt, *op. cit.*, pp. 138-139.

[19] Michael Cardinal von Faulhaber, *Judaism, Christianity, and Germany*, trans. Rev. George D. Smith (New York: The Macmillan Co., 1934), pp. 108-109.

tinued to attend confessional schools; Catholic papers which still existed were confiscated if they published pastoral letters critical of the government's attacks on the Church.

One such pastoral letter was issued in June 1934 by the German Episcopate assembled at Fulda. The Bishops protested strongly against the neopagan spirit, the advocacy of a National Church, the stifling of Catholic organizations, and the suppression of the press. The increasing identity of the National Socialist Party with the ideology of Rosenberg was noted, and the high positions awarded to those " who read and disseminate works destructive of the very foundations of religion and Christian morals " were protested. The bishops note the contrast between these awards and the insults " to a prince of the Church whose name stands for the finest religious and moral qualities." Apparently this referred to von Faulhaber.[20]

That Hitler was unimpressed by the position of the Bishops and their warning on neopaganism is clear from his appointment on January 24, 1935 of Rosenberg as Plenipotentiary for *Weltanschauung.* The formation of the " national mind " was now to be in the hands of the most virulent opponent of Christianity in the Third Reich, the author of the *Mythus des 20. Jahrhunderts* already put on the *Index of Forbidden Books* by the Church in February, 1934.

In a challenging sermon at the end of that month, Cardinal Schulte of Cologne attacked directly the underlying concepts of National Socialism.

> It is heathenism and apostasy from Christ and Christianity to see the essential element in religion only in the requirements of alleged Blood and Race. . . . It is heathenism and apostasy from Christ and Christianity that a man should declare to-day that " Blood and Honour " should alone determine the meaning of our earthly life, that for the sacred means of grace, which the divine Redeemer instituted for our salvation and vouchsafes to us through his Church, there could be substituted the maintenance of a particular kind of human blood in its purity.[21]

---

[20] D'Harcourt, *op. cit.*, pp. 157-158.

[21] Nathaniel Micklem, *National Socialism and the Roman Catholic Church*, 1933-38 (N. Y.: Oxford Univ. Press, 1939), p. 104.

March 1935 witnessed the initiation of the famous Currency Law trials, a new attempt on the part of the Nazi government to stifle the clerical opposition. To these were added other grievances, listed by the bishops in their joint pastoral of August 20, 1935: restriction on the Catholic press, curtailment of the right to hold meetings outside of the churches, imprisonment of members of the clergy, and continual defamation of character on the charge of "political Catholicism." [22]

It is interesting to note that in this letter the bishops put clearly before the people the doctrine of passive resistance ". . . when the commands of the State are at variance with natural law and the commands of God, they are not to be obeyed." [23] But the effort to prevent an irreconcilable break with the State had not been abandoned. While refusing obedience to unjust and sinful laws, Catholic citizens must still conform to governmental regulations in other areas.

> Any effort at national revival will find its best ally in the Church. . . . The children from the Catholic schools will be as good servants of the national community and show just as much respect for their compatriots of another religious faith as those from the State schools. . . . As is only right [Catholic youth] will submit, pending new arrangements, to the State regulations concerning the wearing of uniforms and collective demonstrations.[24]

In 1936 the war against the Church was intensified by the Nazis. Resorting to the age-old technique of discrediting the clergy in the eyes of the laity, the government brought charges of immorality against several priests and brothers. Scandalous publicity was given to these trials despite the fact that in only a few cases was there justification for such charges, and, in most of these, ecclesiastical punishment had already been imposed on the guilty members.[25] The bishops attacked the State for its interference in this matter, particularly because of the publication of lurid details in the press which would be a "danger to youth, a source of offence to all

[22] *Ibid.*, p. 133; cf. D'Harcourt, *op. cit.*, pp. 190-191.

[23] *Ibid.*

[24] D'Harcourt, *op. cit.*, pp. 196-197.

[25] Office of Strategic Services, *Handbook of National Socialist Germany*, p. 41. Cf. *Persecution in the Third Reich*, p. 306.

decent-minded people, and an unjust insult to the honour of all innocent members of the Orders concerned."[26]

The year of decision was 1937; from then on the battle between the Church and the German government could not be denied. On Palm Sunday, March 21, the encyclical, *Mit brennender Sorge,* was read from all the pulpits of Germany. This remarkable document had been written in German and smuggled into the country; travelling by an underground route, it had reached all pastors without falling into the hands of the Gestapo. Now, Catholics were officially informed of the true state of persecution which prevailed in Germany.

The fundamental ground on which Pius XI's protest rested was the repeated violations of the Concordat signed in 1933. He wrote:

> In the furrows, where We tried to sow the seed of a sincere peace, other men—the "enemy" of Holy Scripture—oversowed the cockle of distrust, unrest, hatred, defamation, of a determined hostility, overt or veiled, fed from many sources and wielding many tools, against Christ and His Church.[27]

His condemnation of the Nazi philosophy is unrestrained:

> Whoever exalts race, or the people, or the State, or a particular form of State, or the depositories of power, or any other fundamental value of the human community—however necessary and honorable be their function in worldly things—whoever raises these notions above their standard value and divinizes them to an idolatrous level, distorts and perverts an order of the world planned and created by God; . . .
> None but superficial minds could stumble into concepts of a national God, of a national religion; . . .
> Nothing but ignorance and pride could blind one to the treasures of the Old Testament. . . .[28]

The Holy Father boldly describes the anti-Catholic attitude of the Nazi government:

---

[26] Pastoral letter of Bishop Count von Galen, June 21, 1936. Quoted in A. S. Duncan-Jones, *The Struggle for Religious Freedom in Germany* (London: Victor Gollancz, 1938), p. 201.

[27] Pius XI, *Mit brennender Sorge,* March 14, 1937. English translation in *The Catholic Mind,* XXXV (May 8, 1937), 186.

[28] *Ibid.,* pp. 188, 189, 190.

> In your country, Venerable Brethren, voices are swelling into a chorus urging people to leave the Church, and among the leaders there is more than one whose official position is intended to create the impression that this infidelity to Christ the King constitutes a signal and meritorious act of loyalty in the modern State. Secret and open measures of intimidation, the threat of economic and civic disabilities, bear on the loyalty of certain classes of Catholic functionaries, a pressure which violates every human right and dignity.[29]

Resistance to this pressure is urged:

> Our wholehearted paternal sympathy goes out to those who must pay so dearly for their loyalty to Christ and the Church; but directly the highest interests are at stake, with the alternative of spiritual loss, there is but one alternative left, *that of heroism*. . . . As to those who imagine that they can reconcile exterior infidelity and interior fidelity to one and the same Church, let them hear Our Lord's warning:—" He that shall deny me before men shall be denied before the angels of God." (Luke xii: 9)[30]

The encyclical contains a thorough exposé of the errors inherent in the whole " German Christianity " as professed by the Nazis. The misuse of common words such as " revelation," " grace," and " morality " is pointed out, and the correct notions are restated. Most important, perhaps, from the point of view of resistance to tyranny is the explanation of man's natural rights, and the dependence of all law on natural law.

> Human laws in flagrant contradiction with the natural law are vitiated with a taint which no force, no power can mend. In the light of this principle one must judge the axiom, that " right is common utility." . . . The believer has an absolute right to profess his Faith and live according to its dictates. Laws which impede this profession and practice of Faith are against natural law. . . . Parents . . . have a primary right to the education of the children God has given them. . . . Laws and measures which in school questions fail to respect this freedom of the parents go against natural law, and are immoral.[31]

---

[29] *Ibid.*, p. 194.

[30] *Ibid.* Italics are mine.

[31] *Ibid.*, p. 198-199.

Rome had spoken, and the German Catholics could no longer be in doubt of their duty to shun Nazism and to resist unjust legislation. But Rome had scarcely urged open rebellion! Yet, the official position which the Reich chose to adopt was that the Vatican had issued a call to arms which endangered the peace of Germany.

On March 23, 1937 a special delivery letter went to all German bishops from the Reich and Prussian Minister for Ecclesiastical Affairs. Forbidding the printing, reproduction, or dissemination in any form of the encyclical, the letter gave as the reason for suppressing the document that:

> It attempts to diminish the authority of the Reich Government, to harm the interests of the German nation abroad, and, above all, to endanger the internal peace of the community by means of a direct appeal to the Catholic citizens by a party to the treaty with the Reich Government.[32]

The German Ambassador to the Holy See was forbidden to participate in the Easter ceremonies in Rome,[33] and the German diplomatic missions in Europe were notified by the Foreign Ministry of the Reich's indignation. They were informed that the Nuncio in Berlin had been told that the German government "had to consider the Pope's encyclical as a call to battle." According to the Foreign Office, the encyclical ". . . calls upon Catholic citizens to rebel against the authority of the State. . . ."[34]

The Catholic bishops, in the person of the Chairman of the Fulda Conference [Cardinal Bertram], replied to the letter they had received from the Reich and Prussian Minister of Ecclesiastical Affairs. They defended the text of the encyclical, adding their own testimony to that of Pius XI concerning the persecution of the Church. They protested emphatically:

> . . . the efforts, which are becoming more and more pronounced and extensive, to oust the Church from all spheres of public life, of the life of the people, and of youth education, and to

---

[32] *Documents on German Foreign Policy 1918-1945*, Series D, I, 935.

[33] *Ibid.*, p. 937, German Foreign Ministry to the German Embassy to the Holy See, Telegram No. 12, March 25, 1937.

[34] *Ibid.*, pp. 937-938, German Foreign Ministry to Various German Diplomatic Missions, Telegram, March 26, 1937.

render ineffectual even in religious publications the voice of the Church in the life of the people.[35]

Furthermore, the steps taken by the German government to seize copies of the encyclical, close the printing establishments which had printed it, and prohibit publication of the bishops' official statements after the promulgation of the encyclical were strongly protested by the Nuncio.[36]

Charges and countercharges followed one another during the next three months. That the encyclical was not an isolated statement of resistance to the increasing encroachment of the Nazi government on the personal lives of its citizens is clear from the letter of the Papal Secretary of State to the German Ambassador to the Holy See on April 30, 1937. Denying the validity of the criticism which the Third Reich had submitted to the Vatican, Cardinal Pacelli restated the case of the Church.

At the conclusion of his letter he recounted the number of times that the Holy See had protested privately to the Reich before resorting to a papal encyclical. The Secretary of State wrote:

> After 4 long years of vain pressing for a correct observance of the Concordat; after repeated confidential indications that the Holy See would be compelled to take a public stand if the Government continued its tactics; after numerous attempts to substitute a solution defensible for both sides with regard to the Catholic associations in place of the weakening of the Concordat sought by the State in June 1934; after repeated efforts through personal contact by representatives of the Episcopate with high-ranking persons in the Government, to ease the tension that had set in; after many unsuccessful appeals to the conciliation authority provided for in article 33 in the face of precipitate and repeated unilateral Government measures in the field of education and in various other important questions, His Holiness the Pope spoke the Supreme Pastoral Word, in accordance with his official duty and his contractual right.

What was the Vatican seeking?

> The first and essential condition for the attainment of this

[35] *Ibid.*, pp. 938-941.

[36] Memorandum of Acting State Secretary Dieckhoff, April 5, 1937, *Ibid.*, pp. 943-945. The Nuncio at this time was Msgr. Cesare Orsenigo.

> goal [i. e. ". . . the welfare of the Germans as a nation and as members of the Church "] . . . is the release of the leadership of the State, and of the movement sustaining the State, from the ever tightening embrace and the increasing penetration of ideological and anti-Christian currents which draw their strength from the struggle against the Church and which seeks to make of this struggle a law of life and a condition of life for the German State bearing their mark and animated by their spirit.[37]

The indignation of the German Government was further inflamed by the speech of Cardinal Mundelein of Chicago on May 18, 1937, in which he denounced Hitler and exposed his persecution of the Church.[38] The incident itself need not detain us here, except to note that the Vatican refused to censure the Cardinal or to apologize to the Nazis for the insults delivered by His Eminence. Instead, the Reich's protest was answered by a question:

> What has the German Government done, and what does it intend to do in the future against the malicious slander and defamation, against the disgraceful calumnies directed at churches, ecclesiastical institutions, the Pope, the cardinals, bishops, priests etc., which appear day after day in German newspapers and periodicals and in the speeches of prominent personages?

The Cardinal Secretary of State went on:

> I shall facilitate Your Excellency's task by answering the first part of the question myself: The German Government—regardless of all representations—has done nothing against all that. On the contrary, it is itself responsible, since State and Party authorities, and particularly the Propaganda Ministry, organize and direct a large part of this printed and spoken campaign and, as for the rest, they at least favor and in all possible ways at least further it.[39]

---

[37] *Ibid.*, pp. 965-966. That the encyclical had been written only after numerous protests by the Vatican had gone unanswered was reported by the German Ambassador to the Holy See. Cf. his telegram to the Foreign Ministry # 21 of March 24, 1937. *Ibid.*, p. 936.

[38] *Ibid.*, pp. 968-976. The German Foreign Ministry also sought unsuccessfully to obtain redress from the U. S. Dept. of State.

[39] German Ambassador to the Holy See to the Foreign Ministry, May 25, 1937. *Ibid.*, p. 971.

An amplification of the Holy See's position and an itemized account of previous protests, both from the Holy See and the German Episcopate, was given in a letter from Cardinal Pacelli to the German Ambassador to the Holy See on June 24, 1937.[40] Rome was making it clear that the policies of the German State, in so far as they touched on religious problems, were not acceptable.

Meanwhile, within Germany, untiring opposition and open condemnation of the Nazi program came from the pulpits of Cardinal von Faulhaber, Bishop von Preysing, and Bishop Count von Galen—to mention only the best-known. In June 1937, while the Vatican was engaged in its verbal war with the German Foreign Ministry, one of the outstanding anti-Nazi preachers of Cardinal von Faulhaber's diocese was arrested, namely, Father Ruper Mayer, S. J.

On July 4, 1937, although it was forbidden to mention the arrests of priests, the Cardinal spoke to the men of the Munich Sodality, of which Father Mayer had been Chaplain. Asking them not to resort to violence, the Cardinal urged them nevertheless to prove their devotion to Father Mayer by resisting with all their strength the attempts being made to force them to renounce their faith. Their Chaplain had acted, he said, in accordance with the divine command: "We ought to obey God rather than men," for he had refused to abide by the Nazi injunction against his preaching.

The Cardinal announced that he had protested to the State about Father Mayer's arrest several times, but had not even received the favor of a reply. A new Kulturkampf was at hand:

> The decisive hour is at hand; the Son of man has taken the fan into His Hand to separate the wheat from the chaff. Beacons are being fired and one is the arrest of the apostle of the men of Munich.[41]

Protesting the injustices heaped upon the Church by the Nazi government, the Cardinal was not, however, ready to deny the authority of the State.

---

[40] *Ibid.*, pp. 976-981.

[41] Sermon of Cardinal von Faulhaber, July 4, 1937. *The Persecution of the Catholic Church in the Third Reich* (London: Burns Oates, 1940), Appendix III, p. 541.

> We, who are bound in conscience to respect the authority of the State must support that authority whilst the Church's is disregarded and trodden in the dust.[42]

But when the State goes beyond the scope of its authority, as in the case of Father Mayer, then he feels that the time for disobedience has come.

> I formally state that as long as he was forbidden to address meetings outside the church he obeyed the law, but when he was forbidden to preach in a church he obeyed the dictates of his conscience, for there is a time for speech as well as a time for silence and the law of God must come before that of men.[43]

From 1937 on there was little variation in the attitude of the Church. Joint pastoral letters were issued annually and circulated as widely as possible; each one renewed the plea to the government to observe the Concordat and the elementary norms of Christian morality.[44] It is true that there was a difference in degree of opposition to the Nazis among the German bishops even though they all subscribed to these pastoral letters. For a long time, some of them apparently hoped that peaceful " coexistence " with the Nazis was a possibility.

In November 1941, for example, von Hassell noted with dismay that the German hierarchy was not fully united in resistance to the government. He wrote that, according to Father Noppel, former rector of the Collegium Germanicum in Rome:

> The majority, under the leadership of the old pacifist cardinal,

---

[42] *Ibid.*

[43] *Ibid.*, p. 542. Father Mayer was released from prison at the end of 1937, arrested again in January 1938, released in May, and re-arrested shortly after. He was finally released August 7, 1940 on condition that he would live in seclusion. He then stayed at the Benedictine Abbey of Eital under Gestapo surveillance until the end of the war. He returned to Munich in 1945 and died there November 1 of that year. Since his death he has been venerated as a saint by the people of Germany and his cause has been introduced in Rome.

Cf. Testimony of Rupert Mayer, S.J.; Nuremberg Document 3272-PS. Augustine Klaas, S. J., " The Apostle of Munich," *The Catholic Mind*, 51 (Oct. 1933), 599-602.

[44] Despite governmental restrictions and prohibitions, the annual Fulda Pastoral appeared every year except 1939.

> Bishop Bertram of Breslau, was opposed to an open struggle and against "political" rather than religious methods. The proponents of drastic action, Galen and Preysing, were therefore in the minority. People such as Bertram will get nowhere at all with people such as Hitler and Himmler. Bishop Groeber of Freiburg, once dubbed "Brown Konrad," is now completely disillusioned by the regime. . . .[45]

Nevertheless, in their formal letters and protests, the Bishops always attacked racism, reintroduction of German paganism, euthanasia and sterilization laws, attacks on Catholic schools and youth organizations, and general suppression of the people's natural rights. Protests were regularly lodged with the Ministry of Ecclesiastical Affairs by the bishops, and at the Foreign Ministry by the Papal Nuncio.[46]

Many of the remonstrances were concerned with the official policy of murdering the insane. The justification for the bishops' protests regarding such a matter was put rather ingeniously by Cardinal von Faulhaber:

> The formula of the oath of allegiance, unanimously agreed upon, and found in article 16 of the Reichs-Concordat binds the bishops that in the course of their official care for the welfare and in the interest of the German nation they prevent every harm which might threaten it! Thus, the Archbishop of Munich, not only because of the laws of God, the unshakable foundations of every public order, nor because of the popular voice of distress, but because he feels himself in conscience bound by the Reichs-Concordat, makes complaint and lodges charges. . . .[47]

The Cardinal, denouncing "euthanasia" as a violation of the fifth commandment, pointed out that the government's disobedience of the commands of God would result in a lowering of the

[45] Von Hassell, *op. cit.*, p. 223.

[46] Many of these documents were submitted to the International Military Tribunal at Nuremberg and are available at the Dept. of the Army. Among those consulted were: 2129-PS; 1506-PS; 1497-PS; 617-PS; 1511-PS; 2136-PS; 615-PS; 616-PS; 2131-PS; 3266-PS; 2139-PS; von Weizsäcker Defense Document NG-4604 in Document Book 54.

[47] Letter from Cardinal von Faulhaber to Dr. Gürtner, Reich Minister of Justice, Nov. 2, 1940. *Thought* XX (1945), 754-759.

moral standards of the whole people. War time, the prelate said, is no valid excuse for such inhuman action:

> . . . even during war time one may not discard the everlasting foundations of the moral order, nor the fundamental rights of the individual.[48]

The war itself was not apparently a subject for discussion or protest by the bishops. Catholic sentiment may have favored the *Anschluss* because of Austria's large Catholic population. While Thanksgiving services were held in many churches after the settlement at Munich, no official statement was made on the justice or injustice of the Nazi position. The pastoral letters issued during the war years deplore many governmental actions, but never the war itself.

Bishop Count von Galen of Münster was certainly one of the most outspoken foes of the Nazis. He made no secret of his attitude toward Hitler, and disagreed openly with those who considered him Germany's "Saviour." Writing a letter of protest to Reich Minister Dr. Lammers on July 22, 1941, the Bishop expressed his disapproval of the union of both offices, Fuehrer and Chancellor—plus the added title of Commander of the Armed forces—in the person of Hitler. He went on:

> On this assumption, I was not able to decide in the past to give my vote, at the election held for the purpose, for the two offices of President of the Reich and Chancellor of the Reich. *I knew that Adolf Hitler is not a divine being, who, exalted above any carnal limitations, would be capable of keeping everything in mind at once and directing everything.*

The result of this false deification of Hitler is a state of disorder in which the secret police are in virtual control of the country, he said, and when . . .

> . . . in this way, without interference from the officials obligated to protect the legal order, safety under the law is destroyed, consciousness of right is buried, and confidence in the national government is destroyed, then I feel myself called and in duty bound, as a German man . . . to raise my

[48] *Ibid.*, p. 759.

voice aloud, regardless of the consequences that may ensue for me personally. . . .[49]

On December 10, 1941 the German bishops sent a memorandum to the government asking once more that an end be put to the war of the State against the Church. Particularly noted were the violations of the Concordat in regard to education. In this document, more than in previous ones, the bishops placed great stress on the natural rights of men which were being violated: rights of freedom of religion, of personal liberty, of life, property and reputation.

The bishops pleaded for a return of justice, protesting their love for the fatherland, while at the same time stating firmly:

> We must decisively and firmly reject the suggestion that we should show our loyalty towards the fatherland by disloyalty towards Christ and our Church. . . .[50]

Like most of its predecessors, this document also went unanswered.

The sharpness of the conflict between the cross and the swastika was highlighted in the New Year's Eve sermon of Cardinal von Faulhaber on December 31, 1941. Noting that it had now reached the point where the government was demanding that Germans "Leave the Church or lose your job!", His Eminence begged for a strong "No" in reply.

> When the question comes: "Are you willing, through exemplary fulfillment of your duties and through a spirit of sacrifice, to show your loyalty to the Fatherland?" our answer will be: "Yes and thrice yes." But when that other question comes: "Are you willing to leave the Church?" our answer will be just as decisive: "No, and thrice no." [51]

A few scattered reports give us an idea of the bishops' attitude during the subsequent years. In June 1942 Archbishop Frings of Cologne made the remark that the damage done to Cologne by

[49] A copy of the German text and an English translation were forwarded to the Dept. of State. MS, FW 740.0011 E w/9-2641. Italics are mine.

[50] Statement of the German bishops May 4, 1942 making public their memorandum to the Government of Dec. 10, 1941. Dept. of State. MS, 862.404/362.

[51] NCWC News Service, Mimeographed copy, April 13, 1942. NCWC files, Washington, D. C.

the attack of 1000 Allied bombers was comparable only to the damage done by the Nazis to religious and ecclesiastical life.[52] In December of that year, a memorandum of the bishops denounced Nazi policy in Germany and the occupied territories as "ruthless." [53] Finally, in February 1943 there was a report that Archbishop Groeber had denounced Hitler's war as "unjust." [54]

A more detailed study of these later years of the Hitler regime has yet to be made, but available evidence indicates continued protests against government interference in church administration, sudden and unjustified arrests of priests, and serious invasion of personal rights. Although contact was established with members of the active Resistance Movement, there is no indication that the weight of the Catholic hierarchy was put on the side of incitement to rebellion. The resistance offered was rather that of civil disobedience to unjust laws, the use of legal weapons of protest, and ceaseless efforts to strengthen the faith of the people against the onslaught of Nazi neopaganism. In many cases, their protests apparently caused the government to alter its strategy,—as in 1936 when crucifixes were restored in Oldenberg after the protest of Bishop von Galen [55]—but unfortunately they never brought about a true conversion of heart.

What of the Protestant Resistance? The antagonism between the Nazi way of life and Roman Catholicism had been more evident from the beginning of the National Socialist Party than had the incompatibility of the new doctrine with that of German Evangelicalism. But it was not long before German Protestantism found itself face to face with an enemy that could not be ignored.

There were, in 1933, some twenty-eight *Landeskirchen*, united in a loose confederation but possessing a good share of autonomy; the estimated number of members was over 40,000,000—roughly two-thirds of the German nation.[56] The Nazis were not slow to discover the advantages that greater unity among these churches would

[52] IDS report 133, February 11, 1943. OSS files # 16110. National Archives.

[53] IDS report 250, May 12, 1943. OSS files # 41640.

[54] IDS report 135, Feb. 12, 1943. OSS files # 16168.

[55] OSS, *Handbook on National Socialist Germany*, Appendix on Religion, p. 41.

[56] *Ibid.*, p. 25.

have in "solving" the church question. There would be a single *Reichsbischof* with whom the State would deal; theoretically he would be elected by the various representatives of the individual churches but as time would show, Hitler would direct the "election" carefully.

The so-called "German Christians" [a sect which sought to unite Christianity with Aryan doctrines on race] favored the union of the churches under a single *Reichsbishof* and in April 1933 put forth a plan for the formation of a single German Church based on Nazi doctrine. As protector of the "German Christians" and as his confidential advisor on religious matters Hitler appointed Ludwig Mueller. On September 21, 1933 Mueller was elected *Reichsbischof* by the German National Synod voting under great pressure from the Fuehrer. The struggle which ensued within the Protestant Church between the German-Christian faction and the group which evolved into the Confessional Church (*Bekennende Kirche*) would be a long and interesting story in itself. However, the very formation of the Confessional Church, in direct opposition to the expressed views of Hitler, certainly constituted a form of resistance.

That Protestant ministers preached the possible necessity of resistance to National Socialism as early as 1933 is shown by the sermon of Dr. Otto Dibelius to the members of the Reichstag in the presence of President Hindenburg.

> We do not resist authority since to do so is anarchy and thus irreligious. . . . But as soon as the state demands to be the church, and strives to assume power to rule the souls of men . . . then we are asked by Luther's words to exercise resistance in the name of God.[57]

The doctrine of Aryanism was repudiated at an early date; it was this which led to the suspension of Pastor Niemoeller and others in November 1933. In 1934 Niemoeller was arrested, but by that time the Confessional Church which had grown out of his *Pfarrernotbund* had gotten underway. Early in 1934 there were about 4,000 Ministers (about one-fourth of the German pastorate) who

[57] *Time,* April 6, 1953, p. 67.

had cast their lot in with the group opposed to the state-dominated *Reichsbischof*.[58]

Their first synod was held in January 1934 in Barmen, Westphalia, an area where Protestantism was predominantly "Reformed" or Calvinistic. The main address was given by Karl Barth, the Swiss theologian who was soon to be exiled from Germany for his anti-Nazi views.[59] The Synod issued a statement affirming the teaching that no human power could claim complete obedience from the individual, that the government should not be permitted to interfere with the administration of the church, and that a totalitarian state could not be reconciled with the message of the Gospel.[60]

In the middle of July 1935 Hitler appointed a strong Nazi, Hans Kerrl, to the new post of Reich Minister for Church Affairs. The Confessional Church thereupon refused to deal with the administration set up by Kerrl. Similarly, when a decree was issued making the Reich Church the sole source of legislation for the churches of Bavaria and Wurttemberg, the pastors refused to comply with it and stood by their bishops.[61]

A protest against heathenism in education had already caused the arrest of the 700 pastors who had read it publicly, while 5,000 others received warnings from the government not to read it. Nevertheless, they defied the government and did so.[62] In 1936 the pastors of the Confessional Church read from their pulpits an outright refusal to recognize the spiritual or ecclesiastical authority of Kerrl.[63] In February 1936 there was another synod, this time

[58] McClasky, *op. cit.*, p. 9.

[59] Karl Barth had been a professor of theology at the University of Bonn. His criticism of the "subjectivity" of German Protestantism prepared the ground for the fight to preserve the church's independence of the state. He was expelled from Germany in the fall of 1935. Evaluating his influence on the Confessional Movement, Duncan-Jones writes: ". . . when the crisis came it was Barth more than anyone else who clarified the issue by insisting that it was impossible to resist a philosophy which was sectional, racial, materialist, except by a direct negative, which appealed, not to man's judgment, but to God's." *Op. cit.*, p. 41.

[60] OSS, *Handbook*, "Appendix on Religion," p. 30.

[61] *Ibid.*, pp. 31, 32.

[62] *Ibid.*, p. 32.

[63] *Ibid.*, p. 33.

at Bad Oeynhausen. Then, at Whitsuntide, a secret memorandum was addressed to Hitler, asking pointedly whether or not the government was supporting the attempt to de-Christianize the German people.

This "Memorial to Chancellor Hitler of Ten Leaders of the Confessional Movement of the German Evangelical Church" protested the teachings of Dr. Ley, Dr. Goebbels, and Herr Rosenberg. The Protestant leaders denied the authority of the *Reichsbischof* and condemned the interference of the state in church matters. As to the race theory, they stated:

> When blood, race, nationality and honor are thus raised to the rank of qualities that guarantee eternity the Evangelical Christian is bound, by the first commandment, to reject the assumption. When the "Aryan" human being is glorified, God's Word bears witness to the sinfulness of all men. When, within the compass of the National Socialist view of life, an anti-Semitism is forced on the Christian that binds him to hatred of the Jew, the Christian injunction to love one's neighbor still stands for him opposed to it.[64]

The courageous signers of this protest were Asmussen, Lucking, Middendorff, Niemoeller, and von Thadden as members of the Council of the German Evangelical Church.

As in the case of so many Catholic protests, Hitler made no effort to answer the Memorandum. However, in July 1936 the secret protest was made public and appeared in the foreign press; subsequently it was read in thousands of Evangelical churches. The publication of this document abroad apparently came as a surprise to the Confessionals, but once done, they felt it would be wise to read it at home to their parishes. Defending this action, they stated in part:

> Things have come to such a pass that the honor of German citizens is dragged through the mud because they are Christians. The Christian population of Germany note with strong emotion and indignation that they are jeered at and mocked in every way (press, theatre, public meetings) because of their faith in Jesus Christ.[65]

---

[64] James F. Pollock, *op. cit.*, p. 151.

[65] OSS, *Handbook*, p. 34.

During 1937 restrictions were placed by the government on university attendance which effectively excluded the students of the Confessional Ministry. The latter avoided open conflict by going to the University of Basle where Karl Barth's instruction had a profound influence on them. There were increasingly frequent arrests of Confessional pastors; from February to October of that year over 500 went to jail or concentration camp.[66]

On October 31, Bishop Marahrens, representing the leaders of the remaining *Landeskirchen,* Pastor Muller of Dahlem representing the Council of Brethren of the Confessional Church, and Dr. Breit of Munich, representing the Council of the Lutheran Churches of Germany, issued a formal protest against the teaching of Rosenberg. His demand that the German nation give up its Christian faith was condemned, and it was asked if the Nazi Party intended to protect the right of the churches to serve as places of worship ". . . without exposing preachers and hearers to the danger of being suspected as traitors and enemies of the state." [67]

The incompatibility of Nazism and Christianity became increasingly clear as time went on. When the Chairman of the Reich Church Committee, Dr. Zoellner, was forced to resign in February 1937 Minister Kerrl explained it thus:

> Bishop von Galen and Dr. Zoellner wanted to bring home to me what Christianity really was, namely that it was a question of the acknowledgement of Jesus as the Son of God. That is ridiculous, quite unessential. . . . There has now arisen a new authority concerning what Christ and Christianity really is. This new authority is Adolf Hitler.[68]

This speech provoked an open letter to Minister Kerrl from Dr. Otto Dibelius. Baldly he contradicted the statement made by the Reich Minister:

> . . . the words that Jesus Christ is the Son of God is not a doctrinal clause invented by man, but the fundamental principle of Holy Scripture. Our Faith depends on this teaching.[69]

---

[66] *Ibid.*

[67] OSS, Nazi Master Plan: Annex 4 "The Persecution of the Christian Churches," R&A # 3114.4, p. 67.

[68] Duncan-Jones, *op. cit.*, Appendix D, p. 300.

[69] *Ibid.*, Appendix E, p. 304.

Dibelius expressed opposition to Rosenberg's *Mythus,* and denounced Kerrl's rejection of Sacred Scriptures. Moreover, he accused him of violating his oath of ordination (to preach nothing except what is found in God's clear word in Scriptures) by preaching that the will of God is "in our blood."

That the State was interfering not only in the Church's external life but also with her teaching was a proposition upheld by Dr. Dibelius. The root of the Church-State conflict, in his opinion, was that the State was interfering in censoring the subject matter of sermons and creed.

> The struggle will never come to an end until the State has realized its limits. Luther has said that we, loyal to God's Word, must serve the State, as long as it is a State, with body and life. Adolf Hitler's State too, can rely on the readiness of the Evangelical Christians of Germany. It would be unworthy if we were to assure him of that again in all solemnity. But the moment the State wishes to be the Church, and have power over the souls of men and over the preaching of the Church, we are, in accordance with Luther's words, bound to offer resistance in God's name; we shall most certainly do so.[70]

In 1938, at the time of the Munich crisis, the Confessional Church issued an order for a Service of Prayer for Peace. This was considered a treasonable act, and the Reich Minister for Ecclesiastical Affairs ordered that the salaries of such Confessional leaders be stopped and that they be removed from their parishes.[71]

Meanwhile, the outstanding figure in German Protestant circles, Pastor Niemoeller, had been imprisoned. His last sermon was preached to his people at Dahlem on June 27, 1937. Developing the analogy with the persecution of the early Christians recorded in the *Acts* (V: 34-42), Dr. Niemoeller's sentiment was one of patient acceptance of suffering in the confidence of a favorable solution and judgment by Almighty God.[72]

If this farewell sermon can be taken as the key to his conception of "opposition" to the state, it seems safe to conclude that he would never have been a member of an active resistance group. The

[70] *Ibid.*, pp. 307-308.

[71] OSS, "Nazi Master Plan," p. 56.

[72] Duncan-Jones, *op. cit.*, Appendix I, pp. 271-276.

present writer finds it hard to agree with Gisevius in his estimate of the role Niemoeller would have played if he had not been imprisoned. He wrote:

> To my mind Niemoeller's incarceration removed the last personality around whom any sort of civilian revolt movement might have gathered. . . . At last, by arresting Niemoeller after they had succeeded in isolating him, the Nazis quelled the last chance for a real popular opposition movement.[73]

Nevertheless, Niemoeller's courage in defense of the rights of the church was a source of inspiration to many of his compatriots, and his name became a rallying cry for those who refused to submit to the Nazi policies. His forced departure from the ranks of the Confessional Church made cohesion within the movement difficult, but his message was carried forth by such churchmen as Dr. Dibelius and Bishop Wurm of Wurttemberg.

The latter wrote a sharp letter of protest to Hitler in December 1940 about the killing of the insane and an equally strong letter of general opposition on July 16, 1943. Among other things, he denounced particularly the persecution of the Jews, the "constant sidetracking of the influence of parents and Christian institutions" on youth, and the iniquity of the concentration camps. All of these he considered violations of ". . . the God-given right to live as human beings and with due regard to human values."[74]

Von Hassell considered this "highly courageous action" of the eldest Evangelical bishop very important because it placed the church on record as definitely opposed to the policies of the regime.[75]

From another point of view, this letter is of special interest. In it Dr. Wurm makes a strong plea in defense of what scholastics would term "natural rights." Some who have written on the resistance of the churches to Hitler have pointed out that the objection of the Protestants was based solely on the state's interference with the internal organization and administration of the churches,

[73] Gisevius, *op. cit.*, p. 216. Rothfels points out quite correctly that such a statement contradicts the "whole tenor" of Gisevius's account. Rothfels, *op. cit.*, p. 44, n. 45.

[74] McClasky, *op. cit.*, p. 11.

[75] Von Hassell, *op. cit.*, p. 310.

while Catholics fought against the paganism of Rosenberg and the Nazi infringement on natural rights. It is implied that this resulted from their varying attitudes toward natural law.

Such a distinction appears to the writer as somewhat arbitrary and unsound. While it is true that the original complaints of the Confessionals were directed against the forced election of Mueller as *Reichsbischof,* it was not long before their opposition to the fundamental principles of National Socialism became evident. On the other hand, the early condemnation of 1930 which forbade Catholics to accept membership in the NSDAP gave way in the period 1933-1937 to a restrained defense of the jurisdiction of the Church as defined in the Concordat, with only secondary emphasis on the repudiation of Nazi neopaganism.

Therefore, the true picture would seem to be that both confessions objected to State interference in the ecclesiastical province and also—and in the long run, more seriously—to the State's attempt to de-Christianize Germany.

It was indeed the realization that the Nazi attacks on the churches had this basic aim which, during the Hitler era, drew the members of the two confessions closer together than ever before. Although such movements as the *Una Sancta* had already done much to remove bigotry or strong partisanship, Bishop von Preysing was able to declare in 1937: ". . . never before . . . have we been so deeply linked in love and sympathy with our brothers who differ from us in creed." [76]

This greater unity, in so far as it was effected by mutual efforts at resistance to Hitler, was a product not so much of deliberate cooperation at the top levels of Church leadership as of increasing understanding and mutual sharing of ideals and dangers at the lower levels. In the various cells of active resistance, which we have described at length, there was a happy intermingling of Catholics and Protestants. So easily were confessional lines erased in the joint effort against the Nazis that it is now extremely difficult to discover the religious affiliation of individual conspirators.

Yet, it seems valid to maintain that while the men of the Resistance had strong religious sentiments and, in some cases, definite

[76] Duncan-Jones, *op. cit.*, p. 254.

and close connections with Church leaders, the particular confession to which a man belonged made little or no difference in his decision to fight against Hitler. A tentative list of the men referred to frequently in connection with the Resistance Movement indicates that each group had representatives of both confessions.

Catholic	*Protestant*
Father Alfred Delp, S. J.	Col. General Ludwig Beck
Karl Ludwig von Guttenberg	Claus Bonhoeffer
Theodore Haecker	Pastor Dietrich Bonhoeffer
Paulus van Husen	Pastor Eugen Gerstenmaier
Jacob Kaiser	Hans Gisevius
Erich Kordt	Carl Goerdeler
Theo Kordt	Ulrich von Hassell
Father König, S. J.	Albrecht von Kessel
Paul Lejune-Jung	Helmuth von Moltke
Bernard Letterhaus	Gen. Friedrich Olbricht
Msgr. Bernard Lichtenberg	Major General Hans Oster
Hans Lukaschek	Pastor Harald Poelchau
Joseph Mueller	Fabian von Schlabrendorff
Karl Muth	Theodore Steltzer
Father Roesch, S. J.	Gen. Georg Thomas
Col. Count von Stauffenberg	Major Gen. Henning von Tresckow
	Ernst von Weizsäcker
	Field Marshal Erwin von Witzleben
	Perter Yorck von Wartenburg

While not pretending to be a complete roll-call, this gives us an idea of the cooperation among persons of different faiths in the common cause. Actually, the problems connected with religion and especially the future outlook for Church-State relations concerned them very much.

The Kreisau circle was particularly important in this regard. Both von Moltke and Yorck von Wartenburg were very hopeful that a new unity of the churches would emerge from the Nazi chaos. According to a Catholic member of their group, they were:

. . . devout evangelical Christians, and by their education,

[77] In addition to available printed materials, the writer is indebted for information regarding the religious affiliation of several of the above persons to Major General H. J. von Witzleben. Personal letter to the writer, July 13, 1954.

> their intellectual and cultural standard and their intellectual position they were particularly well placed to take up the leadership, since they could rely on a willing response in both Christian camps.[78]

Von Hassell also hoped for the unity of the churches, but did not see it as a possibility in the near future. In November 1942 he recorded that he had been to an excellent inter-faith discussion on the significance of the "image" in religion. Of the speakers, he said:

> The most effective, because the most primitively religious, was an orthodox priest. The whole affair was refreshing; it was proof that an effective Christianity is still alive. The one holy church, however, is still far away.[79]

Again, in March 1943 he wrote of a "theological afternoon" attended by Guardini, August Winnig, Gertrud Baumer and clergymen of the three faiths: "Theme: 'Evangelism,' that is, how can the gospel be brought to people today?"[80]

Personal conversations were held by members of the Resistance groups with Bishop von Preysing, Cardinal von Faulhaber, Bishop Wurm, Bishop Bertram, and the bishops of Fulda and Salzburg. Two Protestant clergymen, Harald Poelchau and Eugen Gerstenmaier, and three Jesuits, Fathers Delp, König, and Roesch, are listed among the members of the Kreisau circle. They took an active part in the discussions held on Church-State relations, development of liturgical worship among Protestants, the social action program of the papal encyclicals, and the role of the family and the school in a Christian society.[81]

Out of these discussions emerged concrete post-war plans which, as we have seen, were subscribed to by the Beck-Goerdeler group

[78] Paulus van Husen, "The 20th of July and the German Catholics," p. 4.

[79] Von Hassell, *op. cit.*, p. 272.

[80] *Ibid.*, p. 295.

[81] These conversations and discussions were described in detail in the RSHA reports: August 7, 1944, 105/22; August 16, 1944, 105/23; Sept. 15, 1944, 105/25; Oct. 4, 1944, 105/26; Jan. 9, 1945, 105/31.

A valuable account by a member of the Kreisau group is Theodor Steltzer, *op. cit.* The plans formulated by the group are given in an Appendix, pp. 154-169.

and incorporated in the program of the government as it was to have been promulgated after the coup of July 20, 1944.[82] Individual natural rights were stressed, the need for sound family structure was upheld, and the desire for inter-confessional harmony and Church-State cooperation expressed. The Concordat would have been reaffirmed, and state schools would have been obliged to provide religious instruction for the adherents of both confessions. These plans show the steady effort made by their authors to integrate Christian principles in the total framework of national life.

The members of the German Opposition watched the hierarchy closely for an indication of leadership in the fight against Hitler, or, at least, for an implication of sympathy and support in the direction of active resistance. Every protest which the bishops made, every forceful anti-Nazi sermon, every ecclesiastical circumvention of state policy encouraged the men in the oppositional circles.

In December 1940, for example, von Hassell noted with joy that "Bishop Wurm of Wurttemberg had had the admirable courage to take a firm stand . . ." against the "unrestrained mass slaughter of the so-called incurably insane."[83] In July 1941 he wrote of a meeting with Bishop Haekel who, although he had collaborated earlier with the Nazis, had now realized the incompatibility of the two institutions—National Socialism and the Church.[84] He is cheered by the continual protests of Bishop Count von Galen[85] and by those submitted by the Evangelical Pastors Association.[86]

A member of the Kreisau circle, Rudolph Pechel, indicated the inspiration received from both Pastor Niemoeller and Bishop Count von Galen. Speaking of the latter, he wrote:

> Through his sermons and pastoral letters which were secretly distributed from hand to hand throughout the whole of Germany he gave comfort and strength to millions of Germans. This brave and resolute man belonged to the entire German people, in so far as they confessed Christ, just as Pastor Niemoeller on the Evangelical side was respected as a model also by the Catholics.[87]

---

[82] *Supra*, pp. 71-72.

[83] Von Hassell, *op. cit.*, p. 161.

[84] *Ibid.*, p. 201.

[85] *Ibid.*, pp. 210, 223.

[86] *Ibid.*, p. 223.

[87] Pechel, *op. cit.*, p. 58. Translation mine.

A report from the local Gestapo in Dusseldorf to the Inspectors of the SS might be cited in confirmation of this evaluation of the influence of Bishop Count von Galen:

> Catholics see in Clemens August the strong and energetic man before whom National Socialism has come to a stop.[88]

Hans Scholl, the young leader of the student resistance group in Munich, attributed the inspiration for their secret publication and distribution of *Die Weisse Rose* to the courage of Bishop von Galen.[89] There is conflicting evidence on the religious confession to which the Scholls belonged, but their deeply religious spirit is noticeable in the pamphlets they wrote. It is reported of Sophie Scholl that her last words, as she mounted the scaffold were: " But when these things begin to come to pass, look up and lift up your heads, because your redemption is at hand." (Luke: 21:28)[90]

The religious faith and the personal love of God of many of the men involved in the Resistance Movement is evident in their writings and recorded statements. It was testified to unwittingly by the Nazis when a special decree was issued by Hitler forbidding any religious consolation for those sentenced to death after the July 20, 1944 affair. Nevertheless, the chaplains at the Plotenzee prison, where so many of them were incarcerated, were themselves sympathetic with the Resistance and managed to get to them.[91] There were also the clergymen who had been arrested with the conspirators, and the prisoners managed to read the Scriptures together from time to time.[92]

We have already mentioned von Moltke's complete concern with eternal verities during his last days in jail. His letters to his wife are filled with Scriptural quotations, and reveal daily growth in detachment from earthly concerns. Everything, he felt,

[88] Heinrich Portmann, *Dokumente um den Bischof von Münster* (Münster: Aschendorff, 1948), II, 100. Translation mine.

[89] Inge Scholl, *op. cit.*, pp. 23-25.

[90] Heinrich Hermelink, *Kirche im Kampf: Dokumente des Widerstands und des Aufbaus in der evangelischen Kirche Deutschlands von 1933 bis 1945* (Tübingen: R. Wundenlich, 1950), pp. 666-667.

[91] Statement made by Fr. Buchholz in a radio broadcast. Cf. "Ihre Letzten Stunden," *Das Parlament*, July 20, 1952.

[92] Letters of Moltke to his wife. Moltke, *op. cit.*, p. 27 ff.

had been a grace for him, a grace for which he was very grateful to God. He begged his wife to pray only that he would persevere in grace until the end.

He wrote that he had felt the presence of God with him all during his trial—as it is described in Isaias 43:2:

> When thou shalt pass through the waters, I will be with thee, and the rivers shall not cover thee; when thou shalt walk in the fire, thou shalt not be burnt, and the flames shall not burn in thee.

Moltke's wife, Freya, who was also counted among the active members of the Kreisau circle, had a similarly supernatural outlook on the tragedy which had overtaken them. On January 6, 1945, while her husband was in jail awaiting trial, she visited Ruth Andreas-Friedrich of the "Uncle Emil" circle. The latter quotes her as having said:

> We must carry the spark through time. If one carries the spark, everything takes on meaning—living and dying. Yes, even dying. I've thought about it often. Perhaps that's the miracle of the Deluge story, and the secret of the Wise Men from the East. . . . That they save the Ark above the waters and carry gold through the desert—the Wise Men of the old civilizations to the child of the new. . . . It's a blessing to be allowed to carry the spark and a sacred duty. Let us take it as our duty. Somewhere, beyond the desert, the Child is waiting for us.[93]

Peter Yorck von Wartenburg, in a farewell letter to his mother before his execution, said that he was confident of finding in God a gracious judge . . . for his actions had been inspired not by a desire for power but by love of his fatherland.[94] The meditations composed by Father Delp between the time of his arrest and his death are eloquent testimony to the intense spiritual life of this participant in the Resistance Movement.[95] Converting his prison cell into a place of prayer and study, Dietrich Bonhoeffer also spent his last days on earth in a truly admirable manner.[96]

[93] Ruth Andreas Friedrich, *op. cit.*, pp. 185-186.

[94] RSHA report, Oct. 25, 1944. 105/34.

[95] Alfred Delp, S. J., *op. cit.*, passim.

[96] Dietrich Bonhoeffer, *Letters and Papers from Prison.* Ed. Eberhard Bethge, trans. Reginald H. Fuller (London: SCM Press, 1953), passim.

As more material of a personal nature becomes available to scholars, this religious aspect of the Resistance Movement may become even clearer. But the place of religion as a factor in the struggle against Hitler already admits of some evaluation.

The churches relied largely on the weapons of noncompliance, of protest, and of repeated repudiation of the theological errors inherent in the Nazi teaching. Several of their leaders were heroic and courageous in their fearless and outspoken criticism of the regime, but at no time did they publicly urge a *putsch* by the anti-Hitler forces. If they did so privately, there is as yet no available evidence of it.

The indirect effect of religious forces was, however, even greater. The men of the Resistance Movement were obviously concerned about the defense of ecclesiastical independence in matters of doctrine and administration and were also working toward a better Church-State relationship for the future than had existed in the past. Their whole outlook on life was a living repudiation of the Nazi neo-paganism, and the post-war plans which they have left us indicate a sincere desire not only to restore the practice of Christianity to Germany but to build a "new" Germany based on solid Christian principles.

Although the countless executions following July 20, 1944 indicated a complete victory of the Swastika over the Cross, the battle had not ended. The debacle following the vanquishment of Hitler may have obscured the victory of those Germans who had long worked and prayed for his defeat, but it is to be hoped that, in the long run, the quotation used by von Kessel in the dedication of his diary may be vindicated.

> . . . unless the grain of wheat falls into the ground and dies, it remains alone. But if it dies, it brings forth much fruit.[97]
>
> (John 12: 24-25)

[97] Albrecht von Kessel, unpublished diary.

CONCLUSION

If the seed sown by the German Resistance Movement is to fructify there must be an honest confrontation of the problems involved in offering violent resistance to the modern totalitarian state. First of all we must recognize the physical obstacles to successful resistance: brutal police power equipped with modern weapons, courts which no longer protect the rights of the individual, state regulations which make necessary organization almost impossible, and the disappearance of free media of communication. To expect resistance under such circumstances is to expect courage of a superior degree.

But even more important than the recognition of such physical difficulties, is the necessity of attempting an analysis of the moral problems which obscure and often conceal the right of offering such resistance. Unless a man is convinced of the justice of his cause, the call to heroism will go unanswered. The writer of this dissertation has tried to show that the attainment of such a conviction, on the part of those who lived in Hitler Germany, was not an easy achievement.

Every characteristic of the milieu of the modern German militated against it. The inborn sense of duty, of fidelity to a leader, of loyalty to fatherland, of obedience to all authority, and especially of filial submission to a paternalistic government, were his most outstanding virtues. Strong Lutheran teaching, with its dichotomy of temporal affairs and the Kingdom of Heaven, influenced, in the course of four centuries, not only those who were members of that confession but also those of the Calvinist and Catholic churches.

Furthermore, to maintain that the Germans should have spared the world the horrors of World War II by getting rid of Hitler themselves is to ignore, not only the fact that such a feat could not be accomplished easily, but, more importantly, the fact that Nazi propaganda was singularly efficient and effective. The very people who should have been the natural enemies of the Brown

Shirt dictatorship were lulled into a false security by the oft repeated insistence of the Nazis on the necessity of a united crusade against Bolshevism.

Nothing so blinds high-principled men to the steady undermining of their own liberties as a boldly proclaimed " crusade " against an obviously intolerable foe. In capitalizing on the danger from Communist Russia, the Nazis were able to forestall an attack on their own totalitarian regime and its paganistic ideology. Concentration on the future persecution which they would suffer if Communism succeeded caused the Germans to allow a more imminent danger to encompass them.

The men who formed the German Resistance Movement were unique among their countrymen in that they grasped at an early date the true issues at stake. Representing, as they did, all walks of life—military, civil service, diplomatic corps, professors, clergymen, large landowners, and trade union leaders—they found unity not in defending any particular " interests " but in fighting to preserve or restore fundamental Christian values.

Truths which every American schoolboy learns are " self-evident " in his study of the Declaration of Independence—". . . that all men are created equal, that they are endowed by their Creator with certain unalienable rights. . ."—are a part of the Christian ethic which formed Europe, and therefore Germany. Yet, reliance on positive law had gradually obscured for the Germans the true origin of these " rights " and caused them to forget the principle that one who violated their " unalienable " character was no longer fit to govern.

We have tried to show in this dissertation that the neglect of the teaching on natural law and the lack of clarity in theological views on the right of resistance made a decision in this matter extremely difficult. Even those who surmounted the difficulty reached their decision more from an instinctive repudiation of a leader who did not abide by standards of decency and honor than from a well-thought out analysis of the right to defend one's natural rights.

One might have expected Catholics and Calvinists to have been more ardent in resistance than Lutherans. Theoretical support for the doctrine of active resistance can be found more easily in the writings of their theologians; nevertheless, the actual case study of the German Resistance shows that religious belief was not the determining factor in the individual's decision to fight against Hitler.

Discussions now taking place in Germany, like those of the *Europäische Publikation* group in Munich, are re-examining and re-interpreting Luther's teachings and discovering that under such circumstances as existed in Nazi Germany violent resistance could have been justified. But this represents a departure from the traditional interpretations of Luther, and was not available to the men of the Resistance. Similarly, the writings of Father Max Pribilla, S. J., approach the Catholic teaching on resistance from a new point of view—at least among German theologians—and give strong arguments to uphold rebellion against a tyrannical ruler as consonant with both Scripture and tradition.

The time is ripe for a full length study of the problem of resistance in the modern totalitarian state by both the philosophical and theological schools. Earlier justifications of resistance and opinions in regard to tyrannicide, such as those by John of Salisbury, the unknown author of the *Vindiciae contra tyrannos*, Buchanan, Knox, and Mariana, were written within a monarchical and ecclesiastical framework of reference. In the case of the Catholic authors there was usually a supposition that an unjust or heretical king could be declared deposed by the pope, a sufficient alternative to a popular revolution. The Calvinist writers were also concerned with an "heretical" monarch, and therefore their arguments now need reevaluation and restatement.

Today, the problem concerns rather a ruler duly elected by the people or whose seizure of power has been welcomed by the people in a time of internal chaos or external danger. His authority has come to him legally, and it is set within explicit or implicit constitutional limitations. If he subverts the rights of the people, terrorizes them into submission, and rules the country as if it were his personal domain, has he not so exceeded the limits of his authority as to have destroyed the authority itself? Deprived of legal means of redress, what course of action would modern moralists suggest as the appropriate means of promoting the common good?

This whole fundamental question of the right of violent resistance, so badly in need of a definitive answer, was the foremost ethical factor involved in the German Resistance Movement. The second major problem was the choice of means to be used in overthrowing Hitler. This involved, in turn, two major considerations: "Was it ethically permissible to remain in office under the dictatorship in order to work against the regime?", and "To what extent could information and aid be given to potential or real enemies of Germany in order to bring about the downfall of the Nazis?" These are the problems with which we have dealt in chapters three, four, and five.

The answer to the first of these questions, as given by the men of the Resistance, was affirmative. None questioned the right, and even the advantage, of staying in an important office in order to prevent a Nazi from taking it. They considered it a means of securing information of value to the Resistance Movement and of retaining at least partial control of some areas of government, thus being prepared to assume command in the event of a successful *coup*. The most notable case of this, which has been discussed at length, was that of the State Secretary in the Foreign Office, Ernst von Weizsäcker.

The men of the Resistance were not as unanimous in regard to the other question. Some justified giving information to the Western countries in an effort to avoid what happened at Munich in 1938 but found it "treasonable" to give military information to them once the war had begun. Others saw both steps as "means" to the one end which they were seeking—the overthrow of the Nazis—and considered such actions as true patriotism. We have noted that the latter point of view has been upheld by post-war German courts, and we submit that it was done on solid ethical and legal grounds. Loyalty to one's country must not be identified with passive acceptance of domestic tyranny and an aggressive war policy. Rather, the fearless rejection of such a ruler for the sake of the common good would be true patriotism.

The question of tyrannicide was also considered. Although many of the men of the German Resistance finally decided that no method other than the assassination of Hitler would be successful, there were some who consistently opposed it. A few regarded it as immoral to kill even a tyrant; others felt it would be a grave psychological error which would result in a new stab-in-the-back legend. It is, of course, a problem resting ultimately on the more basic question of a right to employ violent means of resistance, for in the modern police state the peaceful arrest of a criminal ruler is virtually impossible. In Germany the search for a satisfactory solution was further impeded by the moral and psychological implications in the oath of loyalty taken to Hitler. The attempted assassination on July 20, 1944 was, therefore, an event in German history of deep and lasting significance.

The Church and Political Resistance

That the churches—both Catholic and Protestant—"resisted" the Hitler government's arbitrary rule and its persecution of the churches can be proved beyond question. It was a fact accepted by the occupation authorities; the churches were to be considered "one of the most important instruments for the reorientation of German society," for, on the whole, the record of the churches in resisting the Nazis was "a very good one."[1] But it seems to be equally clear that the German hierarchy at no time, either individually or collectively, publicly or privately, urged revolution against the Nazi government; in fact, there was repeated admonition to German Catholics to avoid violence, demonstrations, conspiracy, and outright revolution. In addition, no encouragement or support was given to the men who attempted to kill Hitler and bring about a revolution on July 20, 1944.

In dealing with this aspect of resistance in Nazi Germany, there are then two basic areas of study: 1) the opposition of the Catholic Church to Nazism, as demonstrated in the teaching of her bishops and priests; and 2) the attitude of the Church toward the use of revolution as a solution to the problems they faced, and, in particular, toward the specific revolution attempted on July 20, 1944, which presupposed and demanded tyrannicide as its means.

That this historical problem has more than merely academic interest is evident; the bishops in Eastern Europe, in South

[1] Beryl R. McClasky, *The History of United States Policy and Program in the Field of Religious Affairs Under the Office of the U.S. High Commissioner for Germany.* U.S. High Commissioner for Germany, Office of the Executive Secretary: Historical Division. Research Project No. 104, 1951. Introduction, p. 1.

America, and in the Far East are faced now with circumstances similar to those of the German bishops from 1933 to 1945. In 1948, Cardinal Mindszenty of Hungary referred to this parallel:

> The old battle against materialism and totalitarianism continues unabated. We are only taking up the torch which the Cardinals Faulhaber and Preysing bravely held so high in their fight against the Nazi regime.[2]

And recent statements of bishops in South America, in Cuba, in the Congo and elsewhere raise the question anew: "What is the role of the bishops in relation to the political life of a nation, especially under a totalitarian form of government?"

The incompatibility of National Socialism and Roman Catholicism was formally stated even before the Nazi rise to political power. On September 30, 1930, a parish priest in Kirschhausen in Hesse, Father Weber, gave a sermon in which he stated:

> 1. Every Catholic is forbidden to be a member of the Nazi Party.
> 2. No members of the Hitler Party are allowed to attend funerals or other church services in group formation.
> 3. As long as a Catholic is a member of the Hitler Party, he cannot be admitted to the Sacraments.[3]

Quick to seize such an opportunity, the Gauleiter of Hesse asked for an explanation or repudiation of this sermon from the Bishop of Mainz. In answer, he received what was the first official statement of opposition on the part of the Catholic Church to the fundamental principles of Nazism.[4] His Excellency said that the parish priest had been acting on instructions from him, and that the reason for his opposition could be found in Article 24 of the Nazi program:

> We demand the freedom of all religious beliefs in the State insofar as they are no danger to the public weal and do not

---

[2] Msgr. DDR. Joseph Weissthanner, *Michael Kardinal Faulhaber, 80 Yahre* (Verlag Katholische Kirche Bayerns, 1949), p. 117.

[3] John Mason Brown, *Hitler's First Foes* (Minneapolis; Minn.: Burgess, 1936), p. 92.

[4] *Ibid.*, pp. 93-94.

> offend against the ethical and moral sense of the German race.[5]

The Bishop held that such phraseology was, at best, ambiguous, and denied that the "ethical and moral sense of the German race" could be the criterion of religious belief. Furthermore, the Ordinary of Mainz denounced the "positive Christianity" of the Nazis, a concept intimately bound up with the racial ideology of the Party. The Bishop continued:

> Through this conception of religion the National Socialists fall into a position inimical to the Catholic Church. It is for that reason that National Socialist speakers have repeatedly expressed the idea in public meetings: "Our fight is against Judaism and Rome." Hitler, to be sure, has written in his book *Mein Kampf* some words of acknowledgment about the Christian religion and Catholic institutions, but that does not deceive us about the fact that the cultural policies of National Socialism are in contradiction to Catholic Christianity.[6]

In February, 1931, the Bishops of Bavaria condemned these same doctrines and also forbade Catholic priests to work in any way with the National Socialist movement.[7] A month earlier, the outstanding member of this episcopal group—Cardinal von Faulhaber—had already in his Lenten pastoral attacked those who were currently denying the Christian virtues of meekness and obedience, calling them passive and not active virtues—an obvious reference to the propagators of the super-man theory. The Cardinal insisted that true heroism was still to be found in the cross and in martyrdom, and urged his people to use Lent as a time for deciding whether their "Weltanschauung" would be Christian or pagan. A characteristic note is struck in his teaching: "And still to suffer wrong is morally greater than to do wrong."[8]

---

[5] Quoted in Joseph F. Thorning, S.J., "The German Bishops and Hitlerism," *America*, 46 (January 9, 1932), pp. 333-334.

[6] Brown, *op. cit.*, p. 94.

[7] Letter of the Bavarian Bishops in *Amtsblatt für die Erzdiocese München und Freising* No. 4 (1931), February 10, 1931, Beilage.

[8] Michael Cardinal von Faulhaber, "*Fastenhirtenbrief*," January 25, 1931, in *Amtsblatt* No. 3 (1931), February 9, 1931, pp. 29-36.

The unanimity of the bishops at this early time in their repudiation of Nazism may well have been responsible for the failure of the Third Reich to bring about a schism in the Catholic Church. That the masters of Nazi Germany hoped to do so is well documented by the papers they left behind them.[9] Innumerable attempts were made to divide the bishops from the pope and the priests and people from the bishops. Although the bishops expressly limited themselves in the matter of interference—"It lies far from us to interfere with the political goals of National Socialism; we ask only what attitude it has toward Catholic Christianity,"[10]—yet they spoke strongly against any attempt to form a National German Church. In September, 1932, the Bavarian bishops stated:

> In the fight against the "cosmopolitical powers" are concealed a new Kulturkampf and a new attempt to strike the Catholic church in Germany in the heart by founding a national church. We will in this fight not be less strong and faithful than were our fathers and predecessors in the Kulturkampf.[11]

The year 1933 is perhaps the most significant in the story of the Church in Germany under the Third Reich. It is the year in which Hitler came into power (January 20), had his power confirmed by election (March 5), and, as Chancellor, approved the Concordat with the Holy See (July 20). How did the Church react to these events?

In this year of 1933 Cardinal von Faulhaber did not retreat at all from his former position with regard to the Nazis. In his Lenten pastoral of February 10 he considered the topic: "On the Rights and Duties of the State and the Citizen."[12] Basing his remarks on the principles enunciated by Pope Leo XIII in *Immortale Dei* and *Sapientiae Christianae,* the Cardinal stressed

---

[9] Cf. Johann Neuhausler, *Kreuz und Hakenkreuz* (Verlag Katholische Kirche Bayerns, 1946).

[10] Bavarian Bishops in *Amtsblatt* No. 4 (1931), February 10, 1931, p. 15.

[11] Bavarian Bishops, September 7, 1932, in *Amtsblatt* No. 4 (1932), October 6, 1932, p. 167.

[12] Von Faulhaber, "Fastenhirtenbrief," February 10, 1933, *Amtsblatt* No. 5 (1933), February 21, 1933, pp. 57-64.

the fact that although the forms of the state can vary, the source of its authority can never change. All authority is ordained of God and therefore, the Cardinal maintained, Article I of the Constitution of the Reich is erroneous for it holds that the power of the state comes from the people. On the contrary:

> A state without God or, even more, against God has thrown away the best evidence for its own authority, has renounced the religious binding of the citizen's conscience and therewith has laid the axe at the root of its own continuation.[13]

Rather should the state have as its guiding principle the moral order and as its highest goal the care of the public welfare; in fulfilling this duty, moreover, the state must respect the rights of the family and the Church, and must never legislate in opposition to natural law and the commandments of God. Finally, in urging the citizens to pray for the state, the Cardinal delivered a sharp blow to the Fuehrer principle with this plea: "Let us pray that the men at the peak of the state will not say 'We are the State.' "[14]

This letter, and similar words from the other bishops, should have acted as a check on the Catholic vote for Hitler, but apparently it did not. Only five and one-half million out of the twelve and one-half million voted for the Center Party.[15] But, Hitler knew that the bishops were opposed to him. On March 21 he and Goebbels refused to attend the Mass offered in celebration of the opening of the Reichstag and gave as the reason:

> The German Catholic Bishops have quite recently in a series of public declarations on which the clergy have not hesitated to act, stigmatized the leaders of the National Socialist Party as traitors who should be refused the sacraments. These instructions have not been withdrawn and are still being carried out. In these circumstances the Chancellor is reluctantly compelled to remain away from the Catholic service at Potsdam.[16]

---

[13] *Ibid.*, p. 58.

[14] *Ibid.*, p. 64.

[15] Robert D'Harcourt, *The German Catholics*, trans. Reginald J. Dingle (London: Burns, Oates, and Washbourne, 1939), p. 70.

[16] *Ibid.*, p. 72.

Yet, in a seemingly contradictory speech two days later in the Reichstag, Hitler pledged himself to support religion:

> While the Government is determined to carry through the political and moral purging of our public life, it is creating and insuring prerequisites for a truly religious life. The Government sees in both Christian confessions the most important factors for the maintenance of our folkdom. It will respect agreements concluded between them and the States. However, it expects that its work will meet with a similar appreciation. The Government will treat all other denominations with equal objective justice. It can never condone, though, that belonging to a certain denomination or to a certain race might be regarded as a license to commit or tolerate crimes. The Government will devote its care to the sincere living together of Church and State.[17]

That the German bishops were impressed by this speech is obvious from the repeated references in subsequent years to Hitler's statement ". . . both Christian confessions [are] the most important factors for the maintenance of our folkdom." Did they really believe that Hitler was sincere, or was it merely an attempt to get him to live up to his own words by reminding him of them in public? At the time, his words seemed to have a somewhat soothing effect on them for they relaxed slightly on the question of party membership. Soon, however, they renewed their warnings against any attempt to set up a national Catholic church or to stifle the activities of the Catholic press, youth groups, etc. The Bavarian Bishops' pastoral letter of May 5, 1933 struck a conciliatory note in sympathizing with the difficult task of the new government and pointing out that it was the time for all to work together for the fatherland and put an end to the inner conflict:

> Therefore, we bishops cry out in deep love for our fatherland, from a sincere compassion with the army of unemployed and hungry and in great anxiety about the future of our German homeland, to the people of our dioceses no more to direct their gaze to the past, nor from that to see what divided us, but rather what unites us, and therefore to reach out our hand and in a magnanimous spirit of

---

[17] Nuremberg Document No. 3387-PS. Translation of the speech as quoted in *Völkischer Beobachter*, March 24, 1933.

> sacrifice to use our united powers to prevent the frightful misery, the continuing decline, and the unhappy unrest.[18]

At the same time they made it quite clear that they refuted the claims of the totalitarian state to control all areas of man's life and were relying on Hitler's promise to respect the rights of the Church:

> But we hope that the regime will not sanction the endeavor and the procedure of those who wish, as a matter of principle, to establish a different standard of what is right, or to employ the word "Gleichschaltung" in a way which contradicts the guarantee of the Herr Reich Chancellor that he will give equality before the law to all who work together for the nation and who do not deny their support to the government.[19]

This thought was echoed in the annual letter of the German hierarchy assembled at Fulda June 5, 1933.[20] They reaffirmed their love for their fatherland and said they did not wish to put obstacles in the way of the national re-awakening, but [and always there is this "but"] they felt it their solemn duty to caution against the state's infringement on the rights of the Church and its intrusion into the area of human freedom. They, indeed, welcomed the goal of the government—"freedom for the people"—and approved of its desire to restore Germany to an honorable place among the nations of the world, but denounced a spirit of revenge and a forced unity of the people through "Blutsgleichheit."

That the bishops welcomed such a goal and went on record as approving the government's desire to restore the national honor might seem at first glance to be open support for the Hitler regime. Seen, however, within the context of the Pastoral letter, it is weakened by the insistence of the bishops on the rights of the individual and of the Church which must not be ignored in the drive toward this goal.

Cardinal von Faulhaber, in his letter of February 10, 1933[21]

---

[18] Bavarian Bishops, May 5, 1933, *Amtsblatt* No. 8 (1933), p. 101.

[19] *Ibid.*, p. 104.

[20] German Bishops, June 5, 1933, *Amtsblatt* No. 10 (1933), June 9, 1933, pp. 125-135.

[21] Von Faulhaber, "Fastenhirtenbrief," February 10, 1933, *Amtsblatt* No. 5 (1933), February 21, 1933, pp. 57-64.

had made it clear that Catholics had a duty in conscience to be loyal members of the state, but he qualified this duty by insisting that the obedience must be the obedience of free men. In this statement we find the essential note of the type of "resistance" which, according to the Cardinal, should be offered by the Catholic citizen in Nazi Germany.

> The Catechism says about the fourth commandment: "We owe respect and obedience to the secular authority." Respect and obedience to the laws and ordinances so long as nothing is commanded contrary to the commands of God and the Church. Respect and obedience, also, at a time when the present form of the state and its system does not please us. . . . The obedience which the Catechism requires is the obedience of a free man, who never takes part in violent revolution or upheavals, but who cannot, because of that, call disorder, order or madness, truth.[22]

Clearly, this is the path which he himself followed for fifteen years: no error was allowed to go unrefuted; no immoral law was obeyed or countenanced; no arbitrary exercise of power was accepted without protest. But, also, no attempt to overthrow the government was supported.

Fearlessly, the Cardinal gave his famous series of Advent sermons in 1933 in which the Nazi racial ideology, with its vicious anti-Semitism, was refuted by a scholarly—and simultaneously deeply-moving—treatment of the Old Testament.[23] Nothing could have been a more obvious challenge to the Nazis than this exhortation to meditate on the beauties of the Jewish religion and its deep inner relationship to Christianity. The Nazis recognized this challenge and prohibited the printing and distribution of the sermons. In addition they made it obvious that they were watching those who attended the sermons; yet the crowds were so great that loud speakers had to be installed in two neighboring churches. The courage of their Cardinal was, throughout the Hitler period, a source of inspiration for the people of his archdiocese.

---

[22] *Ibid.*, p. 62.

[23] Von Faulhaber, *Judaism, Christianity, and Germany*, trans. Rev. George D. Smith (New York: The Macmillan Co., 1934).

Had the Concordat, signed by the Third Reich with the Vatican, weakened the position of the German hierarchy in their battle against Nazism? When one first discusses this question, even today, with many Germans, the affirmative view is often expressed. Yet, an analysis of the episcopal letters and sermons indicates, rather, the hierarchy's wholehearted defense of the Concordat and a readiness to use it as a legal basis for their claims against state infringement on the rights of the Church. Scrupulous adherence to Article 32, by which clerics were forbidden to enter into the political arena, was urged repeatedly by the bishops and one cannot but think that this was in order to strengthen their own position when they insisted on the government's fulfilling the guarantees it had given in the agreement. The fear, too, that the old charge of "political Catholicism" would be revived inclined the bishops to remark on several occasions that they were speaking, not from political motives or interests, but as guardians of faith and morals. Their agreement to abstain from membership in political parties seemed a small concession to make in return for all the freedom guaranteed in the Concordat and summed up in Article I:

> The German Reich guarantees the freedom of the profession and the public exercise of the Catholic religion. It recognizes the right of the Catholic Church, within the limits of the general laws in force, to regulate and to administer freely her own affairs and to proclaim in the field of her competence laws and ordinances binding upon her members.[24]

Basing their arguments on this public recognition by the government of the Church's competence in her own affairs, the bishops in later sermons and letters constantly referred to the Concordat. Thus it was viewed by them not as a handicap but as a useful legal instrument with which they hoped to force Hitler into acknowledging the rights of the Church.[25]

[24] NCWC text of the Concordat reprinted in Walter Consuelo Langsam (ed.) *Documents and Readings in the History of Europe Since 1918* (New York: Lippincott Co., 1951), pp. 722-728.

[25] Cf. the discussion of this point in Michael Freund, "Hitler und der Papst. Kurie u. Reich in d. Jahren 1930 bis 1945," *Gegenwart*, 11 (1956), pp. 237-242.

Unfortunately, the years of 1934 and 1935 gave irrefutable evidence that the Nazis had no intention of abiding by the terms of the Concordat. Priests were arrested; Gestapo agents frequently interfered with church services; children and their parents were intimidated and openly threatened if they continued to attend confessional schools; every effort was made to force the youth into the German Nazi Youth group; Catholic newspapers were under constant threat of suspension (where they still existed at all).

In his Lenten Pastoral, February 1, 1934,[26] Cardinal von Faulhaber chose as his topic, ''The Moral Teaching of the Catholic Church.'' In it he denounced current errors—based in part on the Nazi interpretation of Nietzsche—on the nature of the state. He warned that without God there can be no true moral order; it cannot be based solely on ''what serves the people.'' If the state promotes moral evils such as abortion, birth control, and euthanasia, then ''Man must obey God rather than men.'' In pointing out that Catholic moral teaching is based on four fundamental truths: 1) that there is a natural law; 2) that man has a conscience; 3) that the human will is free; and 4) that we need the grace of God, Cardinal von Faulhaber clearly refuted the Nazi ideology, with its concern for positive law only, for blind obedience, and its confidence in the super-man who needs not the grace of God. The conflict was basic and it was clear.

On February 9, 1934, the ''Bible'' of Nazi racial teaching, *Der Mythus des 20. Jahrhunderts*, by Alfred Rosenberg, was placed on the Index of Forbidden books.[27] Retaliation came swiftly in the form of increased attacks on Catholic prelates, particularly von Faulhaber. Although Rosenberg, in the introduction to his work, had insisted that it represented his personal views and was not an official party program, the support given him by the government clearly contradicted such a state-

---

[26] Von Faulhaber, ''Fastenhirtenbrief,'' February 1, 1934, *Amtsblatt* No. 2 (1934), February 6, 1934, pp. 17-24.

[27] *Amtsblatt* No. 2 (1934), p. 40. There was further explanation of the errors in this work given in *Amtsblatt* No. 20 (1934), November 15, 1934 and No. 3 (1935), February 11, 1935.

ment.[28] And Hitler's appointment of him as Plenipotentiary for Weltanschauung on January 24, 1935, confirmed the relationship.

The tempo of the fight increased in 1935. On the tenth of February the Cardinal preached a masterful sermon on "The Freedom of the Church." The subtlety of his approach (he began by referring to the persecution of the Church in Mexico) should not obscure for us the fact that he was speaking of the persecution of the Church in Germany as well. In what, he asked, does the necessary freedom of the Church consist?

1. Freedom to exercise the Catholic religion as guaranteed in the Concordat;
2. Freedom to preach the Catholic religion (again the Concordat is quoted and also Hitler's speech in the Reichstag March 31, 1933);
3. Freedom to defend the Catholic religion against such false teaching as that of Rosenberg;
4. Freedom to answer questions of conscience—such as that of parents regarding the Confessional schools.

The Cardinal went so far as to suggest that martyrdom might be called for in defending these freedoms, placing before his people the heroic example of St. Thomas More, the 400th anniversary of whose death was being celebrated. The English martyrs, declared the Cardinal pointedly, died to "uphold the authority of the pope over the king."

He then went on to explain that the current dispute over the schools was not between Catholics and Protestants but rather between Christianity and paganism. He hinted at possible political repercussions when he suggested the adverse effect such actions as the recent dissolution of a parents' organization (January 24, 1935) [because it had sponsored a talk on "Education for Honor and Obedience"] would have on the people of the Saar (annexed ten days before). On the 13th of February there was to be a vote on the school question and the Cardinal concluded with what was probably a hope rather than a belief:

---

[28] Cf. Neuhausler, *op. cit.*, Part I, pp. 257 ff.

"Der Fuehrer hat seine Zustimmung zum Konkordat gegeben, der Fuehrer wird sein Wort nicht brechen."[29]

The same theme was amplified in his Lenten Pastoral, February 22nd, on "The Moral Teaching of the Gospel,"[30] and here emphasis was placed on the Scriptural basis for the Church's teaching. In the same month Cardinal Schulte of Cologne again lashed out at the racial teaching of Nazism:

> It is heathenism and apostasy from Christ and Christianity to see the essential element in religion only in the requirements of alleged Blood and Race. . . . It is heathenism and apostasy from Christ and Christianity that a man should declare today that "Blood and Honour" should alone determine the meaning of our earthly life, that for the sacred means of grace, which the divine Redeemer instituted for our salvation and vouchsafes to us through His Church, there could be substituted the maintenance of a particular kind of human blood in its purity.[31]

Meanwhile, the violations of the Concordat—with respect to the guarantee of freedom for workers' groups—were increasing weekly. In June, 1935, Cardinal von Faulhaber issued a special letter to Catholic workers, warning them not to surrender to Nazi pressure to join the "Strength through Joy" movement, because it promoted strongly anti-Catholic views. The Cardinal quoted earlier protests by Bishop Bertram, in the name of all the bishops, and that of Bishop Bares of Berlin insisting that the workers had had their right to their own organizations guaranteed by the Concordat. Yet, let us note the word of caution:

> Just so must we raise a third demand, that the activities of the workers' organizations in no way must cause a disturbance through terroristic agitators and should rather relish the state protection guaranteed in the Concordat.[32]

This same parallel construction—defense of the rights of the Church as defined in the Concordat and a warning against

[29] *Amtsblatt* No. 3 (1935), February 11, 1935, pp. 1-7.

[30] *Amtsblatt* No. 4 (1935), February 26, 1935, pp. 45-52.

[31] Nathaniel Micklem, *National Socialism and the Roman Catholic Church, 1933-38* (New York: Oxford University Press, 1939), p. 104.

[32] *Amtsblatt* No. 12 (1935), June 4, 1935.

revolution—is clearly evident in the annual pastoral letter issued at Fulda by the German bishops on August 20, 1935.[33] There is no minimizing of the conflict between church and state; it was the "decisive hour" in which the German people must strengthen their souls "against the propaganda of a new paganism." The very essence of Christianity was under attack, and the promotion by the state of unmarried mothers was roundly condemned. Attacks on the Catholic press were protested and the bishops insisted that the state was obliged to act in accordance with the moral law. They announced that they had sent a memorandum to the Chancellor defending the primary rights of the parents in the education of their children, and denied that such action on their part constituted "political action" or came under the heading of the old charge of "political Catholicism." Rather, it was their duty to remind the individual Catholic of his obligation to refuse obedience to laws contrary to the natural law and the commandments of God. Indeed it was a time "to obey God rather than man."

Yet, we see only half the picture if we fail to note that side by side with this forceful denunciation of the Nazi state was an equally strong injunction to avoid revolution.

> German Catholics! Preserve peace and order! Do not repay evil with evil! As far as lies within you, live in peace with all men. You have often heard it asked in recent weeks: Must then we Catholics let all these things happen in our own fatherland? May we be labeled as traitors to our country and to our people even though in World War I we brought bloody sacrifices in good measure? It is not forbidden you, yes, it can become a duty, peacefully to render an account of your faith in firm words, and to ask, "Why strikest thou us?" The spirit of Christ fights according to other laws and comes to victory with other weapons than those of the spirit of the world. You may not call down fire from heaven. Yes, you must forgive and pray for your enemy. "Do not be overcome by evil," or by wrath or desire of revenge! "Overcome evil by good!" *Catholics make no revolt and offer no violent resistance.* That is so well known that from time immemorial such a one who would win an easy victory has fallen first on the

[33] *Amtsblatt* No. 17 (1935), August 29, 1935, pp. 195-205.

> Catholics. Set a watch on your mouth and let yourself not be drawn into rash talk!—Set a watch on your ears and hear not the wild rumors which are spread against civil authority and fear the sin of repeating such rumors. The eighth commandment forbids not merely lies and calumny. Thus, you will help to mitigate the rough tone which at present is struck in the public discussion. Moreover, that will be the best answer to all accusations, if the Catholics are distinguished by conscientiousness in their calling and by the spirit of sacrifice and are examples of Christian fatherhood and dutiful civil servants.[34]

There is no example of the German bishops' teaching which better illustrates the practical difficulty which confronted the German Catholic. If he followed this teaching he would have avoided all conspiracy and revolution, all involvement in such groups as the Beck-Goerdeler circle, and would have remained at a good distance from the men who combined their efforts in the *attentat* of July 20, 1944. For men of honor, men who wished to rid Germany of the godless and inhuman party that controlled it, what alternative was there? Was the only course of "resistance" that of refusal to obey unjust laws, open protest against governmental injustice, consequent arrest, imprisonment, and possibly death? Such would seem to be the declared position of the German hierarchy. This position, put forward so clearly in 1935, seems to have undergone no change in the years that followed. The bishops' resistance to the state continued to be brave, even heroically courageous, but no evidence has been uncovered which would point to their acceptance of revolution as a desirable and legitimate means to the end they hoped for.

In December, 1935, Cardinal von Faulhaber continued his attacks on the Nazis, speaking eloquently of the *true* "Weltanschauung"—the world view of the Christian—and insisting that the word cannot be taken over by evil forces and given only a bad meaning.[35] Again in February he asserted his duty, as bishop, to defend the rights of the Church[36] and delivered a

---

[34] *Ibid.*, p. 202. Italics mine.

[35] *Amtsblatt*, January 15, 1936, Beilage No. 1, pp. 1-8.

[36] Von Faulhaber, "Fastenhirtenbrief," February 6, 1936, *Amtsblatt* No. 5 (1936), February 12, 1936, pp. 37-44.

strong defense of the papacy.[37] In the latter sermon he gave specific examples of the "stones" being hurled at the pope and exposed them as lies and propaganda.

Apparently the Cardinal had no intention of retreating before the enemy. People who were close to him in those days insist that he had no fear that the Nazis would ever seize him personally; what did hold him back on occasion was the knowledge that they might retaliate by sending one or more of his priests to concentration camps — which happened on several occasions. His sermons and pastoral letters were reproduced on a mimeograph machine kept in the cardinal's residence so that no one else might be incriminated if it were discovered. Scores of brave, but unknown, Catholic lay men and women delivered them to pastors and religious superiors, and thus the Cardinal continued to lead and inspire his priests and people.

But again we strike a puzzling note in the attitude of the bishops when we read a statement sent by the Archbishop of Munich to his priests in the *Amtsblatt* of March 21, 1936.[38] It has reference to the coming plebiscite (March 29th) concerning which, the Cardinal felt, German Catholics would obviously have a conflict in conscience. They should be advised that they could vote "Yes" in support of the government without signifying support of its action in those things contrary to conscience. Why should they vote "Yes"? ". . . so as to stand before all the world for the honor, freedom, and security of our German fatherland." He said that it was understandable that the German Catholics wished, in this hour of national decision, ". . . to make known to the whole world their loyalty to the fatherland." But, was this not to mislead the rest of the world? And, later, did not the German opposition complain that foreign nations were so slow to recognize the evil of the Hitler regime? Why, then, did the bishops want to present a united front to the rest of the world?

Again, in June of 1936, Cardinal von Faulhaber protested

---

[37] Sermon, February 9, 1936, *Amtsblatt* No. 6 (1936), February 18, 1936, Beilage II.

[38] *Amtsblatt,* No. 8 (1936), March 21, 1936, p. 71.

the order to cancel a procession on Trinity Sunday and held it in spite of the order.[39] In addressing the men who took part in it, he insisted that this was not a demonstration against the government, but an open profession of faith in the same spirit shown by their fathers ("... and we are told to hold as holy the blood of our fathers, so why not their spirit?"). Claiming that he was acting within the rights guaranteed by the Concordat, the Cardinal then went on to enumerate recent transgressions of that agreement by the state. Are Catholics really free, he asked, when in the next month nearly 600 teachers will be put out of their cloisters? He reviewed the actions of the state in the infamous "morality trials" and its repeated interference with Catholic youth groups, condemning such intrusion of the state into the areas of ecclesiastical jurisdiction. Yet, the Cardinal concluded on a note of loyalty to that same government:

> A German newspaper reported about two weeks ago that a man in Switzerland had in another newspaper urged the children to pray for the death of the Fuehrer. A madman abroad has had an attack of insanity—may therefore all German Catholics be suspected? You all bear me witness that at all the principal services on Sundays and feastdays in all our churches we pray for the Fuehrer—as we promised in the Concordat.

And then, at the end of the service: "... we shall say the Our Father for the life of the Fuehrer."

The annual Pastoral letter of the German hierarchy in August, 1936,[40] was concerned with the evils of communism, but with the pointed reminder that one can only fight communism successfully by building on solid religious principles. The bishops spoke of the lessons to be learned from the Spanish Civil War then raging, and remarked that they were determined to fight similar persecution of the Church, whatever the source might be. They, as followers of the apostle Boniface, would protect and defend the rights and freedoms guaranteed them by natural and positive law in the interest of the entire German people.

[39] *Amtsblatt* No. 16 (1936), June 12, 1936, Beilage, pp. 1-7.
[40] *Amtsblatt* No. 20 (1936), August 27, 1936, pp. 201-207.

In view of the world situation, they pleaded for peace within the nation, maintaining that they remained ready to work for the building up of the country—but not at the price of surrendering to the forces of godlessness.

The bishops repeated their views on communism in a Christmas letter the same year,[41] approving the Fuehrer's fight against it but cautioning him against treating the Church as if it, too, were an enemy of the state.

Nevertheless, such treatment continued, and since the violations of the Concordat, protested over and over again by both the German hierarchy and the Vatican, remained unremedied—as a matter of fact they were usually ignored by the government—the severe condemnation of the Nazi state came in *Mit Brennender Sorge*.[42] Pope Pius XI had had the encyclical written in German, sent into the country and by means of an underground route it reached all pastors with instructions that it be read from their pulpits on Palm Sunday, March 21, 1937. Now, the fight between church and state was openly and officially reviewed, and the world was told clearly and emphatically of the situation in Germany. Coming only a few weeks after the encyclical on atheistic communism, there was no doubt of the Church's repudiation of both ideologies.

> Whoever exalts race, or the people, or the State, or a particular form of State, or the depositories of power, or any other fundamental value of the human community—however necessary and honorable be their function in worldly things—whoever raises these notions above their standard value and divinizes them to an idolatrous level, distorts and perverts an order of the world planned and created by God. . . . None but superficial minds could stumble into concepts of a national God, of a national religion. . . . Nothing but ignorance and pride could blind one to the treasures of the Old Testament.

Moreover, the state, in the hands of those professing such an ideology, had been persecuting the Church and had violated its Concordat with the Vatican:

---

[41] *Amtsblatt*, No. 29 (1936), December 30, 1936, pp. 317-328.

[42] Pius XI, *Mit brennender Sorge*, March 14, 1937. English translation in *The Catholic Mind*, XXXV (May 8, 1937), pp. 185-204.

> Secret and open measures of intimidation, the threat of economic and civic disabilities, bear on the loyalty of certain classes of Catholic functionaries, a pressure which violates every human right and dignity.
> . . . In the furrows, where We tried to sow the seed of a sincere peace, other men—the "enemy" of Holy Scripture—oversowed the cockle of distrust, unrest, hatred, defamation, of a determined hostility, overt or veiled, fed from many sources and wielding many tools, against Christ and His Church.

And the Catholics of the Third Reich were called upon to resist:

> Our wholehearted paternal sympathy goes out to those who must pay so dearly for their loyalty to Christ and the Church; but directly the highest interests are at stake, with the alternative of spiritual loss, there is but one alternative left, that of heroism. . . . As to those who imagine that they can reconcile exterior infidelity and interior fidelity to one and the same Church, let them hear Our Lord's warning:—"He that shall deny me before men shall be denied before the angels of God." (Luke 12:9)

There is in this encyclical a clear demand for Catholics to resist the unjust laws of Nazi Germany, even to the point of heroism, but there is no suggestion that they should attempt to rid themselves of that government. Yet, the government chose to label it a threat to the security of the state:

> It attempts to diminish the authority of the Reich government, to harm the interests of the German nation abroad, and, above all, to endanger the internal peace of the community by means of a direct appeal to the Catholic citizens by a party to the treaty with the Reich government.[43]

According to the Foreign Office in Berlin, the encyclical "... calls upon Catholic citizens to rebel against the authority of the state."[44] But no reading of the document itself can discover any such call to overt rebellion.

Charges and countercharges followed one another during the next three months. In a letter from the Papal Secretary of State

---

[43] *Documents on German Foreign Policy 1918-1945*, Series D, I, 935 (Washington, D.C.: Government Printing Office, 1949).

[44] *Ibid.*, pp. 937-938.

to the German Ambassador to the Holy See, dated April 30, 1937,[45] there is a statement of the goal of the Vatican's protests which comes near to suggesting that the form of government in Germany must be changed if the situation is to be remedied.

> The first and essential condition for the attainment of this goal, [i.e., the "welfare of the Germans as a nation and as members of the Church"] . . . is the *release of the leadership of the State,* and of the movement sustaining the State, from the ever-tightening embrace and the increasing penetration of ideological and anti-Christian currents which draw their strength from the struggle against the Church and which seek to make of the struggle a law of life and a condition of life for the German State bearing their mark and animated by their spirit.

Nevertheless, the "suggestion" is being made by the Vatican to the government itself and not to men who might wish to bring about the release of the leadership by rebellion from without.

In the middle of 1937 came the imprisonment of Father Rupert Mayer, S.J., a priest of the archdiocese of Munich who had devoted himself to preaching to the workers. Today he is venerated by many as a saint and his name is usually the first one mentioned by German Catholics when the question of the resistance of the Church is discussed. Only recently he was described in a press release as "a staunch opponent of Nazism" and as having a "dauntless anti-Nazi attitude."[46] His sermons were so critical of Nazi policy that he was ordered to stop preaching; he ignored the order and was arrested June 5, 1937.[47] In an eloquent sermon in defense of Father Mayer, Cardinal von Faulhaber insisted that the state had no jurisdiction over preachers provided they had permission from their ecclesiastical superiors, and denounced this new violation of the Concordat.[48] It is significant, for our purposes, to note that the Cardinal stresses the fact that there was nothing "political" in the

---

[45] *Ibid.*, pp. 965-966.

[46] Press release, June 3, 1960. Religious News Service.

[47] Cf. *supra*, note 43, p. 180.

[48] Mimeographed copy. Sermon in St. Michael's to the Sodality of the Men of Munich, July 4, 1937.

sermons of Father Mayer and that on May 23 he had specifically rejected revolution: "We reject every self-defense in a revolutionary sense." The Cardinal asked the men to pray for Father Mayer but to refrain from any public demonstration which might lead to violence. In Father Mayer's case it is again the theme: "We must obey God rather than men," but there is certainly nothing suggesting revolution.

In the background of this case, and indeed of the entire history of the Church's resistance to Nazism, hovered always the fear that the actions of the priests and bishops might become liable to the charge of "political Catholicism." The Cardinal denied it with reference to Father Mayer; again in one of his most vehement sermons, February 13, 1938,[49] he went out of his way to refute the charge. The term was no longer being given proper definition or limitation:

> In our state every police official has the right to decide whether something is political or just religious Catholicism. But for the Holy Father and the German bishops one will not recognize the right to judge whether something belongs to religious Catholicism and where political Catholicism begins. To promulgate laws about the moral order, truth and justice, love and fidelity, is religious and not political Catholicism. To put forth and explain the teaching and fundamental laws of the Church is also, according to the Concordat, religious and not political Catholicism. To reject lies and to stand up for truth on the Pope's Sunday—to raise the shield against the calumny directed against the pope is religious, not political Catholicism.

Frequently the Cardinal reminded his priests not to become involved in political questions, and in a letter to Religious Superiors in 1943[50] the same admonition is repeated:

> In political conversations will you never take part. To questions of that kind will you say calmly and decidedly—we are so busy from morning till night with the care of the sick who have been entrusted to us that we have no time for political conversations.

From 1937 to 1942 there is very little documentary evidence

---

[49] Mimeo. copy. Sermon on Pope's Sunday at St. Michael's.

[50] Mimeo. copy. October 9, 1943.

of the Church's attitude. Governmental restriction is obvious in the increasing infrequency with which the diocesan organs were published. A study of the Munich *Amtsblatt* revealed that there was no issue at all from April 7 to June 1 in 1937 (usually it was issued weekly or bi-weekly), very few issues in the following years—containing mostly routine announcements—and that it ceased altogether from March to October 1945. This makes it very difficult to ascertain episcopal "resistance" during the war years.

The only statement concerning the beginning of World War II which appeared in the Munich *Amtsblatt* was that of September 7, 1939.[51]

> The fatherland has entered into a decisive hour of fate. The faithful are called to be adequate to the seriousness of the time, to raise up their hands trustfully to God, the Governor of all destinies, that He will protect the people and the fatherland in need and in danger, that He will stand by their responsible leaders in these hours of vital decisions, that He will strengthen our soldiers and accompany them on their difficult way in battle, that He will uphold the families which are in great anxiety about their relatives and bread-winners, that He will lend His power and help to all who are deeply affected by the hard aftermath of war.
> In such hard times, where all become one, it is imperative that each one in the place where he is stationed fulfill his religious, patriotic, and civil duty and that each one stand at the side of the other in a spirit of close Christian brotherly love and true solidarity.

Unfortunately, the very important question of the German hierarchy's judgment on the justness or unjustness of Hitler's wars cannot be answered from the available documents. It would not be sound, however, to argue from their silence to the conclusion that they supported Hitler's foreign policy (including the war). Here would certainly be a topic readily considered more "political" than "religious" and one, therefore, on which the clergy would have maintained a discreet silence.

---

[51] *Amtsblatt* No. 14 (1939), September 7, 1939, pp. 139-140. Signed by Buchwiester, Gen. Vicar of the Archdiocese.

It is interesting to note, on the other hand, that the Vatican was willing to act as mediator for a peace to be made between England and the German opposition to Hitler in November, 1939.[52] The first condition laid down in the proposed terms was: "The removal of Hitler and the Nazi regime." This can be accepted as tacit approval for an anti-Nazi revolution and, I think, as an insinuation that Hitler was responsible for the war. It seems to be the only approval of the resistance by Church authorities and is, therefore, of great significance.

That the war did not stop the bishops from protesting the state's continued interference with the Church is shown in the sermon given by Cardinal von Faulhaber on March 8, 1942: "Give to the state what is the state's and to the church what is the church's."[53] This statement, he said, is the equivalent in contemporary times of the gospel's: "Render to Caesar that which is Caesar's and to God that which is God's." He denounced once more the efforts of the state to separate German Catholics from Rome by establishing a national church—Christ gave primacy to Peter, not to Pilate; and Peter went to Rome, not to Berlin! He spoke defiantly of the hypocrisy of those who send annual good wishes to the pope, keep an ambassador at the Vatican, and express friendship in a Concordat—and then attack the pope so violently in the German press. The Cardinal reasserted the belief that the authority of the state comes from God and must be respected—but there is a limit: "We are ready to join with civil authority and bring our faith thereto for the common good of the community. We are not willing to become traitors to our Church."

Most of the Cardinal's sermons for 1943-45 which could be located were geared, quite naturally, to the situation caused by the increased tempo of the war.[54] He dealt with the threat of death under which all were living daily, of the need for per-

[52] Cf. *supra*, pp. 112-113. But more recent information from Father Robert Leiber states that point 4 given on p. 113 was not among the terms submitted to him for Pius XII.

[53] Mimeo. copy. Sermon in St. Michael's for Pope's Sunday.

[54] Since these were probably not all reproduced and since no systematic collection of them has yet been undertaken, one can only make a tentative evaluation here based on nineteen sermons that could be located.

fect contrition and steadfastness so as not to give way to the thought of suicide as a means out of the chaos. There were still pointed references to the heathen concept of morality which was being promoted by "men in high places" and to the wrong notions of heroism. In a sermon at a pontifical requiem for victims of an air attack in 1944—when all Nazi propaganda was forcefully turned against the Allied forces carrying out the attacks—the Cardinal courageously insisted that the people must recognize their own guilt, for the sins of each individual were responsible for the frightful times.

Meanwhile, in 1944, a more violent type of resistance was being planned by the group known as the "men of July 20th." It has been well established that these men who attempted to kill Hitler on July 20, 1944 were motivated by religious, patriotic, and humanistic ideals and by the hope that by their last desperate attempt to overthrow the Nazis they might redeem, at least in part, the German fatherland and the whole Christian tradition of their nation. Did they receive support from the Church and its hierarchy, either officially or unofficially, individually or collectively?

The official report on the trials of the men involved in the *attentat* of July 20 [55] hints at a connection between Bishop von Preysing and the man who led the attack, Colonel-General Claus von Stauffenberg, as well as between Cardinal von Faulhaber and an outstanding leader of the resistance for the whole Hitler period, Carl Goerdeler. The Kreisau circle, members of which were involved in the plot, contained two Jesuits—Fathers Delp and Roesch, and in the trials this "subversive" influence was given great prominence, particularly in the case of Helmuth von Moltke. And yet, when the evidence is examined, the case linking the churchmen with the revolutionary attempt falls apart.

The Kreisau circle itself was not established for revolutionary purposes but rather for discussions concerning a Christian

[55] "Reichsicherheitshauptamt Bericht über den 20 Juli." This is the study made by the Reich Security Office for Martin Borman, aide to Hitler. It is now in the Institut für Zeit Geschichte in München and a micro-filmed copy is with the U.S. Department of the Army in Washington.

political and social order. Naturally, it presupposed the end of the Nazi regime before its program could become a reality of the political order, but Moltke specifically denied collaboration with those who favored using violence against Hitler. He was glad that the judge realized this and separated him (together with Delp and Eugen [Gerstenmaier]) from Haubach and Steltzer, recognizing that they "had never had any intention of doing anything concrete. . . ."[56] Even by the court it was stated that this case "differs completely from all others in that during the discussion there was question neither of violence nor of any organization."[57]

It was Moltke who had asked Father Roesch, Provincial of the Jesuits in Bavaria, to assign someone to attend the discussions at Kreisau—a priest who was also a sociologist. To this post went Father Alfred Delp, formerly editor of *Stimmen der Zeit*. Those who knew Father Delp closely remain quite convinced that he knew nothing of the planned *attentat* and that had he known of it he would not have approved of it. We have his own testimony that he was not involved; in his diary January 1, 1945 in prison he wrote: "I am held prisoner here by things I have neither done nor known about."[58] Again, in a letter to his fellow Jesuits on February 2, 1945 (the day he was hanged) he wrote:

> The actual reason for my sentence is that I am and remain a Jesuit. It was not possible to establish any connection with the event of July 20. Neither was the charge of a tie to Stauffenberg upheld.[59]

Delp, it is true, had had a meeting with Stauffenberg early in 1944, but it is reported that the General was furious at the imprudence of Delp in coming to see him and that there was certainly no communication between them regarding the proposed *attentat*. There is no reason to doubt Father Delp's word

---

[56] Letter from von Moltke to his wife, January 11, 1945 in Gollwitzer, Kuhn, and Schneider (eds.) *Dying We Live* (London: Fontana Books, 1958), p. 119.

[57] *Idem.*

[58] *Ibid.*, p. 127.

[59] *Ibid.*, p. 140.

that the first he knew of it was when he was awakened by the news on the morning of July 21st, but some might question his disapproval of it. One author appears to do so when he states that Father Delp reacted to the news by saying: "That, I would never have thought him capable of . . ." and goes on to say that Delp seemed somewhat hurt because he had not been let in on the plans.[60] Yet, this remark finds no corroboration in Delp's own writings after his imprisonment.

As regards the other Jesuit connected with the Kreisau circle, Father Roesch, Provincial of Bavaria, there is even less reason for thinking him sympathetic to the plot of July 20th. He did enter into some of the discussions in Kreisau, travelling there in disguise as a railway worker when it became impossible for priests to travel without a special pass. But those who know him well say that even today he remains unconvinced that the attempted tyrannicide was morally justifiable and denies that he and Father Delp had any knowledge of it. Would he have approved of a revolution without the extreme step of tyrannicide? We do not know, but in 1944 such a possibility was purely academic; the situation was such that no lesser action had any chance of success.

Another priest from the archdiocese of Munich, Chaplain Hermann Wehrle, was called before the People's Court during the trials of the July 20th men. It was he who had been consulted by Major Leonrod, a young officer on Colonel Count Stauffenberg's staff, as to whether or not one might keep secret the knowledge concerning a plot to kill a tyrant. While he agreed that one need not reveal knowledge of the plot, he cautioned Leonrod not to take an active part in it.[61]

What of the bishops mentioned in the RSHA report—von Faulhaber and von Preysing? While it is true that Goerdeler had visited Cardinal von Faulhaber there is no record of their conversation, and since Goerdeler was not an active participant in the 20 July *attentat*, there is no pertinent inference to be drawn from this visit. One wonders, however, if the Cardinal

---

[60] Franz von Tattelbach, "Das entscheidende Gesprach. Zum 10 Todestag P. Alfred Delp," *Stimmen der Zeit.* 80 (1954-55) p. 323.

[61] RSHA report, August 30, 1944, MS 105/24.

was friendly toward the man designated by many as the "heart" of the Resistance movement—a man who had been agitating for "action" against the Hitler regime since 1933. Two close colleagues of the Cardinal insist that he was much too prudent to have committed to writing his thoughts on this dangerous topic; they are certain moreover that he could not have known of the *attentat*—except perhaps as a matter of confession—and that he would not have approved of it; it was "political murder," for while the men had the right goal, they used the wrong means. Yet, one of these same prelates, when asked about the Cardinal's reaction to the news that an attempt had been made to kill Hitler July 20th, said that they had all (including the Cardinal) been "filled with joy." He added that one could gather their attitude also from the fact that requiem Masses had been offered for the victims of the trials that followed. And in 1946 in his Lenten Pastoral, Cardinal von Faulhaber praised the heroism of those who fought against the Hitler tyranny and used as an illustration of such heroism a letter of September 14, 1944 in which a priest from Munich wrote to him: "What a beautiful day—the exaltation of the Cross! I am condemned to death for being the confessor of a man who participated in the *attentat*."[62] How can the men of July 20th be praised for their heroism if what they attempted was "murder"?

This same bewildering ambiguity can be noted in the attitude of the bishop of Berlin, Cardinal von Preysing. Again, the RSHA report mentions a visit which von Stauffenberg paid to the bishop and the report is confirmed by a letter from the late Cardinal to the mother of von Stauffenberg, written in 1949.[63] In this letter, the Cardinal spoke of the visit, adding that as von Stauffenberg left, he had blessed him but not what he was about to do.

Since the end of the war certain theologians, foremost among them Father Pribilla, S.J., have re-examined the question of

[62] *Amtsblatt* No. 2 (1946) Beilage, p. 4.

[63] This letter was not available to the writer but was described by the brother of von Stauffenberg, Professor Alexander Graf Schenk von Stauffenberg in an interview June 14, 1960.

the right of revolution and present a point of view which accepts it as necessary under certain conditions—such as those which existed in Nazi Germany. The urgency of deep study of this problem by our theologians is underscored by Father Pribilla when he writes:

> In view of the frightful seriousness of that day [July 20] which was reddened with the blood of the best and most select of our people, it can only be right if we, in memory of the many victims of the German Resistance, ask ourselves earnestly whether we have rightly recognized and fought actively enough against the germs of the disaster which came to us in the past in order to prevent a new disaster.[64]

The history of the Resistance in Germany makes it clear that the Catholic bishops offered straightforward and courageous opposition to the ideology and tactics of the Nazis, but it also attests to the fact that they offered no encouragement or support to any plans for a revolution by which the Nazis would have been removed from power. Revolution was specifically rejected and denounced by them on several occasions. Yet, the men of July 20th have been praised by a recent theologian as "the best and most select of our people." Are we to conclude then that in such a case the individual citizen must act without the approval—and indeed seemingly with the disapproval—of the Church; that what is objectively and a priori to be condemned is subjectively and a posteriori approved and praised?

At this point the historian must give way to the moral theologian, but in any consideration of the question the facts of the German Resistance are of utmost importance.

---

[64] Max Pribilla, S.J. "Zum 20 Juli 1944: Erkenntnis und Bekenntnis," *Stimmen der Zeit* 154 (1954), p. 242.

BIBLIOGRAPHY

BIBLIOGRAPHICAL AIDS

Braubach, Max. *Der Weg zum 20. Juli 1944; Ein Forschungsbericht.* herausgeben Leo Brandt. Köln: Westdeutscher Verlag, 1953. A critical review of the literature of the Resistance Movement.

Books on Persecution, Terror and Resistance in Nazi Germany. London: Wiener Library, 1953.

Federal Records of World War II. Washington, D. C.: Government Printing Office, 1950. 2 vols. A topical index of source material which gives the present location of each category of documents.

Guide to Captured German Records in the Custody of the Department of the Army Agencies in Washington, D. C., and Vicinity. Washington: Government Printing Office, 1950.

PRIMARY SOURCES

Documents

UNPUBLISHED

Department of the Army:

Documents and affidavits submitted to the Nuremberg Tribunals.

Film of the Trials before the People's Court of those involved in the plot of July 20, 1944. Captured from the Nazis and reassembled into one film by the Office of Strategic Services.

Preliminary interrogations of prisoners and witnesses at Nuremberg.

"Reichsicherheitshauptamt Bericht über den 20 Juli." This is the study made by the Reich Security Office for Martin Borman, aide to Hitler, on the background of the July 20th plot. Used with the necessary caution in view of its origin, it is helpful in corroborating the stories of the various participants.

Transcript of the trials of War Criminals before the Nuremberg Tribunal. This was of particular value in studying the case of Ernst von Weizsäcker, since only portions of the trial appear in the printed version.

Department of State:

"Civil Affairs Guide." A War Department pamphlet on the policy to be followed regarding the revival of old political parties in Germany. No. 31-116 of July 1944. OSS, R&A 1655.1.

"Civil Affairs Handbook: Germany." Compiled July-September 1944. Library of Department of State, HC 58, U5G4.

"Changes in the Reich Government" OSS, R&A 1130; August 26, 1943.

Von Faulhaber, Michael Cardinal, Sermon on December 31, 1941. 862.404/352.

"The Free German Manifesto and the German People." OSS, R&A 1033. August 6, 1943.
Von Galen, Bishop Clement A., Communications with Reich Minister Dr. Lammers forwarded to the Secretary of State. FW 740.0011 E w/0 2641.
"The German Communist Party." OSS, R&A 1550. July 10, 1944.
"The German Political Emigration." OSS, R&A 1568. December 3, 1943.

Germany: Reports from:
Berlin to Washington, February 28, 1933. 862.00/2916.
Berlin to Washington, March 24, 1934. 860.00/3418.
Berlin to Washington, March 29, 1934. 860.00/3419.
Berlin to Washington, April 13, 1934. 860.00/3420.
Berlin to Washington, April 27, 1934. 860.00/3422.
Berlin to Washington, May 2, 1934. 862.00/3252.
Berlin to Washington, September 23, 1935. 862.00/3558.
Berlin to Washington, April 1, 1936. Letter from American Ambassador to President Roosevelt. No serial number.
Berlin to Washington, November 28, 1936. 762.00/140.
Leipzig to Washington, January 11, 1937. 862.00/3640.
Leipzig to Washington, May 28, 1937. 033.6211.
Berlin to Washington, January 27, 1938. 862.002/320.
Berlin to Washington, April 13, 1939. 740.00/794.
Berlin to Washington, September 28, 1939. 862.00/3894.
Berlin to Washington, May 10, 1940. 740.0011/2778.
Berlin to Washington, November 8, 1940. 862.00/3970.
Berlin to Washington, February 17, 1941. 862.00/3991.
Berlin to Washington, February 24, 1941. 862.00/3992.
Berlin to Washington, April 1, 1941. 862.00/4001.
Berlin to Washington, November 17, 1941. 862.021/81.
"Handbook on National Socialist Germany," OSS, R&A 376 and 376-A. Dept. of State Library, 914.3, BX9656.
Letter from the former Consul General in Leipzig to the Secretary of State. August 5, 1944. 862.20200.
Letter from the Milwaukee Council of Churches to the Secretary of State. May 2, 1938. 862.404/263.
Letter from Dr. Henry Smith Leiper, General Secretary of the World Council of Churches to the Assistant Secretary of State. April 6, 1939. 862.00/3842.
Memorandum from the Director of the Office of Strategic Services to the Secretary of State, August 1, 1944. 862.01/8-144.
Memorandum from the Division of Commercial Affairs (Dept. of State) to the Foreign Activity Correlation Office (Dept. of State) re: Carl Goerdeler. January 13, 1943. 862.20200.
Memorandum of a conversation of the Chief of the European Desk with Mr. Federico Stallforth. August 19, 1940. 740.0011; 1939/6061.

Memorandum of a conversation of the Assistant Secretary of State with Mr. Adam von Trott zu Solz. November 20, 1939. 862.20211 Von T/3.

Memorandum of a conversation of the Assistant Secretary of State with Mr. Adam von Trott zu Solz. December 8, 1939. 862.20211 Von T/7.

Monthly Report of the Control Commission for Germany (British Element). Vol. 5, No. 6 (June 1950). J351, R377.

Mooney Report to President Roosevelt. March 11, 1940. No serial number.

"Nazi Master Plan: Annex # 4, The Persecution of the Christian Churches." OSS, R&A 3114.4.

Pastoral Letter of the German Bishops, 1942. May 4, 1942. 862.404/362.

Poole, De Witt C. Interrogations by a special State Dept. Interrogation Mission. No serial number.

"Pre-Fascist Groups in Germany 1918-1933." OSS, R&A 2789.

Report on Religious Affairs by the Office of Military Government for Germany: Education and Religious Affairs Branch. August 1946. 200, AC2791R.

"The Scope and Activities of the National Socialist Party in the German Reich." OSS, R&A 1298. 329.43, AF6161.

Sweden: Reports from:

Stockholm to Washington, November 10, 1942, 862.00/4339.
Stockholm to Washington, June 28, 1943. 740.0011; 1939/29953.
Stockholm to Washington, May 22, 1944. 862.01/639.
Stockholm to Washington, June 26, 1944. 103.918/6-2644.
Stockholm to Washington, August 31, 1944. 862.01/8-3144.
Stockholm to Washington, September 2, 1944. 862.01/9244.
Stockholm to Washington, September 8, 1944. 862.00/9-844.
Stockholm to Washington, September 12, 1944. 740.00119 EW/9-1244.
Stockholm to Washington, September 14, 1944. 862.01/9-1444.
Stockholm to Washington, September 21, 1944. 811.91258/9-2144.
Stockholm to Washington, October 2, 1944. 103.918/10-244.
Stockholm to Washington, October 20, 1944. 858.00/10-2044.
Stockholm to Washington, November 21, 1944. 862.00/11-2144.

Switzerland: Reports from:

Zurich to Washington, January 13, 1941. 862.00/3982.
Bern to Washington, December 5, 1942. 862.20200.
Bern to Washington, January 7, 1943. 862.20200.
Bern to Washington, April 24, 1943. 740.0011; 1939/29150.
Bern to Washington, August 13, 1943. 701.6264/16.
Bern to Washington, September 10, 1944. 862.01/9-1044.
Bern to Washington, October 6, 1944. 862.20254/10-644.

Trott zu Solz, Adam, "Memorandum." November 14, 1939. 862.20211 Von T/1.

"The Underground Movement in Germany." OSS, R&A 992, September 27, 1943. 323.243; AF6025S.

Welles, Sumner. Report of his trip to Germany. 1940. No serial number.

Miscellaneous Reports:

Copenhagen to Washington, April 5, 1930. 701.6260 h/10.
Rome to Washington, November 2, 1932. 701.6265/8.
Paris to Washington, November 23, 1937. 123 Bullitt, Wm. C./382.
Paris to Washington, March 25, 1939. 862.00/3839.
London to Washington, August 21, 1939. 7600.62/906.
Washington to Berlin, December 8, 1939. 862.20211 Von T/8.
Bucharest to Washington, June 6, 1941. 740.0011; 1939/11777.
Vichy to Washington, January 15, 1942. 862.00/4224.
Madrid to Washington, September 17, 1943. 862.01/424.
San Sebastian to Washington, August 27, 1944. 862.01/8-2744.
London to Washington, December 30, 1944. 862.00/12-3044.

Office of Strategic Services:

United States Strategic Bombing Survey, Topical Report # 12: "The Role of the Church," by Dr. Newcomb. OSS 64br (15).

United States Strategic Bombing Survey, "The Size and Composition of the Anti-Nazi Opposition in Germany." OSS 64bt (8).

Carl Goerdeler. Letter to Captain Wiedermann, Adjutant to Hitler. April 24, 1938. Coordinator of Information 6374.

———. Report to Wiedermann on his trip to France, August 1937. COI 6375.

———. Report to Wiedermann on his trip to Belgium, June 1937. COI 6376.

———. Report to Wiedermann on his trip to England, July 1937. COI 6377.

———. Report to Wiedermann on his trip to Canada, Sept. 1937. COI 6378.

———. Report to Wiedermann on his trip to United States, January 1938. COI 6379.

Pastoral of the German Bishops, March 1942, IDS 13, July 20, 1942. 19020.

IDS Report 32, August 20, 1942. 20.67.

Comments on Pastoral letters, OSS report, 22795, Oct. 15, 1942.

Zurich report on Pastoral, Dec. 7, 1942. OSS 33402.

Memorandum of conversation of Lithgow Osborne with T. H. McKittrick, president of the Bank of International Settlements at Basle. For Colonel Wm. Donovan, Chief of OSS, December 14, 1942. OSS 25903.

Comments on Pastoral letters, IDS 133, February 11, 1943. 16110.

Notes on Archbishop Groeber, IDS 135, February 12, 1943. 16168.

Lenten Pastoral of Archbishop Frings and Jaeger, IDS 250, May 12, 1943. 41640.

Pastoral of Bishop von Galen, May 1943. IDS 408, July 24, 1943. 46468.

Report on Father Friedrich Muckermann, S. J., IDS 292, June 8, 1943. 36916.

Report on activities of Albrecht von Kessel. L-48531.

" Study: Morale and Its Maintenance in the German Navy," Series I, Part I, Sect. I. June 1, 1943. OSS 27221.

P/W Interrogation, April 21, 1945. 128182.

PUBLISHED

Bischöfliches Ordinariat Berlin (ed.). *Dokumente.* Berlin: Morus Verlag, 1946. This contains the letters and other episcopal announcements of the Bishop of Berlin for the years 1937-1942.

Carlyle, Margaret (ed.). *Documents on International Affairs 1939-1946. Vol. II.* New York: Oxford University Press, 1954.

Documents on British Foreign Policy 1919-39. Ed. E. L. Woodward and Rohan Butler. London: H.M. Stationery Office. Third Series, vols. II (1949) and VI (1953).

Documents on German Foreign Policy 1918-45. Washington, D. C.: Government Printing Office, 1949.

Faulhaber, Michael Cardinal. " Letter to Dr. Gurtner, Reichs Minister of Justice." *Thought,* XX (1945), 754-759. A strong protest against Euthanasia laws.

Hermelink, Heinrich (ed.). *Kirche im Kampf: Dokumente des Widerstands und des Aufbaus in der evangelischen Kirche Deutschlands von 1933 bis 1945.* Tübingen: R. Wunderlich, 1950.

Hofmann, Dr. Konrad (ed.). *Zeugnis und Kampf des deutschen Episkopats.* Freiburg im Breisgau: Herder, 1946.

Langsam, Walter Consuelo (ed.). *Documents and Readings in the History of Europe Since 1918.* New York: Lippincott Co., 1951.

Leo XIII, Pope. *Diuturnum.*

———. *Immortale Dei.*

———. *Libertas Humana.*

———. *Sapientiae Christianae.*

Parliamentary Debates. House of Commons. Official Reports. Great Britain. Fifth Series. London: H. M. Stationery Office, 1918-1938.

Parliamentary Debates. House of Lords. Official Reports. Great Britain. Fifth Series. London: H. M. Stationery Office, 1918-1938.

Pius XI, Pope. *Acerba Animi.*

———. *Dilectissima nobis.*

———. *Divini Redemptoris.*

———. *Firmissimam constantiam.*

———. *Mit brennender Sorge.*

Pius XII, Pope. "Address to the Sixth International Congress on Penal Law," October 3, 1953.

———. " International Community and Religious Tolerance," December 6, 1953.

———. *Summi Pontificatus.*

Pollock, James F. " Documents on the Nazi Government of Germany," in Rappard et al. *Source Book on European Governments.* New York: D. Van Nostrand Co., 1937.

Pollock, James and Henemen, Harlow J. *The Hitler Decrees.* Ann Arbor, Mich.: George Wahr, 1934.

Portmann, Heinrich. *Dokumente um den Bischof von Münster.* Münster: Verlag Aschenforff, 1948.

Trial of the Major War Criminals Before the International Military Tribunal. 42 vols. Nuremberg: Secretariat of the IMT, 1947-49.

Trials of War Criminals Before the Nuernberg Military Tribunal. 15 vols. Washington, D. C.: Government Printing Office, 1949-53.

Memoirs. Diaries. Sermons. Letters.

UNPUBLISHED.

Von Kessel, Albrecht, "Verborgene Saat, Das 'Andere' Deutschland." The unpublished diary of one of the young Resisters in the German Foreign Office. Covers the period 1933-1944, but was written in 1944-45, so it is a memoir rather than a diary. Excellent source for the spirit of the movement and for an evaluation of the personalities involved.

Mueller, Josef. "Report on conversations at the Vatican and in Rome between November 6th and 12th, 1939." Unpublished typescript made available to the writer by Gen. H. von Witzleben. While this section does not contain the complete story of the attempt to secure British terms through the Vatican, it does record conversations among the leading participants which substantiate the story as recorded by Mr. J. W. Wheeler-Bennett and referred to by Ulrich von Hassell.

PUBLISHED.

Andreas-Friedrich, Ruth. *Berlin Underground 1938-45.* Trans. Barrows Mussey. New York: H. Holt & Co., 1947. A journalistic account of the "Uncle Emil" resistance circle in Berlin. Pseudonyms are used and there is no documentation, but as a first hand account it is interesting and colorful.

[Bell, George], Bishop of Chichester. "The Background of the Hitler Plot," *Contemporary Review* 168 (October 1945), 203-208. Personal account of the Bishop of Chichester's meeting with Pastor Bonhoeffer in the spring of 1942.

Bonhoeffer, Dietrich. *Letters and Papers from Prison.* Ed. Eberhard Bethge. Trans. Reginald H. Fuller. London: SCM Press, 1953. These personal writings of one of the leading churchmen involved in the Resistance Movement are of value in attempting an estimate of the religious attitude of the group.

Bryans, J. Lonsdale. *Blind Victory.* London: Skeffington and Son, 1951. An account of the negotiations carried on with Ulrich von Hassell. Bryans is the "Mr. X" of the von Hassell story, and the two accounts complement each other.

Delp, Alfred, S. J. *Im Angesicht des Todes*, vol. II of *Christ und Gegenwart.* Frankfurt am Main: J. Knecht, 1947. Contains the reflections of

Father Delp during his stay in prison awaiting trial and execution after the failure of the plot of July 20, 1944.

Von Faulhaber, Michael Cardinal. *Judaism, Christianity, and Germany.* Trans. Rev. George D. Smith. New York: The Macmillan Co., 1954. These are the sermons delivered by the Cardinal against the anti-semitic teaching of the Nazis.

Gisevius, Hans Bernd. *To the Bitter End.* Trans. Richard and Clara Winston. Boston: Houghton Mifflin Co., 1947. An essential first-hand account of the Resistance Movement by one of the members of the Beck-Goerdeler group. There are however, notable errors of fact and a tendency to underestimate the contributions of other groups to the movement as a whole.

Goerdeler, Carl Friedrich. *Goerdelers politisches Testament.* herausgeben von Friedrich Krause. New York: F. Krause Verlag, 1945. This summary of Goerdeler's ideas was written by him when he was in the United States in 1937. He left it with a friend to be published after his death. The introduction contains a short biography of Goerdeler.

Von Guttenberg, Elizabeth. *Holding the Stirrup.* New York: Duell, Sloan, and Pearce, 1952. The work of the Resistance Movement as seen through the eyes of the wife of one of the members. As a relative of Claus von Stauffenberg she also gives valuable insights into his character.

Halder, Franz. *Diary, August 14, 1939-September 24, 1942.* Washington, D. C.: Infantry Journal, 1950. 7 vols. The main value of this daily record kept by the Chief of the General Staff lies in the field of operational tactics, but it also sheds light on the personal character of General Halder.

Von Hassell, Ulrich. *The Von Hassell Diaries 1938-44.* New York: Doubleday and Co., Inc., 1947. One of the most valuable sources on the topic. The observations of von Hassell are usually objective and penetrating, and material on the Resistance is set in the framework of contemporary events. Unfortunately some of the valuable notes and appendices in the German edition have been omitted in the translation.

———. *Vom Andern Deutschland.* Zurich: Atlantis Verlag, 1946. The German original of the above.

Kordt, Erich. *Nicht aus den Akten.* Stuttgart: Union Deutsche Verlagsgesellschaft, 1950. Particularly useful for the pre-Munich attempts of the German Resistance to secure British support. Kordt repeats here much that he had given as testimony in the von Weizsäcker trial. On the whole, he agrees with the accounts by the other conspirators. Since he was sent to the Orient in 1941 it is no use for the later conspiracy.

Von Moltke, Helmuth James. *Letzte Briefe aus dem Gefängnis Tegel.* Berlin: K. H. Henssel, 1951. Although parts of this account had been published in the June 1946 *Round Table* and as *A German of the Resistance* (Johannesburg: Central News Agency, 1947), the German work is the more definitive one. Von Moltke's own account of his work as a member of the Resistance and of his trial before the People's Court is the best available source on the Kreisau circle and its spirit.

Niemoeller, Martin. *The Gestapo Defied—Last Twenty-Eight Sermons.* London: W. Hodge and Co., 1942. Niemoeller's sermons, while anti-Nazi in tone, promote the idea of passive rather than active resistance.

Schacht, Hjalmar. *Account Settled.* Trans. Edward Fitzgerald. London: G. Weidenfeld and Nicolson, 1949. Although Schacht assigns himself a leading role in the Resistance Movement, his story remains unconvincing if one is seeking a sincere and consistent opposition based on ethical reasons.

Von Schlabrendorff, Fabian. *They Almost Killed Hitler.* Ed. Gero v.S. Gaevernitz. New York: The Macmillan Co., 1947. One of the officers who survived the July 20 affair tells his version of the preparations for it. There is no effort to magnify his own role in it, and the story is told objectively and well. There is, unfortunately, no documentation so that it is difficult to evaluate some of his statements.

Steltzer, Theodor. *Von deutscher Politik: Documente, Aufsätze und Vorträge.* herausgeben Friedrich Minssen. Frankfurt am Main: J. Knecht, 1949. This brief study by a member of the Kreisau circle is extremely helpful. It contains the texts of the programs agreed to for post-war Germany by that particular group.

Thomas, General Georg. "Gedanken und Ereignisse," *Schweizer Monatshefte* 25 Jahrg. Heft 9 (December 1945), 537-559. This short memoir was written by General Thomas on July 20, 1945 when he was freed from prison. In it he reviews the Resistance Movement and especially his own attempt in 1939 to convince the Army High Command of the folly of war.

Von Weizsäcker, Ernst. *Memoirs.* Trans. John Andrews. Chicago: H. Regnery, 1951. The emphasis here, as at von Weizsäcker's trial, is not on Resistance but on his whole life's dedication to the preservation of peace. Yet there are many useful spots in his autobiography which help us to understand his position and reveal the principles which guided him.

Letters to the Author:

Bryans, J. Lonsdale. November 15, 1954.

Ford, Franklin. January 10, 1954.

Graham, Robert A. S. J. January 22, 1954.

Ritter, Dr. Gerhard. December 29, 1953.

Thompson, Dorothy. December 23, 1953.

Von Witzleben, Generalmajor a.D. H. March 5, March 18, and July 13, 1954.

Personal interviews:

Dulles, Allen. March 6, 1954.

Von Kessel, Albrecht. April 5, 1954.

Murray, John Courtney, S. J. November 20, 1954.

Von Witzleben, Generalmajor a.D. H. February 22, 1954.

Stallforth, Federico. January 19, 1955.

SECONDARY SOURCES

Books

Abshagen, Karl Heinz. *Canaris: Patriot und Weltbürger.* Stuttgart: Union Deutsche Verlagsgesellschaft, 1949. Relied on heavily by Colvin in his work on Canaris, but leaves room still for a definitive work on the former head of ABWEHR.

Allen, J. W. *A History of Political Thought in the Sixteenth Century.* London: Methuen & Co., 1928.

Almond, Gabriel Abraham (ed.). *The Struggle for Democracy in Germany.* Chapel Hill: University of North Carolina Press, 1949.

Alsop, Stewart and Thomas Braden. *Sub Rosa:The OSS and American Espionage.* New York: Reynal and Hitchcock, 1946. A popularly written account of the activities of the Office of Strategic Services. Useful information regarding the acquisition of intelligence from members of the German Resistance.

American Association for a Democratic Germany. *They Fought Hitler First.* New York: 1945. A small pamphlet containing statistics on concentration camps in Germany.

Bayles, William D. *Seven Were Hanged.* London: Victor Gollencz, 1945. A brief account of the Scholl group at the University of Munich. The first names of some of the participants—e. g., "Adrian" Probst and "Maria" Scholl do not agree with those given by Inge Scholl in her account, but otherwise the story seems accurate.

Barth, Karl. *The Church and the Political Problem of Our Day.* New York: C. Scribner's Sons, 1939.

Bell, George. *The Church and Humanity (1939-1946).* New York: Longmans, Green and Co., 1946.

———. *Germany and the Hitlerite State.* London: Victor Gollancz, Ltd., 1944.

Boehm, Eric H. *We Survived.* New Haven: Yale University Press, 1949.

Boesmiller, Franziska. *P. Rupert Mayer, S. J.* München: Verlag Schnell & Steiner, 1946.

Buxton, Mrs. Dorothy (ed.). *I Was in Prison: Letters from German Pastors.* London: Student Christian Movement, 1939. Interesting for the strong current of passivity in the face of persecution.

Calvin, John. *Institutes of the Christian Religion.* Trans. John Allen. Phila.: Presbyterian Board of Christian Education, 1936. 2 vols.

———. *Commentaries on the Epistle of Paul the Apostle to the Romans.* Trans. and ed. Rev. John Owen. Grand Rapids, Mich.. Wm. B. Eerdman's Publishing Co., 1948.

Churchill, Winston. *The Gathering Storm.* Vol. I of *The Second World War.* Boston: Houghton Mifflin Co., 1948.

Colvin, Ian G. *Master Spy.* New York: McGraw-Hill, 1952. The journalistic style and lack of documentation make it difficult to assess the validity of several of Mr. Colvin's statements. His use of material is often misleading, and in some cases quotation out of context actually changes the meaning.

Copleston, Frederick, S. J. *A History of Philosophy.* Westminster, Md.: The Newman Press, 1933, 3 vols.

Cronin, Michael. *The Science of Ethics.* 2nd ed. New York: Benziger Brothers, 1922.

Deuel, Wallace R. *People Under Hitler.* New York: Harcourt, Brace & Co., 1942.

Dictionnaire de théologie Catholique. Ed. A. Vacant, E. Mangenot, E. Armann, et al. Paris: Libraire Letouzey et Ane. 1930-1950.

Dodd, William. *Ambassador Dodd's Diary 1933-1938.* Ed. Wm. Dodd, Jr. and Martha Dodd. New York: Harcourt, Brace and Co., 1941.

Douglass, Paul F. *God Among the Germans.* Phila.: University of Pa. Press, 1935.

Drummond, Andrew. *German Protestantism Since Luther.* London: Epworth Press, 1951.

Dulles, Allen. *Germany's Underground.* New York: The Macmillan Co., 1947. A sympathetic study of the German Resistance by the OSS representative in Berne who was in close touch with the members of it. It verifies from the Allied point of view the claims of the Resistance Movement concerning the passing of intelligence, etc. Dulles feels that the lack of support given the movement was a mistake in Allied policy. Because his main informant was Hans Gisevius, his picture of the movement in some instances is one-sided.

Duncan-Jones, Arthur. *The Struggle for Religious Freedom in Germany.* London: V. Gollancz, Ltd., 1938. Useful for the many documents appended to the text.

Erb, Alfons. *Bernhard Lichtenberg.* Berlin: Morus-Verlag, 1946. A biography of Msgr. Lichtenberg, pastor of St. Hedwig's in Berlin, where services were held in protest against the anti-Semitic outrages of the Nazis.

Fabricius, Cajus. *Positive Christianity in the Third Reich.* Dresden: H. Pueschel, 1937. An interesting example of the extremity to which the "German Christians" went in their attempt to reconcile Nazism with Christianity.

Feiling, Keith. *The Life of Neville Chamberlain.* London: Macmillan & Co., 1946.

Foerster, Wolfgang. *Generaloberst Ludwig Beck.* München: Isar Verlag, 1953. The only biographical study as yet published of the former Chief of Staff who became the leader of the German Resistance. The larger part of the work is made up of the various memoranda drawn up by Beck, and for this reason is of great value.

François-Poncet, André. *The Fateful Years: Memoirs of the French Ambassador in Berlin 1931-38.* New York: Harcourt Brace, 1949.

Fraenkel, Ernst. *The Dual State.* New York: Oxford University Press,

1941. A study of the disintegration of the traditional law-enforcing bodies in Germany.

Glenn, Paul J. *Ethics.* St. Louis, Mo.: B. Herder Book Co., 1951.

Goerlitz, Walter. *History of the German General Staff 1657-1945.* Trans. Brian Battershaw. New York: Praeger, 1953.

Gurian, Waldemar. *Hitler and the Christians.* Trans. E. F. Peeler. New York: Sheed and Ward, 1936.

Haecker, Theodor. *Journal in the Night.* Trans. Alexander Dru. New York: Pantheon Books, 1950. Haecker was a convert to the Catholic Church who was associated with Karl Muth, editor of *Hochland,* and knew the Scholl group. His diary expresses strong anti-Nazi sentiments.

Halder, Fritz. *Gespräche mit Halder.* Compiled by Peter Bor. Wiesbaden: Limes Verlag, 1950.

Harcourt, Robert d'. *The German Catholics.* Trans. Reginald Dingle. London: Burns, Oates and Washbourne, 1939.

Hart, B. H. Liddell. *The German Generals Talk.* New York: Wm. Morrow and Co., 1948. Useful for its analysis of the relationship between Hitler and the General Staff.

Henderson, Neville. *Failure of a Mission.* New York: G. P. Putnam's Sons, 1940.

———. *Water Under the Bridges.* London: Hodder and Staughton, 1945.

Hull, Cordell. *The Memoirs of Cordell Hull.* New York: The Macmillan Co., 1948.

Jackson, Robert H. *The Nürnberg Case.* New York: Alfred A. Knopf, 1947.

Jansen, Jon B. (pseud.). *The Silent War.* Phila.: Lippincott, 1943.

John of Salisbury. *The Statesman's Book of John of Salisbury: being the Fourth, Fifth, Sixth, and Selections of the Seventh and Eighth Books of the "Policraticus."* Trans. John Dickenson. New York: Alfred A. Knopf, 1927.

Jordan, Max. *Beyond All Fronts.* Milwaukee: Bruce, 1944. A first-hand journalistic account of the Hitler period up to 1941 by an American newspaper and radio man. His acquaintance with Carl Goerdeler and Michael Cardinal von Faulhaber makes it useful for our purpose.

Kenny, John Paulinus, O. P. *A Philosophical Study of the International Military Tribunal.* River Forest, Ill.: Ph.D. dissertation, 1949. An attempt is made in this study to analyze the ethical justification for an international trial of war criminals. Unfortunately for our purpose, not enough is said concerning the question of "collective guilt" of the German nation.

Van Kleffens, Eelco Nicolaas. *Juggernaut over Holland.* New York: Columbia Univ. Press, 1940.

Koch, Rev. Antony. *A Handbook of Moral Theology.* Trans. and ed. Arthur Preuss. 4 vols. St. Louis, Mo.: B. Herder Book Co., 1918-1921.

Kramer, Herbert G. *The Indirect Voluntary.* Washington, D. C.: The

Catholic Univ. Press., 1935. A Ph.D. dissertation on this specific ethical problem.

Krzesinski, Andrew J. *National Cultures, Nazism, and the Church.* Boston: Bruce Humphries, Inc., 1945.

Künneth, Walter. *Das Widerstandsrecht als theologisch-ethisches Problem.* München: Claudius Verlag, 1954. A revised Lutheran approach to the problem of resistance by a professor at the University of Erlangen. Dr. Künneth is also a member of the Witzleben group in Munich which has carried on numerous discussions of these basic problems.

Leber, Annedore. *Das Gewissen steht auf.* Berlin: Mosaik Verlag, 1954. A collection of photographs and biographical sketches of various members of the German Resistance. The author is the widow of Julius Leber.

Lend, Evelyn. *The Underground Struggle in Germany.* New York: League for Industrial Democracy, 1938.

Lexicon für Theologie und Kirche. Freiburg-im-Breisgau: Herder and Co., 1938.

Lochner, Louis P. *What about Germany?* New York: Dodd, Mead and Co., 1942. Chapter XVII is of particular value to a study of the resistance movements. Lochner was formerly head of the AP bureau in Berlin, and although his account naturally conceals identities of persons in the " Front of Decent People," it is useful as general confirmation of later accounts.

Lowenstein, Karl. *Hitler's Germany.* New York: The Macmillan Co., 1940.

McClasky, Beryl R. *The History of United States Policy and Program in the Field of Religious Affairs Under the Office of the U. S. High Commissioner for Germany.* U. S. High Commissioner for Germany, Office of the Executive Secretary: Historical Division, Research Project # 104, 1951.

Martin, Hugh et al. *Christian Counter-Attack.* New York: Charles Scribner's Sons, 1944.

Metzger, Max Josef. *Gefangenschaftsbriefe.* herausgeben Dr. Matthias Laros. Meitingen bei Augsburg: Kyrios Verlag, 1947.

Mason, John Brown. *Hitler's First Foes.* Minneapolis: Burgess, 1936.

Michel, Karl *Ost und West, Der Ruf Stauffenbergs.* Zürich: Thomas Verlag, 1947.

Micklem, Nathaniel. *National Socialism and Christianity.* Oxford: Clarendon Press, 1939.

———. *National Socialism and the Roman Catholic Church, 1933-38.* New York: Oxford Univ. Press, 1939.

Mignault, R. P. Albert-Marie, O. P. *La résistance aux lois injustes et la doctrine catholique.* Montreal: Bibliothèque de l'action française, 1921.

Moody, Joseph N. (ed.). *Church and Society.* New York: Arts, Inc., 1953.

Mowrer, Edgar A. *Germany Puts the Clock Back.* New York: W. Morrow & Co., 1933.

Namier, Sir Lewis. *In the Nazi Era.* London: Macmillan & Co., 1952. Decidedly critical of the theory that there was a genuine German Resistance Movement.

Niemoeller, Martin. *From U-boat to Concentration Camp.* London: W. Hodge & Co., 1939.

Paetel, Karl Otto. *Deutsche innere Emigration, anti-nationalsozialistische Zeugnisse aus Deutschland. Gesammelt und erläutert von Karl O. Paetel.* New York: Friedrich Krause, 1946.

Pechel, Rudolf. *Deutscher Widerstand.* Erlenbach-Zürich: E. Rentsch, 1947. An extremely useful and objective account which contains many vital documents of the Resistance groups.

The Persecution of the Catholic Church in the Third Reich. London: Burns Oates, 1940. Continuous history of the development of an anti-Christian attitude by the Nazi government, interspersed with documentary evidence from German contemporary accounts.

Pribilla, Max, S. J. *Deutsche Schicksalsfragen.* Frankfurt am Main: Josef Knecht, 1950. Father Pribilla's book, parts of which were previously published in *Stimmen der Zeit,* is the best indication of current German Catholic concern with the basic problems inherent in the relationship of an individual to the state. The right of resistance is treated in detail. Father Pribilla is also a member of the Witzleben discussion group in Munich.

Pruner, Johann Ev., *Théologie morale,* in *Bibliothèque Théologique du XIX siècle,* 2 vols. Trans. Abbé P. Belet. Genève: Grosset et Tremblay, 1880. Unfortunately the German original of this noted work, *Lehrbuch der katholischen Moraltheologie* (Freiburg im Breisgau, 1875), was not available.

Reuter, Franz. *Der 20 Juli und seine Vorgeschichte.* Berlin: Wedding Verlag, 1946. A small pamphlet telling the events of that fateful day.

Roberts, Stephen H. *The House that Hitler Built.* London: Methuen Publishers, 1937.

Rothfels, Hans. *The German Opposition to Hitler.* Hinsdale, Ill.: Henry Regnery Co., 1948. This small work shows convincing insight into the reality of a continuous anti-Nazi movement within Germany and its basic ethical motivation.

Sabine, George H. *A History of Political Theory.* New York: Henry Holt & Co., rev. ed., 1950.

Scholl, Inge. *Die weisse Rose.* Frankfurt am Main: Verlag der Frankfurter Hefte, 1952. An account of the resistance offered by the Munich students, written by the sister of the two leaders of the group. Full texts of the pamphlets published by them.

Schramm, Wilhelm von. *Der 20. Juli in Paris.* Badwörishofen: Kindler und Schiermeyer, 1953.

Smith, Preserved. *The Age of the Reformation.* New York: Henry Holt & Co., 1920.

Steward, John S. *Sieg des Glaubens.* Zürich: Thomas Verlag, 1946. A documented record of the resistance offered by the religious element of the population. Based largely on the captured files of the Gauleiter in Strasbourg.

Taylor, Telford. *Sword and Swastika.* New York: Simon and Schuster, 1952.

Thomas Aquinas. *De regimine principum.* Trans. Gerald B. Phelan. Toronto: St. Michael's College, 1935.

———. *Summa theologica.* Trans. Fathers of the English Dominican Province. 3 vols. New York: Benziger Brothers, Inc., 1947.

Thompson, Dorothy. *Listen Hans.* Boston: Houghton Mifflin Co., 1942.

Trevor-Roper, H. R. *The Last Days of Hitler.* New York: The Macmillan Co., 1947.

Troeltsch, Ernst. *The Social Teaching of the Christian Churches.* Vol. II. Trans. Olive Wyon. New York: The Macmillan Co., 1931.

Vansittart, Rt. Hon. Lord Robert. *Bones of Contention.* London: Hutchinson and Co., 1945.

———. *Lessons of my Life.* London: Hutchinson and Co., 1943.

Wathen, Sister Mary Antonia, O. S. U. *The Policy of England and France toward the "Anschluss" of 1938.* Washington, D. C.: The Catholic Univ. of America Press, 1954.

Webb, Clement C. *John of Salisbury.* London: Methuen & Co., 1932.

Wheeler-Bennett, John W. *The Nemesis of Power: The German Army in Politics 1918-45.* New York: St. Martin's Press, Inc., 1954.

———. *Munich, Prologue to Tragedy.* New York: Duell, Sloan, and Pearce, 1948.

Wiesenborn, Guenther. *Der lautlose Aufstand.* Hamburg: Rowohlt Verlag, 1953. Based on work begun by Ricardo Huch, this study is largely a collection of pertinent documents illustrating resistance and showing how the different groups finally united in their efforts against Hitler. Useful discussion of fundamental problems.

Zeller, Eberhard. *Geist der Freiheit.* München: Verlag Hermann Rinn, 1952.

Zwischen Eid und Befehl: Revolte um Hitler. Wien: Kühne, 1951. Brief account of the incidents of the July 20 affair.

MAGAZINES AND NEWSPAPERS

Almond, Gabriel A. "The German Resistance Movement," *Current History,* X (1946), 409-419.

Baerwald, Friedrich. "Catholic Resistance in Nazi Germany," *Thought,* XX (1945), 217-234.

Baldwin, Hanson. "The *Caine Mutiny* Issue," *New York Times Magazine,* March 21, 1954.

Bayne, E. A. "Resistance in the German Foreign Office," *Human Events,* III (April 3, 1946), 1-8.

Ford, Franklin L. "The Twentieth of July in the History of the German Resistance," *American Historical Review*, LI (1946), 609-626.

Gurian, Waldemar. "Hitler's Undeclared War on the Catholic Church," *Foreign Affairs*, XVI (1938), 260-271.

Graham, Robert A., S. J. "How Justify Resistance to Tyranny?" *America*, XV (1954), 355-357.

Harcourt, Robert d'. "The Other Germany," *Dublin Review*, 443 (1948), 75-90.

Hopkinson, David. "The Lesson of the German Resistance," *The Contemporary Review*, CLXXV (1949), 17-22.

Van Husen, Paulus. "The 20th of July and the German Catholics," *Dublin Review*, 219 (1946), 1-9.

Klaas, Augustine, S. J. "The Apostle of Munich," *The Catholic Mind*, 51 (1953), 599-602.

Maley, Alex. B. "The Epic of the German Underground," *Human Events*, III (Feb. 27, 1946), 1-8.

Namier, L. B. "Registers After the Event," *History Today*, I (June 1951), 13-22.

Das Parlament, Special edition, 20 Juli 1952.

Poole, De Witt C. "Light on Nazi Foreign Policy," *Foreign Affairs*, XXV (1946), 130-154.

Pribilla, Max, S. J. "Ein grosser Gegenspieler Hitlers," *Stimmen der Zeit*, 149 (January 1950), 254-260.

Reed, Douglas L. "The German Church Conflict," *Foreign Affairs*, XIII (1935), 483-498.

Ritter, Gerhard. "The German Opposition to Hitler," *Contemporary Review*, CLXXVII (1950), 339-345.

Rothfels, Hans. "International Aspects of German Opposition to Hitler," *Measure*, II (1951), 175-190.

———. "Das politische Vermächtnis des deutschen Widerstands," *Vierteljahrshefte für Zeitgeschichte*, 2 Jahrgang (1954), 329-343.

Schorn, Hubert, "Das Widerstandsrecht in sittlicher und rechtlicher Beleuchtung," supplement to *Das Parlament*, January 28, 1953.

Sinsheimer, Hermann. "The German Resistance Movement." *Political Quarterly*, XIX (1948), 356-362.

Thorning, Joseph F., S. J. "The German Bishops and Hitlerism," *America*, 46 (1932), 333-334.

Waasen, Heinrich Maria. "Hie Stauffenberg—Hie Remer," *Die österreichische Furche*, February 7—March 21, 1953.

INDEX

NOTE:—Detailed identifications have been omitted since they have been given in the text.